Everyone Needs a TIMEOUT

Self-Care Strategies for People and Pets

Shaun Davis, PsyD
Charlene A. Derby, MA
Kelsey Weber, CPDT-KA, LFDM-T

Illustrated by
Richard Byron

Text copyright © 2024 by Shaun Davis, Charlene A. Derby, and Kelsey Weber.
All rights reserved.

Illustrations copyright © 2024 Charlene A. Derby. Used by permission.

No part of this book may be used or reproduced in any manner whatsoever without the written permission of the authors except in the case of brief quotations embodied in critical articles and reviews.

Disclaimer:
*Everyone Needs a Timeout: Self-Care Strategies for People and Pet*s is for informational purposes only and does not constitute professional advice. While the authors are professionals and the information provided in this book relates to issues within their areas of expertise, your individual circumstances may call for other solutions. We have done our best to ensure that the information provided in this book and the references and resources suggested herein are accurate and provide valuable information in a general sense; again, your individual circumstances may be such that these resources and information are inappropriate for your needs. The authors expressly recommend that you seek customized advice from qualified professionals as appropriate. Book content shall not be understood or construed as legal, financial, tax, medical, health, or any other professional advice. Neither the authors nor any of the book's contributors shall be held liable or responsible for any errors or omissions in this book or for any damage you may suffer because of failing to seek competent advice from a professional familiar with your situation.

    The content was accurate to the best of the authors' knowledge upon publishing. Any errors will be corrected in future editions.

Illustrator: Richard Byron
Cover illustration: Richard Byron
Book design and production: Drew Stevens
Publisher: The Writing Derby

PRINTED IN THE UNITED STATES OF AMERICA

ISBN: 978-1-948710-18-3

First edition

Praise for *Everyone Needs a Timeout: Self-Care Strategies for People and Pets*

Most of us struggle with finding time for ourselves, yet that impacts our lives and the lives of those around us. This clever book helps you examine ways that a "timeout" will improve the quality of your life and those you live with, including your pets. The suggestions are helpful and allow readers to adapt them to their unique needs. What a great resource.

—DAVID P. MILLIGAN
Owner, Refresh on the Mountain Wellness Center

As a neuroscientist and veterinarian, I highly recommend *Everyone Needs a Timeout: Self-Care Strategies for People and Pets*. It offers science-based, practical, easy-to-follow tips and prompts for improving the well-being of the entire family—people and pets—as one harmonised unit. A must-have for anyone seeking balance and resilience in our increasingly busy lives.

—KATHY MURPHY, DVM, PhD
Founder, Barking Brains Ltd.; CEO, Behavior Vets

Everyone Needs a Timeout: Self-Care Strategies for People and Pets offers foundational and educative information about how important good "timeouts" are for healthy functioning. The discussions of how our bodies and minds evolve establish our changing needs for self-care as we move through developmental stages. It provides an exhaustive compendium of self-care tools for adults, children, and even pets. It is seasoned with self-reflections by the authors which give it relatability and texture. The material in this book is accessible to anyone who wants to put in the work to make positive changes in their lives to reduce stress.

—LINDA BARNHURST, PsyD
Retired Psychoanalytic Psychologist

Everyone Needs a Timeout: Self-Care Strategies for People and Pets is a delightfully creative resource for helping develop healthy habits. It includes suggestions that are clear and inviting as well as being applicable to everyone in the household: adults, children, and pets.

—VALERIE HART, Ph.D., MDiv

In appreciation of my family: Arlin, Heather and Ryan,
Natalie, Danielle, and Aaron, and of course,
my inspirations, Mark, June, Luke, Henry, and Lucy.
—SHAUN DAVIS

To the memory of my mother, Dora M. Lombard,
my earliest and steadfast role model and muse.
—CHARLENE A. DERBY

To all the animals who will never read this book
but whose lessons are embedded throughout its pages.
—KELSEY WEBER

Contents

Why This Book?   ix

Introduction to Timeouts   1

Part 1: Taking the Mystery Out of Timeouts

1. In Your Brain   13
2. In Your Body   20
3. In Your Life   33
4. Your Basic Strategy   38

Part 2: Timeouts for Adults

5. But I'm an Adult, Right?   47
6. Building a Healthy Foundation   59
7. Keeping My Cool   66
8. Enjoying Others   72
9. Fostering Connection   86
10. When Others Depend on Me   96

Part 3: Timeouts for Children and Adolescents

11. Laying the Foundation   105
12. The Developing Human   113
13. Back to Basics   118
14. Don't Look Now, but I Might Be Freaking Out   126
15. Home Is Where the Heart Is   132
16. Peers and Priorities   142
17. Knowing Myself Inside and Out   155

Part 4: Timeouts for Pets

18.	Perks and Perils of Pet Parenting	169
19.	Through the Ages and Stages	180
20.	Balancing Body and Brain	186
21.	Help! I Can't Speak Human!	200
22.	Social Support Equals Social Success	211
23.	From Ownership to Relationship	220

Part 5: Timeout Strategies Everyone Can Use

24.	Finding Your Quiet Place	235
25.	Breathing	239
26.	Relaxing Your Muscles	246
27.	Focusing Your Mind	254
28.	Reciting Mantras and Practicing Meditation	264
29.	Putting Pen to Paper	273
30.	Ending on a Positive Note	283

Bonus for Timeouts   291

Notes   303

Acknowledgments   315

Meet the Authors   319

Why This Book?

The Cartoon that Started it All

In October of 2020, an illustrator friend of Charlene's, Richard Byron, participated in a drawing challenge called Inktober. Each day a prompt was posted by the organizers, and illustrators were asked to interpret it in their black-and-white drawings. For the prompt "dizzy," Richard drew this cartoon and titled it "Dizzy: Mom Needs a Time Out."

What a great example of family chaos! Of course the mom needs a timeout, but so does the dad who is trying to get away from the pets, the child who is chasing the pets, and the pets themselves that may or may not be enjoying the ruckus. Everyone needs a timeout. Voila! A book idea was born.

Creating the Team

Charlene set up a Zoom call with her cousin, Shaun Davis, PsyD, asking her if she'd be interested in collaborating on a book. They'd worked together on a previous project, adding guidance for families navigating holiday stress. Shaun immediately hopped onboard. During brainstorming, the idea came out that pets needed a timeout, too. Shaun suggested we contact Kelsey Weber, the certified pet trainer who had helped her train her goldendoodle puppy for therapy work with children. After learning more about the intent of the project, Kelsey was eager to add her expertise to our team.

As a result of this collaboration, you'll hear each coauthor's voice in the chapters they've written. Each has something unique to contribute to the practice of taking a timeout for self-care and a personal way of presenting it. You'll hear Shaun's perspective in the Introduction, Part 1, and Part 3 as she shares from a therapist's point of view. You'll find her sections reflect her deep respect for the difficult challenges facing parents, caregivers, and children of all ages. Charlene speaks up in Part 2. She draws on her 45-year career in employee training and development to pinpoint easy-to-use techniques for managing the stressors faced by adults. Kelsey advocates for pets in Part 4 as she delves into her experience working with animals of all types. Her years as a dog trainer give her unique insights into the value pets add to our lives and the things we can do to help alleviate any stress they may be experiencing. Part 5 is a collaborative effort where all coauthors share their favorite timeout techniques for reducing stress.

Richard, whose cartoon sparked the initial idea, agreed to illustrate the book. His lively cartoon style supports the content in a lighthearted way.

Addressing the Need for Timeouts

We began our project just as the COVID-19 virus began its steady spread around the globe. We saw stress levels rise for nearly everyone over an 18-month period. And it didn't stop there. Over the three years we've worked on the book, international, national, and local events have continued to add stress to humans and pets alike. Taking a timeout to reduce stress has never felt more urgent. Shaun's therapy schedule is flooded with new clients feeling overwhelmed by unexpected circumstances. Kelsey observes that more people are adopting pets in hopes that a pet will provide them with social interaction and emotional support during times of uncertainty. She is inundated with requests to find and help train pets for families. Charlene empathizes with the pain others feel when she hears stories of those facing personal and professional challenges resulting from current events. She believes additional life skills may help alleviate their distress.

Early research into the effects of the global pandemic showed a dramatic rise in traumatic stress symptoms.[1] Social isolation and fears about the future increased rates of depression and anxiety. Many resorted to unhealthy coping strategies, such as the overindulgence of comfort foods and alcohol. Some relied on Internet sources for information, which increased divisiveness as social media algorithms fed on people's fears and challenged personal ideologies. Even pets suffered from uncertainties. Shaun's therapy dog needed anti-anxiety medicine. After enduring months of quarantine, he—like many humans—became nervous about leaving the house. All in all, we feel the strategies for taking timeouts presented in this book will assist you in creating a positive future and provide a lifetime of benefits.

We've included detailed, evidence-based content and endeavored to present it in easily digestible chunks with lots of special features sprinkled in. We hope it motivates you to develop the habits needed for daily timeouts: for you, your household members, and your pets.

Introduction to Timeouts

"Timeout" isn't a word we typically use when we think of taking care of ourselves and others. We usually think of it as a disciplinary technique used to help young children regulate their emotions by removing them from distressing situations and placing them in a quiet, low-stimulus environment until they calm down.[1] Set that perception aside and get ready to expand your understanding as we explore the ways timeouts can be used for self-care and stress reduction—for you and the people and pets you love.

How Did We Get Here?

McKinsey researchers state "around 50 percent of US consumers now report wellness as a top priority in their day-to-day lives."[2] In *Everyone Needs a Timeout: Self-Care Strategies for People*

and Pets, we offer a pathway for prioritizing wellness needs organized around the physical, emotional, social, and spiritual aspects of life. We call this taking a timeout for self-care. Once you begin to practice the strategies offered in this book, you'll be able to help other family members do the same. We hope you find our approach helpful as well as fun and easy. The goal is to make life better for every member of the family, including the household's pets.

Timeout and Self-Care

Let's begin with a clear understanding of what we mean by timeout. As we've just mentioned, a timeout is frequently associated with childhood discipline, but it pops up in many other contexts. In sports, calling a timeout interrupts a regular period of play so the players may communicate with their coach, adjust their strategy in the game, or inspire morale. When working with electronic devices you may see an error message that a system has timed out, requiring you to relaunch a process. In life, you may feel low on energy and take a break from an activity, a timeout to refuel your physical and emotional reserves.

These common definitions each have something to contribute to the concept of self-care and we have distilled the important features for our purposes. Throughout the book, this is what we mean when we use the terms "timeout" and "self-care."

- **Timeout:** A brief pause to reflect on your current circumstances and deal with the impact of stress on your life.[3]
- **Self-care:** The intentional act of attending to your physical, emotional, social, and spiritual well-being with or without the help of professionals.

Since the adults in a household generally control the family's schedule and resources, the dependents (children, animals, or other household members) may be unable to take timeouts without some assistance. We'll discuss how to set up everyone for success with their own self-care strategies and improve the wellness of the entire household.

Benefits of Taking a Timeout

Stress isn't always a bad thing. We need a certain amount of it to function at an optimal level of energy, arousal, and motivation. Some professionals distinguish between eustress (good stress), and distress (bad stress). The goal is to balance the amount of stress in our lives and the level of physical, emotional, social, and spiritual energy we have available to deal with it. When our needs go unmet or our resources are stretched too thin, stress increases, often to the point where it overwhelms our nervous system.

When our reserves run low, we are more vulnerable to the negative impacts of stress. We increase our health risks. We decrease our ability to manage our emotions and relationships. We lose contact with our deeper values. Self-care is key for keeping us healthy and promoting our well-being.

By taking appropriate timeouts, we increase our ability to live according to the ideals and principles we hold most important. They can be both preventative and responsive in addressing life's stressors and improving overall well-being. Self-care strategies may be simple, but making time to use those strategies is often a challenge. That's why this book describes practical ways to take a timeout for self-care, which in turn allows us to realize the reciprocal nature of relationships. Being our best helps others be their best. We do more than just survive life's stressors—we, and those around us, thrive.

> **WHAT MOTIVATES SELF-CARE?**
>
> Human behavior over the years has demonstrated that self-care increases during times of distress. An example is the global reaction to the COVID-19 pandemic. There was so much unknown about the virus and how it spread or how terminal it might prove to be that anxiety ran high in populations around the world.
>
> Researchers from Kent University found that self-care practices brought mental and physical health benefits even under the immense stress caused by the pandemic.[4] People increased their self-care activities because they felt stressed. Perhaps one of the silver linings of the global pandemic was learning the value of making time for self-care.

Barriers to Taking a Timeout

Self-care is obviously good for us. So why don't we take the time to do it? It might seem too hard or more punishing than beneficial, as if we felt burdened with one more thing we were supposed to be doing in an already busy, demanding, and stressful life. Self-care may feel like another stressor rather than the cure. And now we're saying you should help your family members incorporate self-care strategies, too? That's a lot to ask of anyone.

Here are some common obstacles that keep people from making time for effective self-care activities:[5] [6] [7]

- **Time**. Life is busy, and there are only so many hours in a day to take care of our family, pets, work, appointments, meetings, school, commuting, spiritual practices, and social expectations. When the demands of daily life pile up, self-care is often the first thing we sacrifice. Taking timeouts to relax, exercise, eat nutritional food, and sleep seems impossible. Helping our dependents take self-care timeouts feels doubly impossible. While we can't manufacture more hours in the day, we can find opportunities to take a breath in the busy moments or examine how we manage the time we do have. These are gifts we give ourselves and share with our family members.

- **Negative self-talk.** Usually, we are our own worst enemies. Stigma and gender barriers often lead to negative thoughts. When we consider self-care strategies, we might think, *I've tried that before and never followed through,* or *This is all just psychobabble—it'll never work,* or *Other people are doing just fine without taking timeouts.* Awareness is the first and most important step in scaling the negative self-talk barrier.
- **Perception.** You might equate self-care with strenuous exercise routines, fancy gadgets, an expensive workout wardrobe, gym memberships, or specialized diets. But self-care is as easy as taking a deep breath and as inexpensive as sitting quietly with a cup of tea. Spending time with your pet or enjoying nature is simple and free.
- **Energy.** Stress leads to fatigue. Fatigue becomes more pronounced as stress levels rise and it increases the longer stress is experienced. Add depression or health issues to the mix, and energy quickly becomes depleted. Low energy makes it hard to start a new life habit, particularly if the results aren't immediately rewarding. Good self-care increases energy, motivation, and a positive mood, benefits tough to imagine when you're running on empty. It takes faith in the process to get started, but you won't regret the effort.
- **Lack of knowledge.** Self-care hasn't always been recognized as an important part of leading a healthy life. Educational, medical, and work settings are just now beginning to emphasize self-care as a worthy endeavor. Knowledge is a necessary weapon if you want to increase your commitment to quality self-care. Reading this book is a good starting point.

> **SHAUN SAYS:**
>
> I come from Germanic and Northern European heritage—think Amish and Mennonite farmers. We're known for a stiff upper lip, few words, and placing a high value on hard work. We never discussed taking time to recognize personal needs. Church attendance was expected to maintain good spiritual health. There was no shame in going to the doctor if you were physically sick, but tending to emotional and social needs? Forget it.
>
> Intergenerational transmission of stigma often prevents us from employing strategies that can make us healthier people. How does your family of origin and ancestral heritage impact your view on self-care?

The Barrier Buster

As you read through the list of obstacles to taking timeouts for self-care, identify those that apply to you. Children and pets have similar needs, but they may not have effective ways to ask for help to overcome the barriers. Your time, energy, and money resources are finite, and self-care seems difficult. Barriers don't have to keep you from learning new ways of caring for yourself. See them as opportunities for beginning your journey of change.

> **WHAT SELF-CARE IS NOT**
>
> Society presents many confusing messages about self-care. Advertisements and media bombard us with enticing activities frequently detrimental to self-care. They may suggest indulgence or numbing. These are distractions rather than solutions. Here are a few trends marketed as self-care that result in avoiding our core needs:
>
> - Snacking or emotional eating
> - Retail therapy
> - Happy hour/Miller time/It's five o'clock somewhere
> - Binge watching/Doom scrolling

Taking timeouts for high-quality, effective self-care makes you better able to make good decisions. You can't do that if you're mindlessly eating, spending, partying, or streaming your favorite program. Any activity or behavior used to avoid obligations or unpleasant feelings is not self-care. If the goal is to numb your mind so you don't have to think your thoughts or feel your emotions, that's not self-care.

Escapism and indulgences can be enjoyable in small doses; however, they are not effective in the long term. They might be part of self-care if they're included in an intentional plan for improving overall well-being. The key is being mindful of the reason for engaging in these activities and understanding why you're choosing them.

How to Use This Book

Stress takes a toll on your overall well-being. Identifying and addressing how stressors impact your nervous system is important. Taking frequent timeouts to engage in high-quality self-care activities can become a healthy habit no matter your age, relationship status, gender, race, or economic situation. It even applies to the animals you love. *Everyone Needs a Timeout: Self-Care Strategies for People and Pets* addresses these stressors. Integrated throughout are suggestions for how family members can promote a sense of well-being for one another.

You can read the book from start to finish, or you may want to go straight to the section that addresses your current needs. In either case, we suggest you start by reading Part 1 - Taking the Mystery Out of Timeouts. It provides foundational concepts that are built on throughout the book.

Here's a good analogy. Whenever a commercial airplane takes off, the flight attendant gives passengers safety instructions. "If needed, oxygen masks will be released from the overhead compartments. To start the flow of oxygen, pull the mask toward you. Place it firmly over your nose and mouth, secure the elastic band behind your head, and breathe normally. Be sure to secure

INTRODUCTION TO TIMEOUTS   9

your mask before assisting others." Why do they say that last part? Because if you pass out from loss of oxygen, those who depend on you will also be lost.

The information provided in this book is your oxygen mask. It is supported by the latest research on self-care for humans and animals. You'll find some novel techniques created by the authors with the assurance each one is grounded in solid evidence-based research. Each strategy is based on practices that have been rigorously evaluated in a scientific environment and have been shown to make a positive, statistically significant difference in important outcomes. Taking care of yourself is the first step. So, fasten your seatbelt. It's time to take a timeout.

PART 1

Taking the Mystery Out of Timeouts

Before you can take a timeout for self-care you need to understand what is going on in your brain, your body, and your life. Part 1 introduces the basic concepts needed to address the timeout needs of children, adolescents, adults, and pets, along with a basic strategy you can use when facing stressful situations.

CHAPTER 1

In Your Brain

Your amazing brain regulates every part of your physical, emotional, social, and spiritual self—and most of the time you're not even aware of how hard it's working. This chapter gives an overview of the structural parts of the brain and the role they play in managing the stressors faced by people and their pets. This part may sound technical but stay with us as it lays the foundation for your success down the road.

> **SHAUN SAYS:**
>
> I was a late bloomer. I returned to college thirty years after I began. Learning about the mechanics of the human brain and how it impacts every part of our existence was intimidating, to say the least. However, the more I learned, the more impressed I became with what this mere three pounds of squiggly mush can do. The brain is a truly miraculous organ.
>
> Learning technical information about the brain may not seem like an immediate path to good self-care, but it is the pathway to knowing yourself, your children, your peers, and your animals better. Each part of your marvelous brain plays a role in managing your stressors.

Brain Basics

The brain is the Grand Central Station of the nervous system. It begins forming within days of conception. The structural components of the brain develop from bottom to top and from back to front. The order of that development creates the transition from basic survival needs to the more complex thinking and processing required for higher-order functions.

First, the brain stem develops and connects to the extremities of the human body. Next comes the limbic system, which processes incoming messages and takes meaningful action. Finally, the cerebral cortex wraps around the primitive neural components and manages millions of processes by routing specific tasks to specialized parts of the brain.

Of special interest in understanding the stress response is the amygdala, part of the limbic system. It is a small, almond-shaped structure at the base of the brain. In fact, amygdala is the Latin word for almond. It is sometimes called the primitive brain or the fight-or-flight brain. We'll elaborate on this when we talk about the autonomic nervous system.

By the time humans reach adulthood, the nervous system has grown to more than one hundred billion neurons. Linked together, these neurons would stretch over two million miles. Each neuron is connected to thousands of others; when one is activated, a ripple effect of signals spreads throughout the entire brain and into the rest of the body. In a matter of nanoseconds, the brain processes more signals than the greatest human-made supercomputer—a speed nearly unfathomable. This incredible and complex system is activated when you are under stress.

Brain Neuroplasticity

Early in life, both human and animal brains develop neural pathways that handle stressors using what they perceive as the most effective coping strategies. The nervous system forms its default settings, sometimes called the brain's original wiring. For most of us, these automatic responses are about survival, not necessarily maintaining optimal health. However, brain development is not one and done. The brain has an astonishing ability to develop new neural pathways throughout your life.

You may have heard the saying, "Neurons that fire together wire together." (Or maybe that's just a thing psychologists hear

Cerebral Cortex

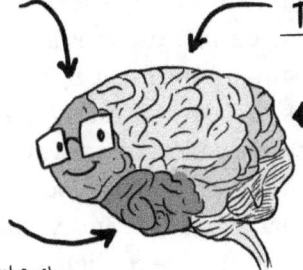

Frontal Lobe
- Attention & focus
- Planning & decisions
- Impulse control
- Emotional control
- Organize thoughts & movement

Parietal Lobe
- Motor function
- Language comprehension
- Monitors skin information (temperature, pressure, shape, etc.)

Temporal Lobe
- Sounds & smells
- Language & speech
- Visual & auditory memories

Occipital Lobe
- Visual processing

Limbic System

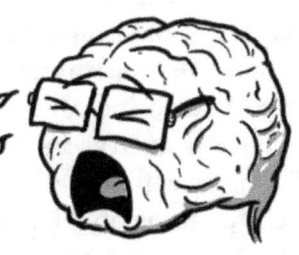

- Meaning & priority for incoming signals
- Stores memories (short/long-term)
- Sounds the alarm (fight, flight, freeze)
- Keeps the body in balance (hormones & neurotransmitters)

Brainstem

- Connects brain and spinal cord
- Directs motor and sensory signals
- Regulates heart and breathing
- Regulates sleep cycle

a lot!) We call this neuroplasticity. It's the nervous system's ability to modify itself both structurally and functionally.

Brain rewiring is possible at any point in life. It happens with the repetition and intensity of experiences. The timeout practices used to counteract stress are literally creating new neural pathways—no brain surgery necessary.

Neuroscience has discovered many exciting examples of damaged brain structures generating new ways to process information. There is still much unknown about the extent of positive outcomes of neuroplasticity. One individual may completely recover from highly traumatic experiences, while another may suffer lifelong neurological and psychological deficits. Nevertheless, every brain will receive some level of benefit from repeated positive experiences.

Neuroplasticity enables us to form new habits that support our ability to respond constructively to stress. Experts say it can take between 21 and 66 days for a new behavior to become a habit. The more difficult the behavior, the more time required. A simple habit, such as taking several deep breaths when you begin to feel anxiety, can be formed in as little as a month. Complex behaviors, such as training yourself to recite a meditation while falling asleep at night, could take as long as eight months to become automatic. The key is to keep at it. Repetition and intensity rewire the brain.

All the techniques discussed in this book will create new experiences that stimulate brain rewriting. If you want to create lasting change in how your nervous system responds to stress, you must practice, practice, practice. It takes intentionality to change the structure of a brain.

At first, rewiring your brain to respond to stress more effectively can feel awkward, clunky, and difficult. It's easier to resort to the go-to tactics you already know. When beginning to use timeout strategies, you may find it helpful to visualize brain rewiring as a curve. You are at a starting point. Trying new strategies may seem difficult at first, lowering your confidence level. Continued practice will pay off and soon you'll have rewired your brain with a new self-care habit.

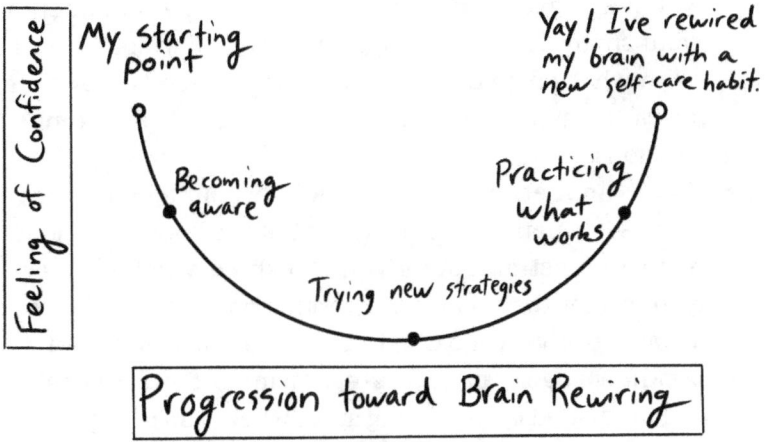

Tips for Brain Rewiring

As you read through this book, take note of the timeout strategies you want to incorporate into your daily life. Here are some ways to lock in the changes that benefit overall well-being:

- **Take time for a timeout.** Our schedules are so full it can be difficult to imagine where to squeeze in self-care. But don't let time be an excuse to skip skill practice. Remember, even a few quick minutes can help you be more balanced, effective, and productive. It's worth it!
- **Practice when you're not stressed.** Stress impairs the cognitive part of the brain and the ability to form new memories. You're unlikely to receive the full benefit of the strategies presented in this book if you use them only when you're in distress. For long-term success, practice when your brain has full capacity for wiring in the benefit of your self-care practices.
- **Start with the basics.** Target simple strategies first. Choose ones that help slow down and relax the physical body. You are more likely to stay motivated for more advanced strategies if you experience success in the early stages of habit formation.
- **Repeat strategies that work for you.** In the beginning,

you may need to make a checklist or set a reminder on your smart device to stop what you're doing and check in with what's happening in your body. Several quick exercises throughout the day are as valuable as extended sessions.
- **Vary the methods.** This book is brimming with ideas. Choose something from any part of the book that piques your interest and suits your lifestyle—whatever helps you master the skill you're working on. (Part 5 - Timeout Strategies Everyone Can Use may be especially helpful.)
- **Acknowledge your successes.** An important part of staying motivated is identifying areas where you're improving. Strive for progress, not perfection.
- **Expand your skills.** Build on your successes to increase your repertoire of stress-reduction strategies.

SHAUN SAYS:

When I first learned to play golf, I wanted to join my husband and our friends on their golf outings. I've never been very coordinated, but graceful movement helps one's golf game. I signed up for ladies' lessons and read books on rules, form, and strategies. (Yes, I'm one of those people who think they can figure out how to do anything by reading enough.) I understood the principles of what I wanted to do, but for the entire first year, I mostly pounded the ground with my clubs instead of hitting the ball.

Things changed when I stopped trying so hard to be good at the game and focused on one skill at a time, like keeping my head down. Then I worked on the next thing: raising my club up behind my head. Eventually, I began to hit the ball more than I missed. I practiced on the putting green, went to the driving range, and played short courses to build my confidence. One summer I drove the snack cart at a local course so I could play for free, and I also treated myself to a pair of pink golf gloves. I'll never make the pros, but I rarely pound the ground anymore. Sometimes I even win a round.

I have come to love a sport I can enjoy with my family and friends. None of this could have happened if I hadn't taken time out of my normal routine to practice and enjoy the process of learning how to play golf.

◆ ◆ ◆

Your brain is an incredible organ built for survival and self-preservation. Understanding how it works is the first step toward building effective self-care habits. Due to neuroplasticity, developing new habits for dealing with stress is possible. It's never too late to take advantage of your amazing ability to rewire your brain.

CHAPTER 2

In Your Body

The word "stress" is often overused, and almost always in a negative way. The fact is a certain amount of stress is needed to function at our best. Without an appropriate amount of eustress (good stress), it would be difficult to get motivated enough to perform the basic tasks of living or to keep ourselves safe when danger shows up.

The problem arises when eustress rises to the level of distress—the kind of stress that makes us feel sick and overwhelmed. Throughout this book, the word stress is used to refer to the unhealthy, excessive state of distress.

Stress is controlled by the central nervous system and is experienced throughout the body. In 1950, Hans Selye proposed the General Adaptation Theory to explain the process of how stress impacts the physical body.[1] The pattern is activated whether we are in true danger or simply running late for an appointment. This response is often referred to as fight, flight, or freeze. By identifying the response, we can engage in effective self-care strategies to mitigate the damage created by chronic activation of our body's alarm system.

> **GENERAL ADAPTATION THEORY**
>
> The General Adaptation Theory describes the three stages a body goes through as it responds to stress as follows:
>
> 1. **Alarm.** Threat is perceived. The adrenal glands release cortisol. Heart rate and blood pressure increase, blood sugar levels rise, breathing becomes shorter and more rapid, muscles tense, perspiration increases, and pupils dilate.

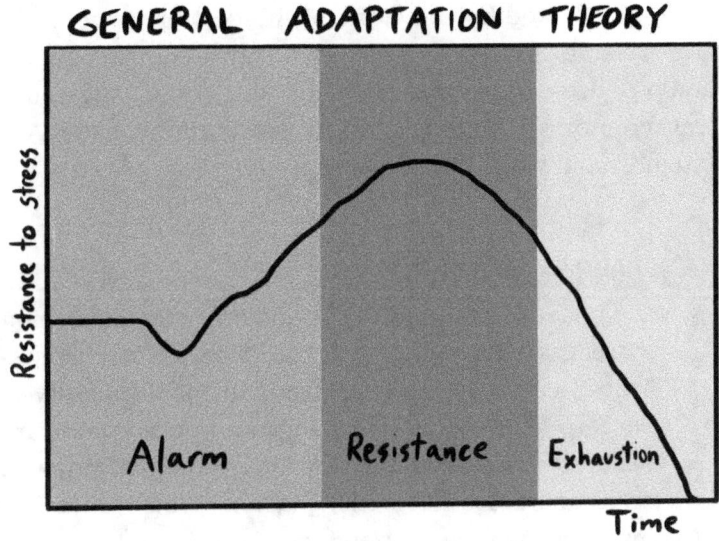

   2. **Resistance.** If the perceived threat continues, the body remains at the heightened metabolic level. If the threat is not addressed, the body will maintain this metabolic level until its resources are depleted.
   3. **Exhaustion.** Prolonged exposure to the stressor results in deterioration of the body's ability to maintain proper functioning. Health issues are likely to occur if effective strategies for resetting the nervous system are not engaged.

Stress and Hormones

Our nervous systems are regulated by hormones, including cortisol and adrenaline. Cortisol is often called the stress hormone. The right amount keeps your heart healthy, supports memory function, wakes you up in the morning, and regulates your blood sugar. Adrenaline is sometimes called the fight or flight hormone. It increases your heart rate, elevates your blood pressure, and boosts energy supplies. Both hormones are released by the adrenal glands, particularly during times of stress.

As illustrated by the General Adaptation Theory, chronic stress results in dysregulated cortisol and adrenaline production and produces many unpleasant and sometimes dangerous physical symptoms, including a suppressed immune system, chronic fatigue, rapid weight gain, and digestive problems.

> **SHAUN SAYS:**
>
> The onset of the COVID-19 pandemic created tremendous challenges in everyday life. Mental health workers like me experienced a dramatic increase in the demand for our services. My clinical psychology training taught me how to monitor my own health so my personal life would not interfere with my work. But it did not prepare me for a long-lasting global event that would impact so many humans and their pets.
>
> During this time, I observed the negative effects of the pandemic and its associated quarantine on the general population. Among them were significant weight gain, increased use of alcohol and other substances, and rising mental health issues. These are typical results of chronic stress and an overtaxed adrenal system. Therapists are not immune from these stresses. Like other front-line workers, I faced the challenges of managing my own fears and frustrations while continuing to care for my patients. I recognized that I needed to be intentional about creating timeouts for self-care, or I would succumb to the pressure.
>
> I suspect we will experience the stress fallout of this for generations to come. It's one reason I feel so passionate about helping people learn to take time to care for all the aspects of their well-being: physical, emotional, social, and spiritual.

Stress and the Nervous System

Your brain partners with your body through a complex nervous system. Many subsystems that regulate your voluntary and involuntary bodily functions all work together to keep you alive and safe. The central nervous system collects sensory information through nerve cells throughout your body that connect to your spinal cord. Those cells send signals to the brain for processing, and your brain decides what to do with them.

The peripheral nervous system is made up of two distinct systems. The somatic nervous system coordinates our voluntary actions by engaging cranial and spinal nerves. The autonomic nervous system regulates our automatic, involuntary actions: breathing, heart rate, blood pressure, digestion, and sexual arousal.[2] This is also the part of the nervous system that helps us recognize the need for a timeout.

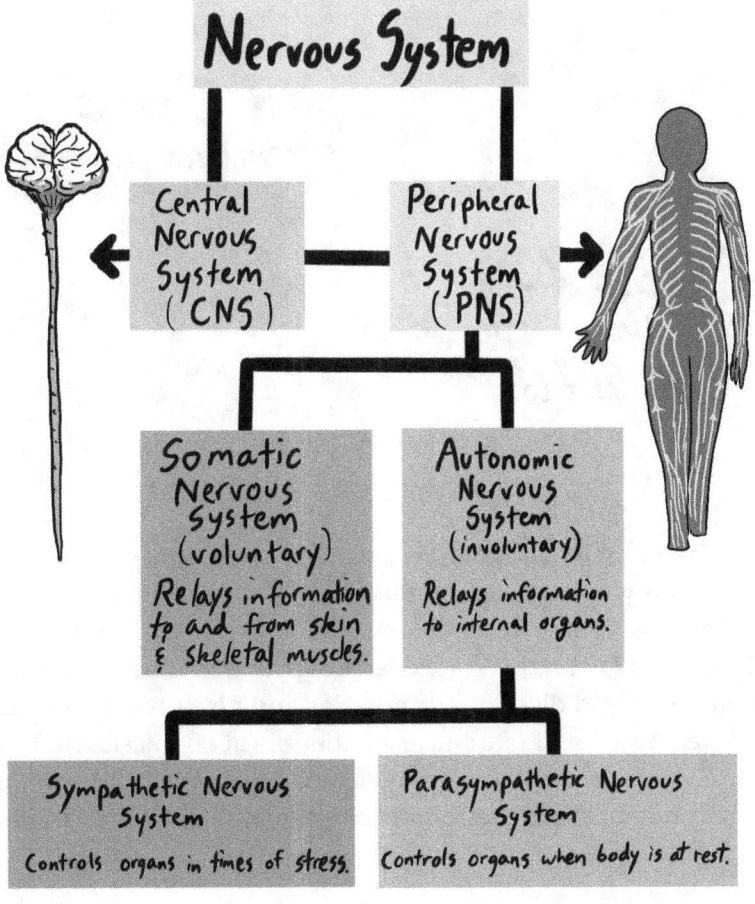

Understanding the Autonomic Nervous System

The autonomic nervous system is controlled by the amygdala. Using the analogy of a thermometer, it regulates the level of stress along a scale from relaxed or cool, to high alert or hot.

Your nervous system temperature rises or falls as you respond to events and environmental clues around you. Depending on the nature of the clues, one of the two subsystems, the sympathetic system or the parasympathetic system, becomes more active.

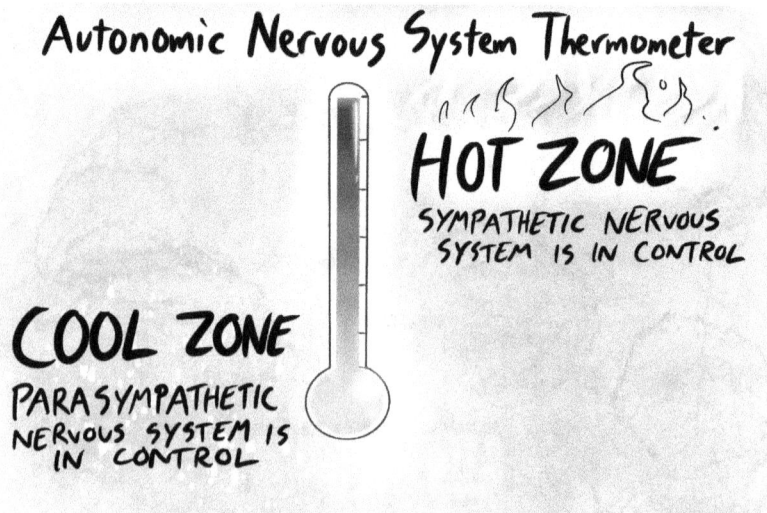

In the Cool Zone—
The Parasympathetic Nervous System in Control

When your autonomic nervous system thermometer is in the cool zone, the parasympathetic nervous system is in control. This is the "just right" state of eustress. In this zone, sometimes called rest and digest, your muscles and digestive system are relaxed. Your heart rate and respiration are at optimal levels. Your pupils are relaxed so you can take in a broad perspective of your environment. Your prefrontal cortex is available for analytical thought and problem solving. This is the state you want to return to when you take a timeout to recover from stressors big and small.

In the Hot Zone—
The Sympathetic Nervous System in Control

When a threat or stressor is detected in the environment, the temperature in the autonomic nervous system thermometer rises into the hot zone. That's when the sympathetic nervous system takes control of your internal organs. It recognizes a need for a protective reaction and sends signals to the brain that scream "Protect me!" Help comes in the form of adrenaline and cortisol that pours into your bloodstream, and tells your body to prepare for fight, flight, or freeze.

The sympathetic nervous system also tells your prefrontal cortex—the reasoning part of your brain—to take a back seat so you can take action to regain safety. Additionally, your heart rate increases, breathing becomes shallow and rapid, eyes dilate (the better to see the threat), muscles tense in readiness for quick defensive action, and blood rushes from your extremities to your internal organs, which may create the sensation of tingling in your hands or feet. Your core temperature may rise, and you might feel physically warm.

All of this happens automatically in a split second, and the change in physical condition may prove necessary if you're faced with a truly dangerous situation. However, you'll also feel it if the threat is a meeting with your boss or a traffic jam that's making you late for an appointment.

Your autonomic nervous system temperature fluctuates between the cool and hot zones throughout the day, depending on what's going on in the environment around you. Your task is to recognize when you're entering the hot zone and determine whether the threat is real or artificial. If there's no logical reason to be in the hot zone, the thermostat analogy comes into play.

Monitoring and Resetting the Autonomic Nervous System

We use thermostats to control the temperature of our indoor environments. We choose a desired setting, and electronic sensors monitor the temperature in the room. When it falls below the setting, sensors turn on the heat. When it rises above the setting, sensors turn on the air-conditioning. When the temperature is at the desired setting, the heating and cooling systems are idle.

The thermostat that monitors your autonomic nervous system temperature acts similarly. The amygdala is activated by perceived threats.[3] Sensors tell your brain that you've reached the hot zone, and you need to take action to keep yourself safe. Or they tell you the threat isn't as big as you imagined, and you need to cool down.

Resetting the thermostat starts with paying attention to how your body responds to events and environmental cues, such as a rapid heartbeat, unsteady breathing, and sweaty palms. Once you recognize these sensors, you can take actions for self-care. Making time for self-care keeps the parasympathetic nervous system in control and your autonomic nervous system in the cool zone.[4]

When you make self-care part of your everyday life, your nervous system does a better job at finding the right balance between the hot and cool zones. When you notice stress pushing you into the hot zone and you've assessed the situation as reasonably safe, press the reset button to intentionally reverse the automatic responses. Slow your breathing and visualize relaxing to lower your nervous system temperature.

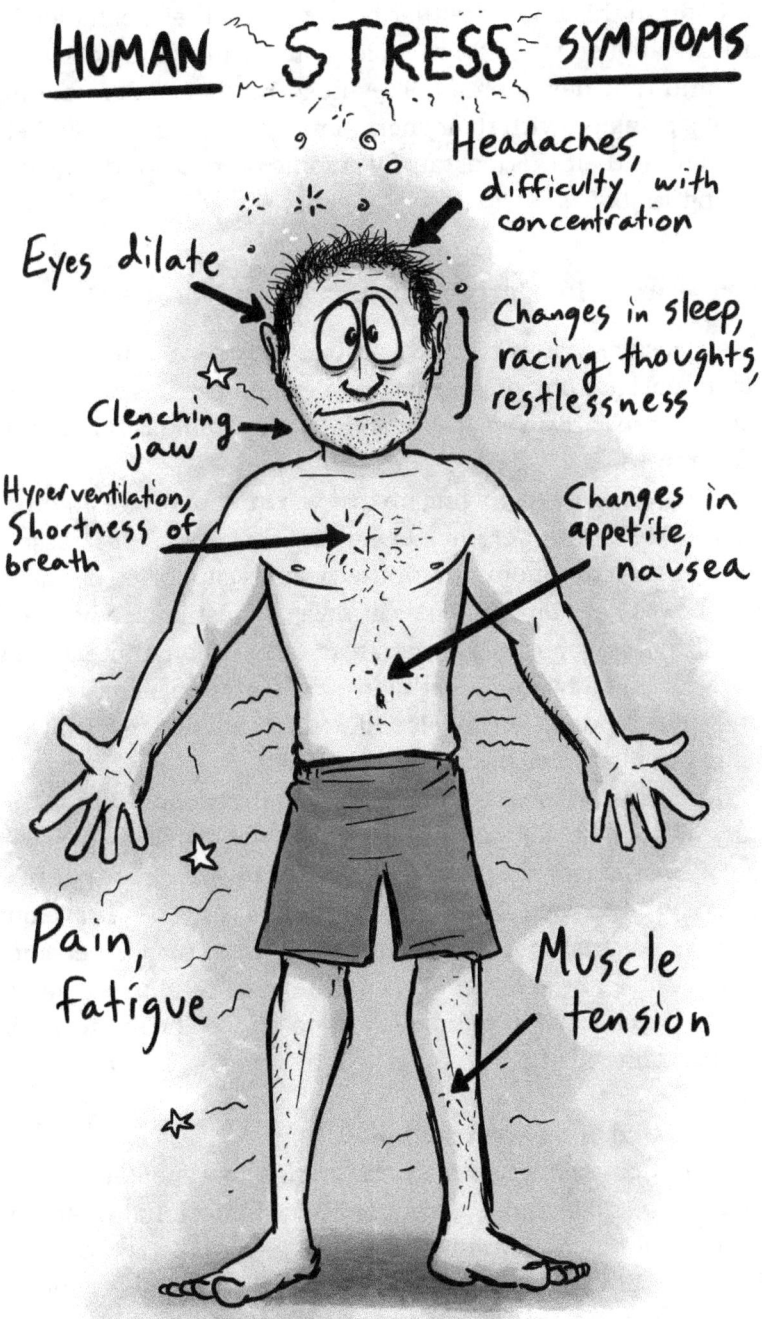

Later in this book, the thermometer and thermostat analogies are applied to children, adolescents, adults, and pets. Keep in mind that developing beings need help in understanding what's going on with their thermometers. Caregivers can help them reset their thermostats by guiding them toward effective coping strategies.

Stress and the Early Emotional Environment

The stress response is wired during early development. The emotional environment during fetal development, as well as that experienced early in life by both humans and animals, influences this process.

Children or pets growing up in a warm, supportive environment will likely experience lower reactivity to mild stressors because their autonomic nervous system is supported by safety and security at home. Their amygdala can distinguish between a bear in the woods and a math test, or between a threatening predator and a balloon floating near the ground. A baseline of emotional moderation developed within a secure environment helps when faced with significant stress.

In contrast, when the brain is exposed to stressors during this early period, the nervous system wires for a high level of sensitivity and develops strategies of reactivity. A child or pet that experiences neglect, abuse, or other trauma early in life develops an amygdala that monitors for threats at every turn. It becomes normal to be in the hot zone. A new normal can be developed, but it takes a lot of intentional work to do so. The strategies in this book provide the resources to make the job easier.

A Pattern of Stress Reactions

Neural connections are strengthened by repeated experiences, especially those associated with emotional intensity. Patterns of repeated trauma or chronic stress teach the amygdala to be always on high alert. This doesn't mean emotional resilience is only possible if we never face stressors. It means that when we do face stressors, big or small, we want our nervous system to interpret them correctly and take appropriate action.

Taking timeouts as effective self-care strategies trains our nervous system to interpret correctly and take appropriate action. Each time we choose to take a timeout for self-care, we provide a positive experience to support our autonomic nervous system's ability to return to the cool zone.

Stress and Stress Reactions

People who have typical childhoods develop patterns of stress reactions based on repeated exposure to relatively mild stressors, combined with inherited biological factors. Moderate to strong stressors result in fight, flight, or freeze reactions. For mild to moderate stressors, we add fidget and fool around to the possible reactions.

Fight, Flight, or Freeze

People may engage all the stress reactions—flight, fight, or freeze—at one time or another, but most of us have a primary strategy to keep ourselves safe. Recognizing your hot zone response equips you to modify your strategies when you notice unhelpful stress reactions.

> **QUIZ: KNOW YOUR HOT-ZONE COPING STRATEGY**
>
> Pay attention to your gut response as you read the scenario below.
>
> Imagine you are in an argument with someone important, for example, your parent, partner, or boss. They yell at you. Which of the following are your most likely responses?
>
> 1. You feel your muscles tighten. Ready to stand your ground, you yell back and try to appear bigger. (Fight.)
> 2. Your stomach churns and you feel shaky. You shrink back and leave as soon as possible. (Flight.)

> 3. Your brain goes blank, and you feel like a deer caught in the headlights. You get quiet and hope they stop soon. (Freeze.)
>
> Can you identify the primary hot zone coping strategies of the people and animals in your life by observing their behaviors?

Fidget and Fool Around

Mild stressors can result in fidget and fool around responses. Both behaviors indicate discomfort is building.

Fidgeting

Humans sometimes fidget when they experience mild anxiety. Fidgeting is a self-soothing behavior that releases stress with bodily movement.

Think about a time when you were asked a question you didn't know the answer to, or when your attention span in a meeting began to wane. Did you tap your fingers, jiggle a knee, click a ballpoint pen? Fidgeting helps you lower your stress level and refocus your attention.

Children and animals fidget when they're in new situations or when they don't know what's expected of them. Pets may scratch, chew, sniff, self-groom, or vocalize. All sorts of toys are marketed toward helping humans fidget. Toys marketed to pet fidgeters include food puzzles and items that can be safely shredded or chewed.

Everyone fidgets. It's one of the ways the nervous system tries to displace the stress to move your nervous system back toward the cool zone.

Fooling Around

Fooling around releases stress by diverting attention away from the stressor. Making a joke to diffuse tension, responding with nervous laughter, or changing the subject to a safer topic are all forms of fooling around.

Have you ever noticed your pet become overly excitable in

stressful situations? A puppy may jump up to excessively lick your face, or a kitten may do zoomies around the living room. That's your pet's form of fooling around.

For humans or pets, it's important to recognize what's going on so you can respond appropriately.

An Initial Response to Stress Reactions

When you feel yourself moving into fight, flight, freeze, fidget, or fool around mode, you need to be mindful of your heart rate, your muscle tension, and your breathing to de-stress. You can use the **THRIVE** strategy to enforce a brief pause so you can create an effective timeout. Use the letters in **THRIVE** to remind you of the following:

- **Take time.** Even thirty seconds can make a huge difference.
- **Hear your heart.** Tune in to your heart rate and listen as it slows down.
- **Relax your muscles.** Release the tension in your shoulders, chest, and neck.
- **Inhale.** Slowly inhale through your nose, filling your lungs until you notice your abdomen expand.
- **Visualize.** Picture oxygen entering your body and reaching all the way to your fingers and toes.
- **Exhale.** Slowly exhale through your mouth, letting every part of your body feel the release of breath and tension.

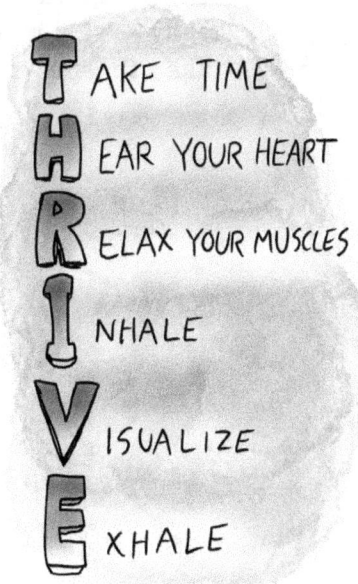

Continue to use **THRIVE** until your nervous system temperature decreases enough for you to think clearly. Once that is accomplished, you're ready to attend to other signals, such as physical symptoms and behavioral changes to create additional awareness of the source of your stress and determine how to best deal with it.

◆ ◆ ◆

Did this chapter feel a bit like a lesson in anatomy? If so, you've aced the test. Yes, the nervous system is complicated, but understanding it is easier using the thermometer and thermostat analogies. Effectively managing life's stressors requires you to recognize your nervous system's temperature and reset it as needed. Applying the **THRIVE** strategy is an excellent way to do this. Get ready to learn more about what causes stress and how to take a timeout from it in the upcoming chapters.

CHAPTER 3

In Your Life

Now that we know what's going on with our brains and our bodies, we can turn to understanding the aspects of life affected by a stress response. By our definition, self-care is the intentional act of attending to our physical, emotional, social, and spiritual well-being with or without the help of professionals. Here's a basic description of each of these aspects.

Physical

Basic physical needs can create stress. Hunger, hydration, and sleep move the nervous system temperature up or down depending on how well they are met.

If physical symptoms or sensations point to a basic need, consider how to meet that need. Is a healthy snack required to

recharge the body's fuel cells? More water? Maybe a quick nap or a good night's sleep is in order. Would physical activity or at least increased movement or stretching help? Rest and relaxation? Would a breathing exercise be helpful?

When you engage in timeouts to address physical needs, you derive an immediate benefit that helps return your nervous system temperature to the cool zone.

Emotional

Fear, anxiety, anger, irritability, and negativity are frequent emotional responses to stressful situations. These feelings are fueled by the adrenal flood that happens in times of stress. A prolonged stressor can result in depression, apathy, and cynicism.

To address these stressors, choose a timeout activity that specifically focuses on improving that emotional state. For example, if your teenager feels sad for underperforming on an important math test, an appropriate timeout option may include one-on-one time with you to talk about the disappointment, or perhaps some play time with a trusted animal companion.

Emotions are neither good nor bad. They are a normal part of everyday life. It's the response to emotion that influences overall well-being. A timeout for emotional care is not so much about making an emotion go away as working through it effectively.

> **SHAUN SAYS:**
>
> After my mother died unexpectedly in 2017, I felt intense grief. I was completing my professional training and had obligations that could not be postponed. One of my dear friends offered to take me to the Oregon coast for a day of walking and crying. It proved to be the best kind of self-care timeout I could have imagined.
>
> I will never stop grieving the loss of my mother. However, I make time for the tears when they show up and honor my mom

> by maintaining some of her favorite traditions, such as making fudge at Christmas and completing crafts with my daughters. These timeouts for self-care allow me to find the joy of living day to day, just as my mother did.

Social

Social situations can be the source of stress and part of the cure. When our nervous system temperature is in the hot zone, we tend to push others away with negative behaviors, withdraw, or overwhelm those around us with too much closeness, neediness, or exuberance.

The way we view ourselves can make us hide at home or lash out in frustration at our children, our animals, and ourselves. An introvert may avoid family members or guests. An extrovert may not be able to contain their enthusiasm when greeting other people. (Wait... are we talking about people or animals? Both!)

When social stress sends a child into the hot zone, they might act disrespectfully. A pet might behave with aggression. It's easy to respond to these behaviors with judgment, but it's important to recognize the source: an unmet need or increased stress because of the social situation.

Consider which timeout options could help reduce social stress. Perhaps some quiet alone time? Or a few hours with a good friend? Expanding one's social environment could be invigorating and exciting.

Are there boundaries that need to be established with certain people or situations to reduce their impact on your overall well-being? Are there social activities that could reduce stress by stimulating intellectual, physical, or spiritual health?

Positive, connected relationships calm the nervous system. Interactions with supportive people are part of maintaining a healthy nervous system temperature. As you evaluate timeout options to address social needs, consider whether the situation could be improved by including a friend.

Spiritual

Spirituality means different things to different people. The authors of this book engaged in many discussions about why and how to include spiritual well-being. Research organizations report that more than 80 percent of people throughout the world identify with a specific religion.[1] Most cultures believe that faith, religious beliefs, or spirituality play an important role in overall well-being.[2][3] So it seems like a no-brainer to address the impact of stress on faith beliefs and spirituality.

A deeper dive into the research revealed that more than half of people in the Western world said that religion plays a smaller role in their life today than twenty years ago.[4] What about those who don't identify with any organized religion? And for a bigger challenge, how would this apply to pets? Thankfully, many people have come up with insights to these questions.

For our discussion, we're using the definition Dr. Brown introduced in *The Gifts of Imperfection*. (If you haven't read this book, make it a timeout priority.) "Spirituality is recognizing and celebrating that we are all inextricably connected to each other by a power greater than all of us, and that our connection to that power and to one another is grounded in love and compassion. Practicing spirituality brings a sense of perspective, meaning, and purpose to our lives."[5]

Stress makes the body hurt. It tanks the emotional system. It tells us to keep people at a distance. Sometimes the stress of everyday life makes it difficult to engage in spiritual practices. In more extreme situations, it can challenge core beliefs.

Research shows that faith—and spirituality in a broader sense—is a resilience factor in managing persistent stress. When you notice changes in your spiritual life, you have a choice: act or drift into apathy. Making time for spiritual self-care is another way to press the reset button and return your nervous system temperature to the cool zone.

Take a moment to reflect on spiritual factors that could be contributing to stress in your life. Are you feeling disconnected from things that provide meaning and purpose? Do you sense a break in connection with the beauty of the world around you? Is there a rift in your relationship with yourself, others, or your pets? Would time set aside for spiritual practices help reduce your feelings of stress?

◆ ◆ ◆

Stressors may impact any aspect of life: physical, emotional, social, or spiritual. You may find that you need to take a timeout for self-care to attend to one or more aspects multiple times a day. You will be your best self when you care for all aspects.

CHAPTER 4

Your Basic Strategy

Becoming aware of stressors and responding to them appropriately involves assessing the central nervous system's temperature and resetting your thermostat by engaging effective self-care habits. In this chapter, we offer a basic tool for evaluating the physical, emotional, social, and spiritual aspects of life that impact your overall well-being. We call it the **A+ Model**.[1] We refer to this model throughout the book to help you apply the strategies you're learning. We've provided an A+ worksheet for you in Bonus for Timeouts. Here's a summary of the steps:

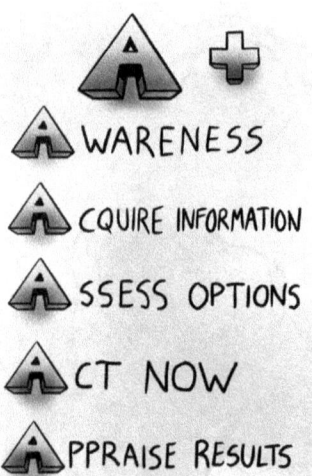

- **Awareness** of internal state (yours, your children's, your pet's).
- **Acquire** information (by collecting observable, objective, specific facts).
- **Assess** your options (what tools are available to address the situation or need).
- **Act** now (implement one or more of the options).
- **Appraise** the results and adjust if necessary.

Here are some guidelines for applying the **A+ Model**.

Awareness of Internal State

In this step, take note of what is happening inside you, your child, or your pet in the given moment. Being aware of your internal state is an important first step in determining the appropriate preventative measure or responding to the circumstance causing you stress.

Check Your Temperature

When you and your loved ones are in the cool zone, everyone feels calm and life goes smoothly. When you become overwhelmed by stress, you move into the hot zone. The same is true for all family members.

Let's say it's October, and you're feeling good about your organized routine. The kids have adjusted to school, your job is going well, the house is clean, and your dog loves going on daily walks with you. Holidays are coming up and that will mean additional demands on your time, resulting in tension and fatigue for you and your human and animal family members. Schedules will become chaotic, finances stretched, and guests coming and going will stress out everyone, all of which will get in the way of fully enjoying the season. Your nervous system temperature is warm but not overheating—yet. Assuming history repeats itself, you know that by the second week of December, you'll be in the hot zone.

October and December offer different situations, so different types of timeouts are needed. Autumn is a good time to practice preventative timeouts so you can enter the holiday season ready for the escalating stressors. If you wait until the stress level rises, you will need immediate relief, but your brain may not be working well enough to take positive action.

When you're in the hot zone, you won't be able to use the **A+ Model** effectively. If a bear is chasing you in the woods, you don't need a timeout for self-care; you need to run! In non-life-threatening situations, it's imperative to cool down the temperature before taking the next step. This brings your prefrontal cortex back online, helping you make good decisions.

Identify Physical Symptoms

Physical sensors provide clues that a timeout is needed. These include a change in heart rate, altered breathing, muscle tension across the jaw, neck, and shoulders, increased skin moisture, a churning stomach, body aches and pains. The body scan, described in Chapter 26 -Relaxing Your Muscles, is a good technique for identifying physical stressors.

While physical symptoms are often easy to identify, you may also notice mood changes. An overloaded nervous system often causes irritability, irrational anger, anxiety, depression, apathy, a sense of dread, increased negativity, pessimism, or cynicism.

To assess the physical stress level of a family member or pet, you may need to rely on nonverbal clues. Animals and very young children can't use words to let their caregivers know when they're feeling stressed. Their body language is the primary indicator that it's time to press the reset button to return to a more relaxed state.

Observe Behavioral Changes

How are you or your family members acting? Are there tantrums or emotional outbursts? Increased clinginess or aloofness? Unusually high or low energy levels? Hyperactivity or lethargy? Too much or too little excitement? All these signal that something is going on with the internal state.

What about social interactions? Are you feeling withdrawn or avoiding social contact? Are your children acting out in their relationships? Does your pet's behavior change when other people or animals are present? Are family members talking too much or too little? Interrupting? Acting impulsively? Are pets barking, meowing, or neighing incessantly? If so, check the reading on the nervous system thermometer.

Acquire Information

Now that you're noticing what's happening internally, you need to collect data to create an effective timeout for self-care that's appropriate for the situation.

Where is the stress coming from and how can it be addressed? For example, if your grandchild is having a meltdown because he didn't eat his cereal at breakfast, putting him down for a nap will probably end up in more tears and tantrums. A more effective solution would be to provide a nutritional snack.

Here are some questions to help you collect the correct information:

- What situations, activities, expectations, or other factors typically send the person's or pet's nervous system into the hot zone?
- Is there a basic physical need that needs attention, such as hunger or sleep?
- Are there too many, too little, or inappropriate social expectations or interactions?
- Are there specific people or animals that impact stress, both positively and negatively?
- How many commitments, responsibilities, activities, and events are scheduled? Is this a reasonable expectation?
- Is there financial pressure associated with the situation?
- Are there emotional needs or responses to be considered?
- Is the stress a response to painful memories or traumatic events?
- Have spiritual needs been met? Is there a need for connection to self or others?

Assess Your Options

Now that you've collected as much information as you can, you're equipped to determine what your options are. Ask yourself: *What can I do to help myself, my family members, or my pets take a timeout for self-care? What strategies are available to me?* Determine what type of intervention will be most helpful in your current situation. Do you need immediate stress relief so you can think more clearly? Are you hoping to establish a lifelong habit? Many of the suggestions in this book are even more beneficial when used daily. This helps reduce or prevent the reactivity that results in a return to stress. The repetition of an effective timeout for self-care leads to a lifetime of improved well-being.

Act Now

This is where you try various strategies to determine what works best for you and your family members. When in doubt, the **THRIVE** strategy is always a great place to start.

When you take timeouts for self-care as part of your daily routine, you recalibrate your nervous system to decrease the level of reactivity to low-level stressors. As you repeat these practices, they rewire your brain and become lifelong habits. This is the ultimate in preventative care.

Appraise the Results and Adjust if Necessary

Some strategies work short-term and others long-term. For example, if you take a deep breath, you experience an instant cooling down of your nervous system's temperature. This provides immediate relief. Other practices, such as repeating positive affirmations, may take a while to learn on the road to becoming beneficial lifelong habits.

Look at the information you acquired and used to choose a timeout option. Did the strategy change things for the better? Have the physical signs of distress lessened? Do you feel better prepared for future stressors? Are subsequent behaviors more aligned with a cooler temperature? Did the strategy address the correct source of stress? Answering these questions helps you determine the effectiveness of the option(s) you selected.

If the timeout you chose didn't quite hit the mark, try again. You may need several repetitions of the **A+ Model** to develop effective timeouts that work for you, your family, and your pets, but it will be worth it. Give yourself and your family members permission to try new things. Everyone will benefit.

> An A+ worksheet is provided for you in Bonus for Timeouts. Use it to apply the timeout strategies discussed in the upcoming chapters.

Using the **A+ Model** is an effective way to begin your self-care journey. It guides you to attend to what's happening inside and outside your body so you can choose the most effective strategy for your timeout. Think of it as a life skill. Once you get the hang of it, it will become an automatic problem-solving approach. A big bonus is that it can be a powerful tool for the whole family.

PART 1 WRAP-UP

Part 1 explored how the brain and body work together to manage stress. We discussed how to pay attention to the nervous system's temperature so we know when to take a timeout. We acknowledged how stress affects all aspects of our lives: physically, emotionally, socially, and spiritually. We introduced the **A+ Model** for creating and using effective timeouts.

Now it's time to look at specific stressors for adults, children, adolescents, and pets, and the unique timeout needs for each group.

PART 2
Timeouts for Adults

We're diving into timeouts for adults as an extension of the theme of buckling up and securing your oxygen mask first. Calm, respectful, and purposeful interactions with others are based on engaging the parasympathetic nervous system, which allows access to higher-order thinking. The resulting creativity and problem-solving abilities are tools adults need to respond to life's stressors. Later in the book we'll talk about facilitating timeouts for children, adolescents, and pets, all of which require adult supervision and perspective.

Part 2—Timeouts for Adults builds on the basics presented in Part 1. It looks at the stressors faced in adulthood and suggests timeout strategies that allow you to reset and return your nervous system temperature to the cool zone—exactly what's needed to help you live a healthier life overall.

CHAPTER 5

But I'm an Adult, Right?

The adult years span approximately seven decades and include a variety of life tasks. It's a broad category—perhaps too broad when considering our need for timeouts. We grow and develop both mentally and physically throughout life. Our reasons for taking timeouts remain constant, yet the circumstances that prompt them change as we age.

To provide a more nuanced look at what it means to be an adult, we'll break adulthood down into five stages: emerging adulthood, early adulthood, middle adulthood, late adulthood, and elderhood. We'll touch on the physical, emotional, social, and spiritual characteristics along with the common stressors associated with the life tasks of each stage.

You'll probably slot yourself into a specific stage, and in addition, we're certain the information from the other stages will help you better understand those around you. Let's get started.

Emerging Adulthood (ages 18-25)

This is an energetic and exciting time of life. Individuals in this category are generally healthy and looking forward to exercising the independence they longed for during their teen years. This stage coincides with the maturation of the human brain, particularly the frontal lobe, which provides the ability to make thoughtful decisions, inhibit problematic behaviors, and manage one's emotions.

One key psychosocial question[1] asked during this stage is "Who am I?" This question is answered as emerging adults continue to differentiate from their family of origin while refining their likes, dislikes, and values. Their political and spiritual views face challenges from exposure to a broader worldview. A growing sense of purpose may be shaped by a deeper understanding of the human condition and a desire to make the world a better place.

Another important question faced by emerging adults is "Will I be loved?" Enlarging their social circles through job and college experiences provides opportunities to answer this question. Friends may become more important than the family of origin. Emerging adults begin to establish committed relationships and look forward to the perks of adulthood, including making their own decisions about life and establishing homes of their own.

Yet the life tasks in this formative stage come with their own unique stressors. Many emerging adults encounter the costs and responsibilities of independent living for the first time. Finding

work that supports their interests, abilities, and aptitudes may be challenging. Financial stressors may include finding a way to pay for a college education or to start a family. A childhood pet may come to the end of its life about this time. Losing a pet who has been a companion during childhood and adolescence adds grief and loss of nostalgic connections to childhood to the responsibilities of emerging adulthood.

Taking a timeout during these years may mean finding ways to deal with the stress of meeting short-term goals as well as taking the time to reflect and focus on one's skills and abilities for achieving long-term goals. Getting into the habit of taking timeouts now builds the foundation for taking timeouts later and provides lifelong benefits.

Early Adulthood (ages 25-45)

Early adults are typically focused on work, relationships, and families. This is the stage when many begin to achieve their goals of establishing a career and building a home and family of their own. During early adulthood, physical health remains stable, allowing individuals to focus on other needs. However, as they approach their forties, the effects of aging become more apparent.

The adult brain has completed its most dramatic growth, the nervous system has developed a set of coping strategies for dealing with adult responsibilities, and yet the brain remains capable of meaningful change. New skills are learned, and new thought patterns continue to develop. Early adults seek out activities that bring meaning and purpose.

The questions "Who am I?" and "Will I be loved?" remain important, but the answers are becoming clearer. Social relationships expand to include people from their romantic partner's circle and the parents of their children's friends. The community provides additional opportunities for interaction through shared activities, religious gatherings, and work assignments.

During this stage, many people choose to bring pets into their lives for companionship and reliable relationships. This choice should be based on the knowledge that the pet is a good fit for both family and lifestyle. The time, expense, and energy needed to care for the pet are key factors in this decision.

> **KELSEY SAYS:**
>
> As a dog trainer, I work with dog owners from all stages of life, including children. Sometimes my own perceptions get in the way by thinking people in a certain life stage shouldn't get a dog. Then I meet fantastic owners who prove me wrong.
>
> Criteria like age, schedule, physical ability, familial status, etc. don't determine whether you should get a pet. Rather, they determine which pet would be the best fit for you.
>
> Many animal species cohabitate nicely with humans. They differ in the amount of physical strength and coordination required to manage them. They also differ in the financial resources and habitat setup needed to support them. There's a lot to consider. On the plus side, a pet will add companionship, responsibility, enrichment, and connection with other animal enthusiasts into your daily life. On the minus side, a pet will introduce elements of physical, emotional, social, and financial stress.
>
> The best advice I can offer for when to get a pet is to evaluate what you have to give to a pet and research which ones would appreciate that level of care. If your pet is happy and healthy, and you are providing care within your means, you're likely to have a fulfilling relationship with your animal.

While achieving the goals of early adulthood can be immensely satisfying, the life tasks of this stage bring their own unique stressors. Adulting becomes real. Living expenses may increase through the purchase of a home, new vehicles, or the latest technology.

These are the primary child-raising years—from birth through high school graduation. They may come with the stress of ensuring that children receive an appropriate education along with encouraging their involvement in extracurricular activities. There may be an added financial burden to save for a child's college education or to begin retirement financial planning.

During this time, some adults become part of a demographic known as the sandwich generation with responsibility for both their children and aging family members. Divorce or separation may disrupt family relationships.

Additionally, it's important to recognize the shifts in attitudes toward marriage over the past several years. University professor Peter McGraw asserts "the societal narrative presenting marriage as a pathway to fulfillment overlooks the rich diversity of life choices."[2] He further distinguishes between singles still looking for Mr. or Ms. Right and those he calls "solos" who celebrate their autonomy while remaining connected to those around them.[3] At this stage of life, he encourages singles to "take care of the foundational elements that make up well-being: health, [financial security], and social connections."[4]

Columnist Jean Guerreto of the *Los Angeles Times* echoes McGraw's themes. She dreads going home for the holidays due to family pressure to marry and have children. While rejecting the shame her family attempts to place on her for remaining single, she affirms the value of a single lifestyle. She states, "Women without kids have more time, energy, and financial resources to fight the many threats we face . . . [we] are prioritizing larger society."[5]

The stressors of early adulthood highlight the need for timeouts. This may mean setting aside time to practice self-care strategies that help prevent one from feeling overwhelmed by life's demands. The concept of work/life balance comes into play here. Implementing timeout strategies during this stage reduces stress later in life.

WHEN ARE YOU GOING TO...
"When are you going to get married?"
"When are you going to have children?"

People ask these questions out of concern, curiosity, or just to make small talk. To the recipient they can feel intrusive and demanding. Culturally, we are indoctrinated from early childhood about expected sequences of life tasks. Remember the childhood rhyme "First comes love, then comes marriage, then comes the baby in a baby carriage"? That's how life is "supposed" to be done, and it has held true for many generations. Yet 2020 census data show an emerging alternative.[6]

Many women in the Generation X and Millennial categories prioritize personal and career goals over starting a family. As more individuals question the financial, logistical, and philosophical aspects of having children, they marry later and have children later. This deviation from the expected pattern may create conflict with those who are at a different stage of life.

Overall, those in the emerging and early stages of adulthood deal with economic and social circumstances that are vastly different today than they were a few decades ago, and this influences their ability and desire to meet expected cultural milestones.

It's important to respect the decisions others make about their lives even if you don't understand or agree with them. For those in a later stage of adulthood, this may involve loss of the future you envisioned for your loved ones. Accept that they are living their values and managing their lives to the best of their ability. Ask about their interests and goals but avoid communicating disappointment if they haven't followed cultural norms.

Middle Adulthood (ages 46-66)

This stage provides opportunities to look back and forward.

In the physical realm, this is when many begin to experience the effects of aging. Some may exhibit symptoms of mild cognitive decline.

Psychosocial success involves answering the questions: "Am I making a difference in the world?" "Have I invested myself in the right priorities?" and "Have I made adequate progress toward achieving my life's goals?" Answering these questions requires carving out time to reflect on who the person wanted to be, where they wanted to go, and their progress toward these goals. It also means contemplating the deeper meaning of life.

With or without children, those in midlife encounter a variety of stressors. Retirement is looming, but financial concerns come from other sources as well. Economic uncertainties may disrupt savings plans. Health issues may impact careers and hobbies. Remaining flexible is key to keeping your nervous system in the cool zone during this time.

For those who chose to have children, empty-nest syndrome may challenge spousal relationships as focus on the children pivots to focus on each other. Now there is time to resume activities the couple enjoyed before having children or find new interests to appreciate together. Some partners continue to feel the squeeze of the sandwich generation, attending to the needs of both their aging parents and their maturing children. Entering a second marriage may create additional stress.

Taking a timeout in this stage means addressing practical daily needs, such as nutrition, rest, and relaxation. It includes "me" time, family time, and vacation time. Many find a renewed interest in fitness activities and a heart-healthy diet. Work/life balance remains important. They may also continue to implement the timeout strategies developed during the earlier stages of life.

Late Adulthood (ages 66+)

Viewing late adulthood as a new adventure is a positive way to approach this stage. Many are leaving the workforce and looking forward to an extended period of leisure. Reinventing themselves outside their careers is where the adventure begins. With more time, self-knowledge, and hopefully, wisdom, late adulthood can be an immensely satisfying time of life. On a more serious note, the transition to retirement may be accompanied by a sense of loss—of structure, identity, friendships, and purpose.

Adults in this stage may ask "Did I live a meaningful life?" and "Am I leaving a legacy?" Answering these questions means reflecting on important events and relationships. It requires reassessing one's interests, abilities, and aptitudes, and determining how to apply them in this stage of life. It means sharing wisdom and knowledge with the next generation through family stories, volunteering, or scrapbooking. Some may enjoy a second career based on a hobby they enjoyed prior to entering the workforce.

Life tasks in late adulthood include end-of-life planning and preparation of documents such as a will, advance-care directives, and living trusts. Empty-nest couples may move from a family home into a retirement community. Older adults living alone may rely on pets for companionship. Some retirees become caregivers for grandchildren or aging parents. (See Chapter 10 – When Others Depend on Me for tips on managing these responsibilities.)

By late adulthood, the brain and nervous system pathways are more rigid. However, thanks to neuroplasticity, people in this stage can maintain cognitive health by continuing to learn new things and staying physically active. The National Institutes of Health recommends staying socially connected and managing stress.[7]

A study by The National Institutes of Health, "Growing Older in America," suggests that maintaining a healthy lifestyle is important to both happiness and longevity after retirement.[8] Good sleep and nutrition habits contribute to quality of life during late adulthood. Even when older adults have been in fair to excellent health overall, they are more likely to experience serious illnesses in this stage.[9] Emotional problems as well as cognitive decline may surface. Attending to one's physical and mental health remains important.

Retirement may feel like one big timeout from adult responsibilities; however, self-care in late adulthood means creating opportunities for mental and social stimulation. Finding an exercise program that accommodates the physical changes of aging is a good strategy. Timeouts for physical and mental well-being will be most beneficial when they create a renewed sense of purpose and meaning.

> **SHAUN SAYS:**
>
> A certain amount of aging is dependent on one's mindset. Both of my grandmothers, Sugar Cookie Grandma and Grandma Bessie, played important roles in my childhood. I loved them both, and I knew they loved me unconditionally.
>
> They taught me things I have taken into my Mema role with my own grandchildren. My grandkids sit on the countertop while making sugar cookies, and we always taste the dough before cutting out the shapes. I take my grandkids camping and share puzzles and crafts with them, (although I have yet to put a worm on a fishing hook as Grandma Bessie did so patiently). This is the legacy shared from generation to generation by loving grandmothers.
>
> My two grandmothers lived very different lives. When I was in first grade, Sugar Cookie Grandma told me, "I just don't know how much of me is left." She lived fifty more years believing her time was almost up. Grandma Bessie, on the other hand, laughed easily and was fearless. She danced at her eightieth birthday party and loved the family trip to Hawaii. Even when hospitalized for the stomach cancer that eventually ended her life, she was an encouragement to the people around her.
>
> My grandmas faced many of the same challenges. They were single for most of their adult lives. They lived on a fixed income. They had good but not perfect health. They held strong faith beliefs and were deeply loved by their families. One held a fixed mindset, the other a growth mindset. I prefer to choose growth. Live well, think big, and embrace adventure!

Elderhood (loss of independent living)

Late adulthood mingles into elderhood when people reach a point in life where they need assisted living or memory care. During this stage they may come face-to-face with their mortality. This is a time for looking back and letting go as they evaluate their relationships, accomplishments, and whether they found purpose during their lives. They are likely to value people, things, and activities that provide physical and emotional comfort.

Social connections remain important during this stage. However, death of a partner, siblings, and longtime friends brings grief and is a reminder of the limited time left on earth. Health problems, cognitive changes, and increased dependence on family members or other caregivers are typical stressors. Therapy animals accompanied by competent handlers may bring comfort during this stage.

Interacting with Someone in a Different Stage

Every season of life brings unique experiences and challenges. Views of the world are significantly dependent on one's current developmental stage. This can lead to what is known as the generation gap. Friction can build when different generations live or work together. Understanding and compassion may reduce these tensions.

> **PRO TIP: DOS AND DON'TS FOR POSITIVE INTERACTIONS**
>
> Do:
> - **Respect those with whom you interact.** Let them be who they are and not what you want them to be.
> - **Provide support rather than advice.** Asking, "What can I do to help?" is better than stating, "You should ..." or "Why don't you ...?"
> - **Foster curiosity.** Showing interest is a way to build empathy.

- **Learn to live with ambiguity.** You can't fix people or manipulate their circumstances to provide favorable outcomes. Whatever will be, will be. Or in the words of the Ray Evans song popularized by Doris Day, "Que Será, Será."
- **Respect others' boundaries.** Let them make the choices they need to manage their lives and those of their families. This can be hard on older adults who want to remain involved in their children's and grandchildren's lives, but it is essential to developing respectful relationships.

Don't:

- **Ask others when they plan to reach certain life milestones.** While the biological clock is always ticking, a general timeline for completing life tasks is much less rigid. Ask instead about current interests and activities.
- **Use judgments when talking about your successes.** There is no "should" here. Others will achieve their own success on their timeframe, not yours. The playing field isn't level, and not everyone enters adulthood with the same advantages or goals. Give others the grace to develop their lives the way they see fit.
- **Give advice unless specifically asked.** Empathy and/or sympathy is always appropriate. Telling others how to live their lives is not.

CHARLENE SAYS:

It's normal for us to feel anxious about our family members. My three sisters and I found mantras an effective way to quell this apprehension. Here is one I used often as my children, nieces, and nephews moved from high school through college and into their first jobs:

> May they find guidance when they are in situations they don't understand.
>
> May they find leadership when they are asked to do things they've never done before.

> May they find direction and insight when the path before them is uncertain.
>
> May solutions present themselves when there are problems that make things difficult.

I have no way of knowing whether this mantra helped any of my family members pass an exam, find a long-term relationship, or land a good job. What I do know is that it gave me a timeout from the anxiety I felt about their situations. The words instilled trust that they had the intelligence, skills, and abilities to make good decisions. As a result, I was able to let go of my stress and enjoy them for who they were.

◆ ◆ ◆

Adulthood involves a progression through many life stages. Each one has its accompanying stressors and needs for timeouts. Thanks to neuroplasticity, the ability to take timeouts can be developed or improved throughout your life and can reduce stress in the process. Commit to a lifestyle that includes timeouts.

CHAPTER 6

Building a Healthy Foundation

There are many things that impact physical well-being. Three areas easy to address are nutrition, sleep, and exercise, and they're also easy to incorporate into any routine or lifestyle. This chapter presents some techniques for taking a timeout when you sense your nervous system temperature rising into the hot zone due to unmet physical needs.

CHARLENE SAYS:

Throughout my life I've been tempted to sacrifice self-care for the sake of earning more money. I suspect this is common.

When I entered the workforce, I quickly learned that working overtime and holidays brought in a few extra dollars. As I began a serious career, I used to eat lunch at my desk and worked overtime to complete my projects ahead of schedule, wanting to look like a stellar employee to my boss. This, of course, left little time for recreation and socializing with friends. I lacked physical exercise, even though I worked for companies with free in-house gyms and proximity to walking trails.

Looking back, I realize I had poor boundaries around the expectations I perceived my bosses had of me as well as the expectations I had of myself. I didn't have to eat lunch at my desk to be thought of as a good employee. And finishing work before a deadline? That was just me trying to outshine my coworkers.

I've come to understand the value of building a healthy foundation for daily living. I give myself permission to eat lunch in a relaxed setting away from work tasks and I may read for a few minutes. I take walks before preparing dinner to transition from the day's tasks to relaxing with family over a meal. Refreshing and restoring my body and soul keeps my nervous system temperature in the cool zone and helps me show up as my best self at work and at home.

Nutrition

Good nutrition supports your body's needs which in turn contributes to a positive mood. It keeps you from becoming "hangry," that is, irritable from hunger. Additional benefits include reduced risk of disease and health-related complications, such as high blood pressure and high cholesterol. Nutrition improves your ability to fight off or recover from illness or injury, and it provides the energy you need for living.[1] Taking time out for nutrition is a high priority.

Because adequate nutrition is a public health concern, the United States Department of Agriculture has established the MyPlate dietary guidelines[2] for consumption of fruits, vegetables, grains, protein, and dairy products. These guidelines work for many people, though those with specific dietary needs may be given different instructions by their physicians.

Following any guideline takes planning. Having a healthy

snack on hand prevents you from picking up whatever is nearby that may be less nutritious. Not skipping meals helps you maintain stable blood glucose levels and adequate energy.

Sleep

Restful sleep is believed to improve memory, generate creativity, reduce the visual effects of aging, and protect against diseases, including Alzheimer's.[3] It also increases your ability to manage stressors, project a positive mood, interact with others more effectively, and maintain a healthy weight.[4] During sleep, your subconscious mind is hard at work transferring information from short-term to long-term memory. It processes daily experiences, sometimes through dreams.

Professionals don't always agree on the optimum hours of sleep, though seven hours is believed to have positive health outcomes for most adults.[5] Be sure to get quality sleep and the right numbers of hours to function at your best.

Specific habits, or sleep hygiene, assist in promoting healthy sleep. See Bonus for Timeouts, Sleep Hygiene for additional tips on getting a good night's sleep.

Exercise and Movement

Our hunter-gatherer ancestors were naturally active. Through urbanization, city folk became more sedentary. Factory and office work are much less strenuous than agricultural labor. Electronics and entertainment options add to a sedentary lifestyle, so we must schedule times to exercise to obtain the same health benefits taken for granted by previous generations.[6]

The benefits of physical exercise include improved cognitive function, better bodily function, restful sleep patterns, and an increased sense of well-being.[7] Exercise is one of the most effective ways to recover from a stressful event, though it can seem challenging at the moment. By engaging in physical exercise on a regular basis, you can discharge built-up stress.

A healthy exercise program need not be arduous. It doesn't require a gym membership or specialized equipment, although some find these helpful. The benefits of exercise can be obtained from a mere thirty minutes of movement a day.[8] A simple walking program is a good place to start. Include a more intensive workout or a fitness class for added benefit if you're feeling up for it.

> **EXERCISING WITH YOGA**
>
> Yoga is a type of exercise that involves intentional fluid movements, balance, and strength. One of its goals is to improve the mind-body connection. Many yoga classes emphasize breathing and guided meditation. While it originated as a meditative practice within the Hindu faith, yoga doesn't require adherence to any religious tradition. Anyone can benefit.
>
> Here are some of the known benefits of yoga:[9]
>
> - Improved strength, balance, and flexibility
> - Relief of back pain
> - Reduced arthritis symptoms
> - Improved heart health
> - Improved sleep
> - Increased energy and brighter moods
> - Reduced stress
> - Connection with community
> - Better self-care
>
> Yoga classes range from easy to strenuous, including chair yoga for those with limited flexibility. Try out a few and see which ones help you reset and restore your mind-body connection.

Exercising in Nature

An exercise routine that includes time outdoors enjoying nature has both physical and psychological benefits. Some of the stress-reducing benefits of exercising outside are:[10]

- **Improved cognition.** Persons exposed to natural environments have better working memory, cognitive flexibility, and attention control.
- **Brighter mood.** Contact with nature is associated with increases in happiness, subjective well-being, positive social interactions, and a sense of meaning and purpose. Exposure to nature includes being outdoors, video and photos of nature, sounds of nature, and even virtual reality.

Exercising with Your Children

Many families schedule playdates for exercise activities, for example, taking children to indoor or outdoor gyms or enrolling them in swim lessons or dance. Youth sports are a big draw once children demonstrate the coordination required to be successful. While the children are performing these activities, the adults frequently supervise from the sidelines, socializing with other parents. If the activity doesn't require parental supervision, adults may use the time to run errands or catch up on household chores.

If you and your children are busy with separate activities, try adding some exercise together. A neighborhood nature walk is a great place to start. Once children have learned to ride bicycles, plan a family outing along a safe route. Visit the local pool or skating rink as a family. Be sure to plan ahead, because everyone is going to want a nutritious snack during or after the outing.

> **SHAUN SAYS:**
>
> Some of my happiest memories are the parents versus children games after soccer practice. We lived in a neighborhood with dozens of families of similar ages, and the team of kiddos was coached by two of the dads. The competition could get quite wild. There's nothing like watching a seven-year-old kid bending it like Beckham to get past the other team's defenders.

Exercising with Your Pets

Many people add an animal to their lives to enhance their exercise routines. Walking with a dog or guiding them through an agility competition are excellent exercise opportunities. Anyone who has animals on acreage knows about the physical labor that goes into the maintenance of packs, flocks, and herds. Some pets don't require human involvement in their exercise routine, but most small animals and indoor pets benefit from engaging in physical activity with you. They provide external motivation for people to get up and get out of the house.

PRO TIP: COMPLEMENTARY EXERCISE NEEDS

When deciding which pet would be the best fit for you, be sure to consider an animal that matches or complements your exercise needs. If you get a pet with high exercise needs because you envision a rigorous fitness program, you may be asking for frustration down the road. Begin building up your own exercise habits to the desired level, and then add a pet that will enjoy participating with you.

Physical Well-Being throughout Your Lifetime

Your basic health and wellness needs will change throughout your lifetime. Good nutrition and sleep are important at any stage; however, your exercise routine may change as you grow older. Seek out age-appropriate routines. When you're ready to retire, use your additional waking hours constructively—don't become a couch potato!

You will find the time and effort needed to develop a healthy foundation is worth it when it leads to a more satisfying life. Repetition solidifies these practices until they become lifelong habits.

Taking a timeout for self-care is important, so be aware of the societal pressure to ignore these needs for other priorities. Yielding to this pressure may reduce your well-being in the long term. Caring for your physical needs keeps up your spirits, increases your energy, and maintains your nervous system temperatures in the cool zone. By taking timeouts to meet your physical needs, you'll lead a healthier and happier life.

> **APPLYING A+ TO BUILDING A HEALTHY FOUNDATION**
>
> Refer to the **A+ Model** discussed in Chapter 4: Your Basic Strategy and use it to map out the various ways you can improve your physical well-being. Use the A+ worksheet provided in Bonus for Timeouts to facilitate this process.

CHAPTER 7

Keeping My Cool

Yup! We're going to go there. We're going to talk about emotions because understanding them is foundational to emotional well-being. The National Institutes of Health describe emotional well-being as the ability to appropriately handle life's stresses, adapt to change, and respond positively to difficult times.[1] It enables you to share your emotions with others, set boundaries without feeling guilty, and relax. A prime benefit is feeling good about who you are.[2] A lack of emotional well-being has serious consequences. It may result in a long-term feeling of dissatisfaction with life and may develop into illnesses such as hypertension, gastrointestinal reflux, and reduced immunity.

In this chapter, we'll define emotion, discuss how to name emotions, and suggest strategies for regulating emotions. In other words, we'll talk about how to keep your cool.

Emotion vs. Feeling

Since the terms "emotions" and "feelings" are frequently used as synonyms, it can be helpful to distinguish between them. Emotions arise from your physiological response to what you're currently experiencing. This happens in a nanosecond as your body tries to tell you something about your environment. It frequently results in a fight, flight, or freeze response. A feeling is your brain making sense of this response.[3] For example, if your heart is racing because you were in a near miss accident, you might label the emotion "fear," and you might feel frightened. In contrast, if it is racing because you're about to welcome a family member home for the holidays, you might label it "anticipation" and you might feel excited. So, the emotion is physical followed by the brain making sense of the situation, helping you understand how you feel. Your body responds to the physical sensation. Your brain interprets it based on the context.

Naming Emotions

Naming emotions contributes to emotional regulation and life satisfaction. American psychologist, Dr. Paul Ekman, who served as a consultant to the Disney PIXAR movie *Inside Out*, has identified seven universal emotions: anger, contempt, disgust, enjoyment, fear, sadness, and surprise.[4] These emotions are always accompanied by physiological changes indicating a shift toward the hot zone. Responses include increased heart rate, rapid breathing, goosebumps, hair rising on the back of one's neck, and sweaty palms, among others. Dr. Ekman's research also confirmed that the facial expressions associated with these feelings are consistent across cultures.

Understandably, the universal emotions exist along a spectrum from mild to intense.[5] For example, anger can range from annoyed to furious and surprise can range from interesting to awe inspiring. Being able to pinpoint an emotion along this spectrum is called "emotional granularity."[6] It enables you to use specific language to describe your experiences. In "Calling Emotions by Name," Katrina McCoy explains, "The more accurately we can describe emotional experience and the context in which the experience is happening, the more information we have to decide what will help."[7] Being specific improves interpersonal interactions and an overall sense of emotional well-being. For example, saying "I feel angry," is more effective than saying, "That really pisses me off."

Regulating Emotions

Strong levels of irritability, anxiety, anger, fear, and negativity can occur in a moment, and before we know it, we're responding out of a fight, flight, or freeze mode. If an emotional stressor is prolonged, depression, apathy, and cynicism may set in. When these emotions are recognized, we can regulate them more effectively. Some strategies used to improve emotional health include building resilience, reducing stress, coping with loss, being mindful, and strengthening social connections. You'll note that these strategies overlap with the physical, social, and spiritual aspects discussed in Part 2.

Any emotional response to life or circumstances may cause your nervous system temperature to move into the hot zone. The ability to recognize and deal with emotional stressors results in a more productive, proactive, and peaceful life. Here, we present **Surf the Wave**, spending time with family and friends, and spending time with pets as antidotes to emotional distress.

Surf the Wave

Surf the Wave is a useful strategy for reducing emotional stress and building resilience. Begin by imagining yourself standing on a beach with your emotions rolling toward you like a strong wave. Depending on your assessment of the wave's strength, your first reaction might be to dig in and remain planted in the sand until the wave passes. If you become overwhelmed by the strength of the wave, your second reaction may be to give up and allow yourself to be swept up by the current and washed out to sea. In either case, you're exhausted!

There's a better option. You can **Surf the Wave** by following these steps:

- **See the wave.** If you recognize the physical symptoms generated by the wave of emotions, you'll feel more in control of the experience.
- **Don't panic.** The physiological symptoms you feel are your body's natural process for dealing with a perceived threat. You might feel overwhelmed now, but like the waves on the ocean, emotions ebb and flow. Your stress response can subside as the wave moves out.
- **Choose the right surfboard.** In ocean surfing, every part of

the board matters: the length, weight, shape, and materials. Each component affects how the board responds to your movements as you skim across the wave. Your emotional surfboard could be an act of altruism, sitting in a sunny spot with your cat, a hug from a loved one, or any of a wide array of timeout activities that help you **Surf the Wave**.

- **Be patient with yourself.** Surfing is hard. You'll need time and practice to master the skill. By the time you're ready for a competition, you'll have fallen off the board many times. Your brain has followed the same neural circuits for responding to stress for many years. Now you're rewiring that response. It will take repetition and intensity to develop a new pathway. When you catch yourself falling, get back on the board and try again.
- **Learn from an expert.** You don't have to learn this skill on your own. By reading this book, you already have a good start. Seek out role models who can show you how surfing the wave works in real life. A communication skills class, a support group, or a therapist may help you identify techniques for staying on your emotional surfboard.

> **SHAUN SAYS:**
>
> Choosing the right emotional surfboard looks different for everyone. My parents had been married for 55 years when my mother died unexpectedly in 2017. Grief hit my father in waves and sometimes overwhelmed him. One of the things that brought him comfort was spending time in the barn with Missy, our aging quarter horse. She rested her head on his shoulder while he sobbed, which helped him through his darkest days.

As with all strategies, **Surf the Wave** takes practice. Soon you'll be able to see the wave coming and experience the exhilaration of riding it to the beach.

Spend Time with Friends and Family

Healthy relationships with friends and family are characterized by positivity, encouragement, trust, compassion, and respect. Caring individuals support us daily, help us celebrate life's milestones, and create traditions around holidays.

Unhealthy relationships are characterized by negativity, criticism, distrust, abuse, and disrespect. These individuals aren't there for you when you need them. They may even cause you emotional, psychological, or physical harm.[8]

Emotional well-being is enhanced by spending time in healthy relationships. Plan activities with others. Share meals. Take walks. Set boundaries around unhealthy relationships to protect your emotional and physical well-being. You'll be given additional suggestions in Chapter 8 – Enjoying Others.

Spend Time with Pets

Designating pets as emotional support animals has gained popularity over the years, but with or without this designation, pets can support human well-being. Studies show that positive interactions with pets impacts the human brain by releasing oxytocin (the neurotransmitter associated with feelings of love and attachment) and dopamine (associated with feelings of pleasure and motivation) and reducing cortisol levels (the primary hormone associated with stress).[9]

For many animal enthusiasts, having pets is an engaging and enriching hobby. There are endless facts to learn when caring for animal companions. This opportunity for mental and emotional growth has positive impacts on well-being as well as relationships with others. Plus, pets are fun! Regardless of the species, spending time with animals can provide entertainment and relief from life's other stressors.

Emotional well-being is based on practices that help you develop resilience when dealing with strong emotions. Specifically naming emotions is a good place to start. Training yourself to see the waves of emotion coming and choosing to surf them is a good timeout strategy. Spending time with loved ones and pets also assists with emotional regulation. Now you have some concrete actions to take when you recognize your internal nervous system temperature is rising into the hot zone. Stay cool!

> **APPLYING A+ TO EMOTIONAL RESILIENCE AND REGULATION**
>
> Refer to the **A+ Model** discussed in Chapter 4: Your Basic Strategy and use it to help you keep your cool when dealing with strong emotions. Use the A+ worksheet provided in Bonus for Timeouts to facilitate this process.

CHAPTER 8

Enjoying Others

To better understand social well-being and to mitigate social stress, let's look at the recent research from social neuroscience. First, experts say our brains are wired for social interaction and our need to be in relationship with others is more basic than our need for food or shelter.[1] Second, the need to belong has been identified as a basic human need.[2] In this context, belonging refers to being part of a group or a sense of fitting in with others.

Given this core need, how can we ensure our social needs are met and social interactions with others are safe and affirming? One way to keep your nervous system in the cool zone is to be aware of your social needs and take a timeout for self-care when needed.

This chapter begins with **Vitality Vowels**, a strategy that summarizes engagement in healthy social relationships, followed by more detail on other behaviors that promote social well-being.

Vitality Vowels

Vitality Vowels is a memory device you can use to remember the behaviors that guide your social wellness.[3] Each behavior is represented by one of the vowels of the English language: A, E, I, O, and U. The **Vitality Vowels** stand for awareness, engagement, identification, openness, and unleashing community.

- **<u>A</u>wareness.** Notice when stress is having a negative impact on your social interactions. Using **THRIVE** (introduced in Chapter 2) may help you see the situation more clearly and respond to it more effectively.

Vitality Vowels

Challenge the social impact of stress.

- **A** Awareness
- **E** Engage with others
- **I** Identify safe people
- **O** Openness
- **U** Unleash community

- **Engagement with others.** Being with other people decreases depression and pauses spiraling emotions.[4] This happens because positive interactions with others causes your brain to release oxytocin, the "love and belonging" neurotransmitter. Place yourself in an environment where human contact will happen, even if it's casual. A pleasant verbal interaction, an appropriate touch (for example, a handshake or hug), or a smile go a long way to soothe a stressed-out nervous system.
- **Identification of safe people.** Who do you feel comfortable interacting with? Consider your friends, family members, coworkers, therapists, or even friendly service providers. Many hairdressers jokingly refer to themselves as therapists, and pet trainers sometimes spend more time empathizing with the owners than working with the animals. The conversations don't need to be deep or reveal personal details to be helpful. It's the human connection that counts. Of course, a conversation with someone who is invested in your well-being is always a bonus.
- **Openness.** Choose at least one person with whom you can authentically share the unfiltered truth of your day-to-day

experience. Being known for who you are is a good antidote for stress-induced social impairment.
- **Unleashing community.** All humans and most pets benefit from being part of a social group. Being in a community provides encouragement and support and promotes the flow of feel-good endorphins. If possible, find a group you can interact with on a weekly basis. In addition to social interaction, you'll receive emotional support for your stage of life.

Even if you don't feel like getting out, it's important for you to see others in person. "Safer at home" may have been useful advice during the global pandemic, but it preconditioned us to limit our activities. When you make your world smaller, it continues to get smaller unless you push back.

Identify things you can do comfortably to get out and about. It can be as simple as taking a walk or as complicated as planning a weekend activity with friends. When face to face isn't feasible, make use of video chat. Personal engagement is the key.

> **SHAUN SAYS:**
>
> Memories of the COVID-19 pandemic provide us with an example of how the **Vitality Vowels** work in unique situations. During the prolonged global quarantine, every person on the planet wondered: *How do we stay connected when it might not be safe to get together?* Fortunately, humans are resilient and creative. Thanks to social networks, video conferencing platforms, and the information technology engineers who created them, we learned to do things in new ways.
>
> Many professions transitioned to virtual meeting platforms. (Oh, boy, you should have heard the psychologists panic about that!) Grocery stores and restaurants focused their energy on pickup and delivery services. Classes were held online. Live streaming replaced in-person gatherings for many organizations. Schools and teachers created online curricula to meet students' learning needs.

Entertainment options abounded due to streaming services. Families and friends learned how to use shared screens through video conferencing to play cooperative games. One of my biggest thrills was having my eighty-year-old mother-in-law use the Marco Polo app to send us videos. (She's a pretty high-tech great grandma!)

Here's how our family applied the **Vitality Vowels** when isolated by the pandemic. We were aware of our stress. We found new ways to engage with others. We all identified safe people to engage with—those who didn't make us feel even more stressed. We opened our lives to each other. Virtual work meetings included children and pets, something that never happened prior to the pandemic. We checked on friends and loved ones to take care of each other and lift our spirits and theirs while unleashing community. Overall, the **Vitality Vowels** were extremely helpful during this time.

The Value of Interpersonal Skills

The skills you learned early in life while interacting with family members are the same ones you bring into your adult relationships. You might be surprised when some of these behaviors don't work as well in adulthood to get you the results you need. Effective social skills can be developed during any stage of life. It just takes practice and a genuine desire to develop positive relationships with others. Learning to negotiate expectations and set boundaries is a big part of this. The communication skills of speaking and listening also play a role. Effective interpersonal skills support your social well-being by forming relationships based on mutual respect.

Negotiating Expectations

When expectations are set appropriately, our lives fall into predictable patterns. Routines make us happy when we know what to expect. They make us feel safe and reduce our stress. An unexpected schedule change, a sick family member, a new job, or even an invitation to a social event may disrupt our expectations.

A possible outcome is that we feel frustrated, anxious, or angry.

Negotiating expectations falls into three categories: your expectations of yourself, your expectations of others, and the expectations others have of you.

Take a good look at what you expect from yourself. Are you trying to be a superhero? Are you doing things you don't enjoy because you're trying to look good to someone else—a parent, boss, or partner? Are you reaching for goals because you think you should or because you want to? Hang up the red cape and examine what you can realistically do. Take a timeout to evaluate what you want for yourself and make a realistic plan for getting there.

Next, clarify what you expect from others. Are your expectations realistic? Do they have the knowledge, skills, abilities, and aptitudes to perform to your standards? Do they even know what you're expecting of them? The best way to clarify expectations is to talk to those impacted by them. (Hint: No one can read your mind, so you need to tell them.) Plan a family meeting or a coffee date. Discuss what you need from them and what happens if your expectation isn't met. Explore what might be getting in the way of the expectation not being fulfilled. For example, if you want your teenager to do the dishes every night after dinner, it would be beneficial to understand their homework load. Maybe they need Tuesday nights off because Wednesday morning's math class is brutal. Once all parties have a good understanding of each other's needs and expectations, a plan can be developed to reduce stress for everyone.

Negotiating other's expectations of you can be the hardest part. If you think someone holds unrealistic expectations of you, talk to them. What are their real expectations? Why do you feel like you can't meet them? It may be reasonable for your boss to expect you to be at your desk by 8:00 a.m., but it may not be reasonable to double your workload after your company has let someone else go. A timeout for a respectful conversation will allow both sides to express their views and feelings. Expectations mutually agreed upon can be freeing to both parties.

You're the one who must take the initiative. You do not have the power to control someone else's thoughts or behaviors. You do have control over your reactions.

Setting Boundaries

A physical boundary may be set by a property description, a fence, a "No Trespassing" sign, or a "No Overnight Parking" notice. Social boundaries are more subtle. They are typically communicated through words, body language, and physical space.[5]

Social boundaries define the parameters of our relationships—the way we extend ourselves to others as well as the actions we take to protect ourselves from others. The strength of your boundary depends on the situation and the people involved in the relationship.

Our society values cooperation. We want to come across to others as pleasant and agreeable, even if that causes us social stress. To avoid being labeled self-centered or branded as not a team player, we may comply with others' expectations of us to appear kind and compassionate.

Healthy relationships begin with your physical and mental health. When you feel pressured to expend time and energy on someone else's behalf, it's time to take a timeout for clear communication and setting personal boundaries.

There are endless ways to express how you will not meet their expectations in a polite, yet firm manner. It is okay to say

no or maybe or that you will think about it. You get to determine whether an expectation is unreasonable.

Clarifying expectations and maintaining positive connections with others decreases the possibility for regret or resentment. It brings you freedom to enjoy all the relationships in your life.

NICE PEOPLE DO SAY NO

You have a right to your own decisions. Give yourself permission to say no to requests for your time and provide limited explanations only if you feel comfortable doing so. People may ask for reasons, but that doesn't mean you have to give them.

You are not required to explain yourself to anyone. You can soften your refusal by saying something like "Thanks for thinking of me, but I don't have the bandwidth right now." If you say you have another commitment that precludes you from accommodating their request, they may try to counter by saying, "Oh, you can do that later," or "Can't you reschedule that?" Some may try to guilt you into doing what they want by saying, "We're all working sixty hours a week to get this stage of the project finished. Come on, be a team player."

Be creative in your reply while exuding self-confidence. You may find others appreciate your clarity.

Communicating to Connect

Effective communication supports all areas of life: physical, emotional, social, and spiritual. Speaking assertively improves social well-being by allowing you to express your viewpoint while respecting the rights and beliefs of others. Assertiveness is not aggressiveness; it's an alternative to passiveness. Assertiveness comes from a place of self-confidence. It maintains honest communication while respecting and empathizing with others. Aggressiveness lacks self-confidence and therefore becomes angry or demanding. Passiveness also lacks self-confidence but hides behind timidity or silence.

Common assertive communication techniques include **Fogging**, **Broken Record**, **Yes/And**, and **"I" Messages**.

- **Fogging.** Fogging is giving a vague response when you choose not to engage. If someone makes a comment you disagree with or tries to bring you into an undesirable conversation, you can stay uninvolved by saying something like, "Yeah, I've heard that from several people," and then change the subject or walk away.

- **Broken Record.** This technique is used when someone repetitively misses your intended message. You simply restate your position until the other person hears you and/or gives up.
- **Yes/And.** This technique is an effective, assertive way to add your thoughts and feelings into a conversation in progress. It shows respect for the person speaking and for their thoughts while demonstrating self-confidence in your own position.

> **WHAT A YES/AND CONVERSATION MAY SOUND LIKE**
>
> Friend: I'm concerned the boss isn't taking our recommendations seriously.
>   You: Yes, and maybe we can ask for a department meeting to elaborate on some of our ideas.
>   Or,
>   Child: I'm not going to play with Smitty anymore. He cheats!
>   You: Yes, and let's talk more about what's going on with your games. Maybe we can come up with ways you can continue to enjoy playing together.

- **"I" Messages.** This is a way to express your point of view and draw the other person into problem solving rather than putting them on the defensive.

    1. Place "I" at the beginning of the statement, not "you." ("You" usually triggers a defensive reaction, and the person might not hear what you're trying to say.)
    2. Describe the situation that concerns you.
    3. Express how you feel about the situation as clearly and specifically as you can. (Examples of basic feelings words are: happy, sad, angry, afraid, and ashamed. There are many levels of these basic emotions. Convey the intensity of your emotion and the other person will have a better understanding. For example, anger spans the range of emotions from annoyed to furious. There's a big difference between the two. Avoid vague, non-emotions, such as "meh.")
    4. Summarize the outcome of the situation.
    5. Ask the other person for help in resolving the situation or make a suggestion.

    > **WHAT AN "I" MESSAGE MAY SOUND LIKE**
    >
    > "When I see dirty dishes piled up in the kitchen, I feel frustrated because that means our goal of having everyone put their own dishes into the dishwasher isn't working. Is there something we can do differently to reach this goal?"
    >
    > Or,
    >
    > "When people arrive late to meetings, I feel frustrated because it wastes our time. What can we do to get meetings started on time and respect everyone's project schedules?"

Using assertiveness techniques may feel awkward at first, but they will become second nature with practice. With repetition and intensity, you'll rewire your brain with new responses and experience reduced stress when communicating with others.

Listening with Intention

Social connection with others requires being open and available to them, and them being open and available to you.[6] This includes spending fun times together, feeling listened to and understood, expressing empathy, and sharing conversations with people who hold similar values and share common interests. Connecting with others increases your longevity, strengthens your immune system, and helps alleviate anxiety and depression.[7]

Listening with intention means coming alongside someone and seeing things from their perspective. You may be tempted to view their experiences through your own lens, but mere sympathy rarely draws people to deeper levels of connection. Empathic listening seeks to understand or learn, which helps both parties return their nervous systems to the cool zone.

Here are behaviors involved in listening with intention:[8]

- **Attending.** Establish eye contact with the speaker. Demonstrate positive body language and provide verbal encouragement to show that you're interested in what they're saying. Nod, smile, and make vocalizations, such as "Um-hum," "Okay," and, "I see."
- **Reserving.** Listen with an open mind to better understand what the speaker is saying. Avoid judging. Focus on the whole message and not just a portion that may be triggering for you.
- **Reflecting.** Ensure you understand by reflecting the speaker's words back to them. Rather than responding with a counter thought, ask open-ended questions to clarify the speaker's meaning and intent. The phrases "Tell me more," "Can you give me an example?" and "I'm wondering what the background is on that" open the conversation and allow you to formulate an appropriate response.
- **Clarifying.** To verify your understanding, ask questions like "Did I get that right?" or "Is there anything else?"
- **Summarizing.** Restate the speaker's points using your own

words. Then ask, "Is that what you're saying?" When the speaker feels they've been heard, you can move to the next phase of the conversation.
- **Sharing.** When the speaker is receptive, begin to share your perspective and experience. Circle back with the speaker to ensure you're on target with their concerns.

Listening with intention shows you value the relationship and allows meaningful conversation to take place.

> **WISDOM FROM JULIA CAMERON**
>
> In *The Listening Path*, author Julia Cameron recounts a conversation with her friend, poet James Navé. During their conversation, Navé commented, "People are hungry to be noticed, hungry to be cared about, hungry to be recognized. True listening does all that.... Listening is an act of love. Giving time is an act of deep caring. Giving time means pausing and allowing the silence to hold emerging thoughts. The core of listening is generosity, empathy, graciousness, and patience. Listening delivers a message of respect to those around you."[9]

Pets and Social Well-Being

In addition to enjoying others, social well-being includes enjoying our pets. Whether a dog looks lovingly into your eyes, a cat purrs on your lap, or a lizard cocks his head at you when you walk by the terrarium, having a pet companion provides comfort. Just as humans need companionship, many animal species have similar social needs.

> **ATTENDING TO A PET'S NEEDS**
>
> During the first year of the COVID-19 pandemic, pet purchases and adoptions skyrocketed to record-setting numbers. When told to shelter in place, millions of people decided to add a pet

to help alleviate the stress of isolation. And for many, that was effective.

Working from home and/or homeschooling the children created a unique opportunity for many families to add a puppy to their lives. The term "pandemic puppy" was quickly coined. However, trainers, groomers, veterinarians, and other animal professionals cringed when massive numbers of puppies were brought home. Pet services became overbooked, limiting the physical, emotional, and social care these dogs needed.

While pets can be a wonderful source of companionship for human well-being, it's critical to consider the pet's needs in all situations, not only during a time of increased family stress. Part 4 – Timeouts for Pets can help you with this.

The social benefit of having a pet doesn't end at home. Outings with pets provide valuable opportunities. Pet playdates connect like-minded animal lovers. Dog parks and riding barns can be great places to meet others with common interests. Even service dogs that are supposed to be ignored by the public remove social barriers for their handlers since they are a conduit for conversation.

◆ ◆ ◆

There are endless enjoyable possibilities to support your social well-being with both the humans and pets in your life. Some are easy to implement. Others take a little effort. The most challenging types of timeouts may be learning how to negotiate expectations and adjusting relational boundaries. Connecting through effective communication is key. All the strategies mentioned in this chapter can help ensure your nervous system temperature remains in—or can quickly return to—the cool zone when you're interacting with others.

APPLYING A+ TO SOCIAL WELL-BEING

Refer to the **A+ Model** discussed in Chapter 4: Your Basic Strategy and use it to improve your social well-being. Use the A+ worksheet provided in Bonus for Timeouts to facilitate this process.

CHAPTER 9

Fostering Connection

We've defined spirituality as a sense of connection to each other and to the world at large. Acknowledging a larger purpose to living provides meaning. Some consider it a connection to the divine; others find a spiritual connection to their family, community, or the natural world.

However you define it, when your spiritual needs are unmet, you will likely feel lonely and powerless to help yourself or others. When your spiritual tank is empty, you might wonder, *What's the point? Why am I here?* Spiritual stress often leaves people feeling apathetic, helpless, or hopeless. Taking a timeout to meet spiritual needs will improve your overall sense of well-being. Connecting to others, self, and nature helps you refine your strengths, values, and sense of purpose. Connecting to others, as discussed in Chapter 8, has spiritually oriented social benefits. This chapter focuses on connection to self and connection to nature.

Connection to Self

It's important to understand who you are, what you believe, and what you're contributing to life. To achieve this connection to self, take a moment to identify your strengths, your chosen values, and the ongoing development that comprises your sense of purpose. Your unique combination of strengths, values, and purpose enables you to pursue and become your best self.

What are My Strengths?

Your strengths are what you're good at. They're a combination of your knowledge, skills, abilities, and character traits. You may think of them as your unique talents or gifts, ones that contribute to your choices in hobbies, careers, and relationships.

In contrast, weaknesses are usually defined as something you're not good at, or an area where others—parents, teachers, or employers—think you should improve. A weakness may indicate either an undeveloped competency or a lack of aptitude. The first type can be remedied by gaining knowledge or developing new skills. In the second case, capitalize on your strengths and allow others to contribute to the areas where you don't excel. Accepting that other people's strengths can compensate for your weaknesses is, in fact, a strength. And recognizing your own weaknesses allows you to have empathy for weakness in others.

> **THE FALLACY OF "YOU CAN BE ANYTHING YOU WANT TO BE."**
>
> Tom Rath, author of *StrengthsFinder 2.0*, suggests that the maxim "You can be anything you want to be if you just try hard enough," is misguided.[1] Society is captivated by stories of those who overcome great odds—the underdogs whose strength of character helps them overcome natural deficits—more than stories of those who maximize their natural talents. Rath suggests a more appropriate maxim: "You cannot be anything you want to be—but you can be a lot more of who you already are."[2] To become your best self, take regular timeouts to better understand your strengths and how to apply them to daily life.

If you've been shamed in the past for your weaknesses, begin by countering those negative voices with positive ones. Your new self-talk will affirm what you're good at, possibly by using a mantra, such as, "I am unique and have many strengths. I'm proud of myself." Then embrace your weaknesses. They make you human; they don't define you. They may provide you with opportunities to connect with others who have complementary strengths.

What Do I Value?

Values are the beliefs you hold about what is most important and meaningful in life.[3] They are influenced by early childhood experiences, the authority figures in your life, the people you admire, your religious training, and your culture. Your values may evolve over time, especially during the phases of life where you differentiate yourself from your family of origin or develop committed, romantic relationships. This is both good and necessary for developing a successful adult life.

Values guide your behavior. For example, an extrovert may value time with others, while an introvert may value time alone. An individual who chooses a career in research may do so because they value contributing to the larger body of knowledge, while an individual who chooses a career in teaching may value passing knowledge on to others.

You experience spiritual stress when your values are out of alignment with the requirements of daily life. For example, someone who values family traditions and get-togethers will feel unhappy if their job requires them to work on holidays. Another individual may value entrepreneurship and independence and

hope to start their own business someday, but when the lack of capital keeps them tied to an eight-to-five job, they experience conflict. For some people, spiritual stress happens when they have difficulty finding the time to attend religious gatherings or engage in the spiritual practices of their faith beliefs.

Your values impact how you think about self-care timeouts and your willingness to make them part of your daily life. Nevertheless, taking a timeout for values clarification and goal setting helps relieve spiritual stress and contributes to your well-being.

Review the values clarification exercise in Bonus for Timeouts. You may enjoy going through it by yourself or with family and friends.

What Is My Purpose?

Your spiritual life thrives when you develop your sense of purpose. Finding it may seem elusive with so many voices telling you what you could or should be. You may have no idea how to mold your strengths and values into your purpose. Or you may have so many ideas it's hard to refine a clear sense of purpose.

Parents may expect you to follow in their footsteps. Academics push you toward professional occupations. Popular media encourages you to follow your heart. Global needs beg you to make a difference in the world. How can you sort through the competing expectations and craft a purpose that best utilizes your strengths and values?

First, take a timeout to answer the question "What is my *why*?" Many people enjoy doing meaningful work, taking responsibility for themselves and their families, living moral and ethical lives, cultivating spirituality, or giving back to society. Without understanding "Why am I here?" humans drift from task to task, relationship to relationship, emotion to emotion, resulting in dissatisfaction with life.

Every timeout you take to better understand your values and purpose brings you to a deeper place of knowing yourself and a fulfilling sense of belonging in your world.

When You Sense a Disconnect

Living with purpose enables you to use your strengths and live your values in your daily activities. However, you may experience a disconnect when you feel you must sacrifice or compromise your dream to take on work that provides adequate financial resources. Flexibility and creativity are needed to pursue your purpose in these areas while you continue taking care of your financial needs.

> **CHARLENE SAYS:**
> My husband and I have many friends talented in music and the visual arts. They have found their purpose while teaching in an educational environment, offering private lessons, and taking part in performance ensembles with their peers. Finding your purpose while participating in the arts doesn't mean you must conform to the starving artist stereotype. My husband, who holds a PhD in music composition, worked day jobs in other fields while exercising his talents in the evenings and on

weekends. Now in retirement, he has many opportunities to promote his work and his compositions have been performed by instrumental groups around the country.

A Dream Deferred

Living a purposeful life is a lifelong pursuit. Late adulthood provides opportunities to reconnect with a sense of purpose that may have been set aside due to the responsibilities of middle adulthood. This can be an excellent time to circle back to the activities you enjoyed as a young adult and reengage with them—perhaps sharing them with grandchildren or mentoring others. You could even return to grad school or take on an entirely new profession. These activities can give you a renewed sense of purpose to support your spiritual well-being.

CHARLENE SAYS:

When I was in high school, I dreamed of being a writer. I read books on creative writing and wrote poetry in my free time. I submitted poems to children's magazines and received my first rejection slips. My first break came when a poem I wrote for Senior English was published in a national anthology.[4] My mother supported my efforts—until it was time to apply for college. Then she said, "You need to become a teacher so you can support yourself." I was disappointed, but I followed her advice.

I earned a BA in English and secondary education. But after I entered the business world, I became interested in the human resources field of employee training and development. Coincidentally, or possibly providentially, this field required a lot of writing. It prompted me to earn an MA in management, and it led to a fulfilling 45-year career. Throughout this time, I continued to write poetry. Several pieces were published in local magazines, and I received two prizes from Poetry.com. With marriage and a child though, other activities became a priority, sidelining my writing goals.

> In my current stage of life, I'm free to pursue writing projects along with other interests. Publishing my books has been a rewarding experience.
>
> Was I living with purpose earlier? Yes. I had an honorable work ethic. I participated in activities that helped other people. I contributed to just causes. I raised a child. I enjoyed doing all these things, and each of these activities contributed to a satisfying life.

Connection with Nature

Connecting with nature supports both physical and spiritual well-being. Scientists agree that green landscapes, including urban parks, are restorative. Blue seascapes are beneficial as are remote landscapes accessible by walking trails or backpacking treks.[5] The National Forest Service recommends "green" exercise, such as walking, gardening, and participating in outdoor sports.[6] Being mindful of the outdoor experience and journaling about it increase the benefits, especially during season changes.

Connecting with nature frequently inspires a sense of awe—a feeling of reverential respect mixed with wonder. For many people this means experiencing vastness: a view from an elevated area—think mountaintop experience or standing at the edge of a natural wonder—like overlooking the Grand Canyon or viewing the distant horizon from an ocean beach. Awe can also be felt by looking at the detail in something intricate or small—think a caterpillar inching its way up a stem or the symmetrical design of a spider's web. Awe is the emotion so elegantly expressed in Lee Ann Womack's song "I Hope You Dance" when she sings, "I hope you never lose your sense of wonder."[7]

The benefits of awe extend beyond spiritual awareness. They are believed to improve health and reduce depression. They may also lead to increased compassion, generosity, and critical thinking ability.[8] Look for awe in your daily experiences and you're likely to find it.

> **PRO TIP: THE 20/5/3 RULE**
>
> How much time should we spend outdoors? Rachel Hopman, PhD and neuroscientist at Northeastern University, recommends the "nature pyramid" or the **20/5/3 Rule**.[9] It works like this:
>
> - **20 minutes.** Spending twenty minutes a day outside at least three times a week (without looking at your phone) is believed to "boost cognition and memory as well as improve feelings of well-being."
> - **5 hours.** Spending five hours each month in semi-wild nature has restful and restorative benefits.
> - **3 days.** Spending three days a year "off grid" in the wild can "reset your thinking, boost creativity, tame burnout and just make you feel better."

Connecting with Pets

Connecting with animals is an excellent way to connect to nature. Mammals and some birds and reptiles behave, emote, and learn similarly to humans. Hamsters experience stress. Cats experience joy. Dogs experience frustration. By recognizing and

appreciating the mental and emotional inner workings of the animals you care for and interact with, you will see the world through a different lens. Like humans, pets are trying to navigate the demanding environments they've been placed in. They need support from others, both human and animal.

Many find the presence of animals complements their spirituality. The tactile component of running your fingers through a pet's fur or feeling their heartbeat while they snuggle on your lap can be grounding and comforting. Exploring new terrain with your dog, listening to the moving water in a fish tank, or watching a reptile crawl through the plant in their terrarium helps you connect with the natural world.

Animals operate in the moment. They don't worry about the future or dwell on past mistakes. Observing animals as they engage with the social and environmental cues around them reminds us to be mindful and reflective in our own lives.

❖ ❖ ❖

Spirituality is part of your humanity, whether you embrace any religion. Focusing on the aspects of spirituality discussed in this chapter enables you to reach a new level of wholeness and connection.

While spiritual well-being looks different for everyone, it typically includes focus on a healthy connection with yourself and nature. Adding the insights for connecting with others from Chapter 8 is a plus. Fostering connection has a positive impact on your overall functioning, including improved mental and physical health and reduced risk of disease. Reflect on your strengths, values, and sense of purpose. Capture a sense of awe. Developing spiritual practices that create connection may feel both exhilarating and daunting, but it is well worth the effort.

APPLYING A+ TO SPIRITUAL WELL-BEING

Refer to the **A+ Model** discussed in Chapter 4: Your Basic Strategy and develop a plan that encourages your spiritual well-being. Use the A+ worksheet provided in Bonus for Time-outs to facilitate this process.

CHAPTER 10

When Others Depend on Me

Taking care of our own self-care needs can feel like plenty, yet many adults are in circumstances where they must care for others. The American Association of Retired Persons reports that more than 20 percent of Americans are caregivers to an adult or child with special needs. That adds up to 53 million adult caregivers. More than 30 million of those caregivers work full-time jobs. In every generation from Baby Boomers to Gen Z, folks are taking care of dependent family members above and beyond typical family and child-raising responsibilities.[1]

There are many situations where adults accept responsibility for the care of someone who is unable to care for themselves. For some, it is part of a life plan associated with one's value system. For example, if you come from a culture where family needs are

emphasized over individual needs, you may be expected to care for your aging parents. Other times, these duties are unexpected and disrupt life goals.

If you become the main caregiver for someone with a terminal illness or significant disability, your life changes dramatically. It may mean the end of a career or postponing retirement. Whether planned or unexpected, taking on a caregiver role comes with inherent stress.

Feeling the Strain

Caregivers experience higher levels of depression and anxiety than other adults.[2] If you bear the ultimate responsibility for the health and well-being of another human being, your own needs are often neglected. You will have less time to take care of personal needs, participate in social interactions, or enjoy leisure activities. Lack of attention to one's self can leave the caregiver vulnerable to negative emotions and health problems and, in turn, lead to poorer care for the dependent family member.

> **SHAUN SAYS:**
> My husband and I are in the sandwich generation. We've had years of living with adult children and an aging parent in our home. Most of the time, our lives carry on well. However, after my father's stroke, the strain of arranging his care, maintaining my newly formed private practice, and tending to the needs of my spouse, children, and grandchildren nearly broke me. I had to ask for help.
>
> I adjusted my work schedule, attended sessions with my therapist, and reached out to my support system. My husband took a huge part of the practical needs off my plate. He installed grab rails in Dad's bathroom, prepared meals, and helped with laundry. My youngest daughter created a master schedule and posted it on the refrigerator so Dad would know who his helper was for the day. She also monitored Dad's activities for safety

(like making sure the stovetop was always turned off). Our church community stepped in to stay with him and drive him to appointments when I had to work.

I shed a lot of tears during that season: tears from feeling overwhelmed, and also tears of gratitude for the people who shared the load. I had to take care of myself before I could meet the challenges associated with caring for my dad. And I asked for help. That was humbling, but it allowed me and my dad to be blessed by the outpouring of love and nurture.

Self-care during these stages is not optional—it's imperative!

Relief in Sight

Taking a timeout for self-care is crucial if you're going to be an effective caregiver without sacrificing your own health. One of the most important factors to how well you will function as a caregiver—while also managing your emotions, organizing your time, and adapting to the changing needs of the person you're caring for—is whether you believe you can do it or not. Self-efficacy is the confidence that you have the resources and abilities to manage the challenges of everyday life and the demands of being a caregiver.[3]

> **PRO TIP: SELF-EFFICACY FOR CAREGIVERS**
>
> Do you lack confidence in your ability to cope with the responsibilities associated with caregiving? You can focus on this with a self-care timeout. Start by making a list of strengths you bring to the caregiving role. If you identify as little as one strength, you can create a positive mantra to build confidence. A mantra is a simple phrase you repeat to yourself when you need a little encouragement. For example, in Shaun's story about caring for her father, she could start with *Even if I can't meet all his needs, I bring love to my father's life. That's enough for today,* or *I don't have to do this alone. I can ask for help.* You can learn more about mantras in Part 5 – Timeout Strategies Everyone Can Use.

In-Home Care and Other Options

Keeping your nervous system temperature in the cool zone as a caregiver takes intentionality and planning. Taking time-outs for self-care can feel like shirking duties. Operating from a deep sense of love and responsibility does not change the ongoing demands that can overwhelm even the most devoted caregiver.

Use the **A+ Model** as a tool to help you determine if in-home care with you as the primary caregiver is feasible. Although most older adults hope they can grow old in their own homes or in the care of their adult children, a time may come when a decision must be made to obtain a higher level of care for your loved one. Health and safety issues, cognitive changes, or financial concerns may suggest a different path. Family caregivers often feel a sense of guilt if the home care setting is no longer working well. Perhaps other responsibilities—work, raising children, or taking care of personal needs—make it difficult. An older adult's failing mental health may require constant supervision. Their inability to complete independent tasks (for example, showering, cooking, or dressing themselves) may reach a point where they need more help than a family member can give.

When considering options, find out what levels of care are available. A comprehensive list of options can be found on the American Association of Retired Persons (AARP) website. While it can be difficult to make the decision to move a dependent from your home, part of being an effective caregiver is making an honest assessment of the situation and researching resources. Sometimes the most compassionate decision you can make is to arrange for a higher level of care.

While health and safety are paramount, the impact on relationships is equally important. Your medical team, as well as your loved one's medical team, can provide support and resources as you make decisions. There are few situations that present a greater need for self-care timeouts than the caregiving journey.

SHAUN SAYS:

I've seen news stories about Alzheimer's patients who wander off and get lost, but I never expected to see a familiar face pop up on my local news. The mother of a close friend, an elderly lady with mild dementia, went for a drive and never returned home. After a terrifying 36 hours, she was located at a hair salon in Portland. The stylist said the mother had shown up for what she thought was her regular appointment, despite never having been to that part of town. When my friend asked her mother where she'd been, her mother looked her in the eye and said, "I was with you, of course."

We'll never know where she was all those hours or how she survived a brutally cold night away from home. My friend and her siblings immediately planned for memory care services. No one wanted that experience again!

❖ ❖ ❖

Using timeout strategies for self-care are crucial for sustaining the role of caregiver and providing the warmth, nurture, and patience your loved ones need. Be open to engaging outside help if they require more support than you can offer.

APPLYING A+ TO CAREGIVER WELL-BEING

Refer to the **A+ Model** discussed in Chapter 4: Your Basic Strategy and use it to evaluate your needs for self-care timeouts as a caregiver. Use the A+ worksheet provided in Bonus for Timeouts to facilitate this process.

PART 2 WRAP-UP

A holistic view of adulthood includes taking timeouts to care for your physical, emotional, social, and spiritual well-being. Your journey is determined by how you see yourself, the values you hold, your goals, and the sense of purpose you find in daily life. You may ease into or be thrust into a situation where you are expected to care for others. Using the strategies presented here in Part 2 will help keep your nervous system temperature in—or return it to—the cool zone.

PART 3
Timeouts for Children and Adolescents

Throughout Part 3 we use the term caregiver to refer to the wide array of adults entrusted with the important task of caring for children and adolescents. If you are a caregiver, Part 3 provides the skills you need to help your young charges take timeouts when facing their stressors. As their brains and bodies mature, they gain the ability to be more responsible for taking care of their own physical, emotional, social, and spiritual needs, yet they continue to need your wisdom and guidance.

Before diving into Part 3, take a moment to reflect on how well you are taking care of yourself. How would you rate your physical, emotional, social, and spiritual health? The best way to teach children the skills they need is to model them. If you need a refresher, go back to Part 2 - Timeouts for Adults and spend a little time taking care of yourself.

CHAPTER 11

Laying the Foundation

Raising children is hard. Type "Parenting is not for . . ." into an Internet browser and look at the words that follow: "the weak," "cowards," "the faint of heart," and "everyone." A search for parenting in an online bookstore generates over sixty thousand hits. Parents are looking for a little magic to help them do better. The magic is simple: prioritize self-care. Everyone in the household, humans and pets, will fare better.

> **SHAUN SAYS:**
>
> The adults in a child's or teen's life are the most influential factor in how well they learn to manage stress. Since self-care for children and teens is more supported care than self-care, much of what you find here are ideas for caregivers. These strategies are a culmination of research, training, and clinical experience. They are a roadmap for diminishing the impact of stress as your child journeys toward adulthood.
>
> Caregivers who function with loving intent tend to harshly judge themselves when they hear new perspectives and ideas about parenting. What you could've or should've done in the past serves no one. Unhelpful negative self-messaging increases shame rather than promoting healthy change.
>
> My children were adults when I began my formal training in child psychology. Boy, do I wish I had done a lot of things differently. They turned out to be terrific human beings despite my imperfect parenting. I encourage you to move forward and try out one or two new ideas. You never know—they might be what you've been looking for.

Let's look at ways to enhance the caregiver-child relationship by laying a foundation for high-quality, effective timeouts for children and adolescents using the **PACE** mindset.

PACE Yourself to Build a Foundation of Sensitive Caregiving

Caregivers play an important role in helping children develop healthy ways of living, including managing stress, regulating emotions, and engaging in prosocial behaviors. Research shows that when caregivers are attuned to their children's attachment needs even 50 percent of the time, their children will grow into secure, well-adjusted adults.[1]

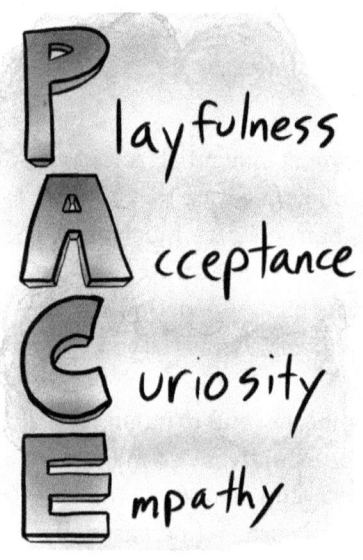

Children learn a lot about caring for themselves and others from their caregivers whose job is to teach, guide, and model the behaviors they want their children to learn. A child who has a stable relationship with their caregiver is better able to regulate their emotions and use timeouts for effective self-care. **PACE** is a good tool for creating security and stability.

The **PACE** approach was developed by Dr. Daniel Hughes.[2] The attributes emphasized in **PACE** foster attachment security and build on the reciprocal relationship (we respond and react to each other) that begins in the parent-infant relationship. Think about the delight you feel when you interact with a giggling infant. You smile. The baby smiles. You smile even broader. Pure joy!

If you can maintain the **PACE** attitude, you will be amazed by the things you discover about your child and how that knowledge draws the two of you closer. Here's an explanation of the **PACE** acronym:

- **Playfulness.** Playfulness is "the positive, unconditional, deep interest in each other and in the act of being together."[3] Responsible caregivers take their job seriously. Too often that seriousness sends unintended negative messages about the child's goodness or badness and makes the caregiver seem less accessible to the child. The underlying messages in every situation should be "I delight in you," "I believe you're doing the best you can with what you have right now," and "I want to know you and the things that are important to you." Playfulness is a way to take the tension out of high-pressure conversations.
    — What playfulness is not: Playfulness is not mocking or sarcastic. It does not use humor to avoid or minimize conflict and distress. It does not demand an explanation for bad behavior. It doesn't make excuses for misbehavior and instead seeks to understand the child's inner world. Playfulness is light, but it does not make light of serious subjects.
- **Acceptance.** Acceptance is the radical, unconditional, nonjudgmental approach to each family member. It does not assign right or wrong to their thoughts, feelings, wishes, intentions, perceptions, beliefs, values, or memories. It establishes open communication between caregivers and children. By separating the child's experience from the undesirable behavior, caregivers relay the message: You can trust me to see all the parts of you because I love and value you.
    — What acceptance is not: Acceptance does not mean allowing bad behaviors. If a child is about to pinch the family dog, a caregiver needs to step in to prevent injury to the child and the dog. Additionally, acceptance does not always mean agreement. A child's perception of a caregiver's decisions will often differ from the original intent. The caregiver can either argue with the perception or demonstrate that they understand how the child sees it. Children

are more receptive to correction and discipline when they believe their caregivers understand the experiences that generated the behaviors.
- **Curiosity.** Curiosity is reflected in a deep desire to understand your child's experience. It is the adventure of learning the story your child has developed to make sense of the events in their life and then joining in. Curiosity enters your child's experiences without knowing what will be found.
  — What curiosity is not: Curiosity is not an interrogation. It's not a method for finding blame or making excuses. It is not a subtle way to teach a lesson.
- **Empathy.** Empathy is the ability to understand and share your child's emotional experience. To be truly empathetic when a child is experiencing big emotions, the caregiver must remain emotionally regulated. Open, responsive empathy requires the caregiver to be with the child in their emotion and resist trying to fix the problem or talk the child out of their feelings. When a child feels empathy from their caregiver, they can lean into the caregiver's regulation and derive the safety needed to regulate their own emotional system.
  — What empathy is not: Empathy does not minimize or excuse behavioral problems. It does not foster weakness or make children dependent on their caregivers for emotion regulation.

Sounds like a big job, right? Think of **PACE** as an aspirational goal. No human hits the goal all the time. (Thank goodness for the research mentioned at the beginning of this section showing that attending at least 50 percent of the time has positive results.) Striving to do your best will be noticed and appreciated even if you don't get to hear the child's gratitude until they're older.

PACE in Practice
This comic strip is a simplistic example of **PACE**, noting important points. Let's dig a little deeper.

In panel 1, Mother has choices. She can react to the crying and immediately correct the child. Or she could use the **PACE** elements of playfulness and curiosity to find out what's really happening. Sibling conflict is never as simple as it seems on the surface. Unless it's a matter of life and death, gather more information first.

In panel 2, Mother uses the closeness of her body to demonstrate equal care for both children—not siding with the "good" child while excluding the "bad" child. Mother uses facial expression and tone of voice to communicate that she understands how upsetting it was for the older child to have her puzzle ruined, accepts the child's experience, and provides empathy for her frustration.

In panel 3, Mother addresses the younger child. She uses facial expression and a soft tone of voice to express that she understands his longing to be part of his sister's activities, demonstrating acceptance and empathy for the younger child's experience.

In panel 4, Mother uses a light tone and inclusive language to tackle the two family rules that were broken. She invites both children to recognize their part in the conflict without shame or blame. Her message conveys she is taking the situation seriously and their behaviors haven't damaged their relationship with her. Instead of giving a solution, Mother uses curiosity to give the children the opportunity to take part in resolving their conflict. She is genuinely open to their ideas.

Panel 5 demonstrates the positive results of Mother's acceptance and empathy. The older child can acknowledge her behavior and apologize. The younger child, following his sister's example, acknowledges his mistake and offers an apology and a helpful solution.

In panel 6, Mother celebrates her children's responses and relationships are repaired—until the next time. Because that's what being in a family is like.

This cartoon portrays how powerful these four caregiving attitudes can be for connecting on a deeper level with your children. This type of relationship is the foundation for teaching the self-care practices that reset the nervous system thermostats for everyone in the household.

◆ ◆ ◆

When family members interact calmly without high levels of tension, life skills are more easily accessed than in times when children are overwhelmed by stress or big emotions. Find ways to incorporate **PACE** into your interactions with children, and then practice, practice, practice!

CHAPTER 12
The Developing Human

Children face unique challenges when it comes to stress because they live in an environment not of their own making and without the benefit of a fully developed prefrontal cortex. Their nervous system temperature can move from the cool to the hot zone so quickly that caregivers hardly have a chance to respond before things feel out of control.

The prefrontal cortex, which manages executive functioning, is not fully developed until around age twenty-five.[1] Caregivers manage a child's executive function abilities until that part of the brain catches up.

The first step in self-care for children and adolescents requires understanding what is within their developmental ability. The caregiver can help by matching self-care timeouts to a child's capacity. In this way, self-care for children and adolescents is supported care.

> **SHAUN SAYS:**
>
> Like many psychologists, I'm always seeking ways to explain my own quirks and trying to better understand those of my family

members. (Some might say I'm trying to fix them, but I know my limits.) My father's parents divorced when he was a toddler. His father (my grandfather) moved away and was out of touch with his children until they were well into adulthood. I wonder how my father's life might have been different if he'd had a stable relationship with his father growing up. By extension, I wonder if these circumstances impacted the way he fathered our family. Another question I think about is my birth order. What if I'd been a middle child instead of the oldest? (Research reports say this is not as important as you might think, but my mother would swear middle children have the most challenging lives.)

As you read this section, take a few moments to celebrate the miracle of human development and the joy of discovering your child's unique needs.

Infancy (ages 0-2)

Infants feel safe and cared for when their needs are met. They know when they're hungry, tired, wet or soiled, or feeling physical distress. Infants are unable to address their own needs, so they do their best to let the adults in their lives know. They reach for us with smiles, coos, cries, arm waving, leg kicking, screams, and other forms of communication.

When the caregiver addresses the infant's needs, oxytocin—the neurotransmitter associated with feeling love—is released and the child's stress level is lowered. The adrenal response associated with distress is reduced and the nervous system is calmed. When an infant's needs are consistently ignored or attended to in a chaotic manner, long-term harm is done to their nervous system.

Taking a timeout for supported care in this stage means spending face-to-face and skin-to-skin time with the infant and providing them with the right amount of stimulation.

Toddlerhood (ages 2-3)

Toddlers need to explore their independence within a safe environment. As they discover the extent of their mobility and freedom, they begin to assert their will. "No" becomes a common word as they choose their favorite—and least favorite—foods, clothing, and toys. They are learning new skills and abilities that can increase their confidence and self-esteem. This is an ideal time to give simple choices, such as "Would you like to wear the red shirt or the blue shirt today?"

Toddlers are often frustrated by the limitations of their skills and the boundaries set by caregivers. They have not learned frustration tolerance, and their response will be fight, flight, or freeze. Their nervous system temperatures soar into the hot zone. Caregivers can help them calm down by celebrating accomplishments and providing comfort and encouragement when mistakes or failures occur. By avoiding criticism and shame, they equip the child to develop the resilience that reduces the impact of future stressors. You will need a lot of **PACE** (introduced in Chapter 11) from this stage on through adolescence.

Taking a timeout for supported care in this stage means creating moments for cuddling, play, praise, and lots of laughter.

Early Childhood (ages 3-6)

Children in this stage slowly develop their self-regulation skills. They often overstep their bounds, which makes the caregiver's job tough. Children make mistakes by being too forceful or selfish as they navigate the back-and-forth of relationships. They depend on their caregivers to recognize when their moods and behaviors indicate a rising nervous system temperature.

Taking a timeout for supported care in this stage means caregivers help children recognize their bodies' signals and use **THRIVE** (introduced in Chapter 2) to assess what they need to calm their nervous system. These children will benefit from breathing and sensory grounding techniques. Practice those skills frequently and demonstrate a good model of self-care.

Middle Childhood (ages 7-12)

Older children are growing in their social skills and their ability to manage more aspects of their lives without help. They begin to attach parts of their identity to specific abilities. Their self-talk may include praise: *I'm the smart one, the pretty one, the athletic one, I'm good at math, terrible at spelling,* or *I'm too shy to speak up in class.*

Taking a timeout for supported care in this stage means caregivers continue to play an important role in helping children recognize signals of stress in their physical bodies and learning how to resolve it. Assist children in this stage by using the **THRIVE** technique (introduced in Chapter 2) and help them practice emotion-regulation skills. This will help them form effective strategies they can use when feeling overwhelmed.

Adolescence (ages 13-19)

Although early research defined adolescence as ages thirteen through nineteen years old, more recent studies have suggested that adolescence begins as early as ten and extends into the mid-twenties.[2] Educators and therapists attest to the definite shift of children approaching adolescence at younger ages seen in behavioral, psychological, and physical manifestations.

The age of pubertal[3] onset has dropped over the last two centuries as much as seven years. Children's bodies are outpacing neural development, which leaves them with hormonal impulses far beyond their ability to moderate. Teaching your child to take timeouts to reset their nervous system temperature gives them the tools they need to give their brains a chance for good decision-making and emotional regulation.

Teenagers can recognize when they need a timeout for self-care and to engage in effective strategies. However, the immense physiological changes in their brains and bodies may lead to erratic application of their knowledge and skills. Caregivers can lend support by giving special attention to basic needs—nutrition, hydration, sleep, and safety—to support the physical changes.

Adolescence is a stressful phase of life, and teens often experience an overloaded nervous system that impacts their physical, emotional, social, and spiritual lives. Encourage teens to engage in timeout strategies for relaxation and stress reduction as part of their daily routines.

◆ ◆ ◆

Children need a high level of caregiver support to teach them how to recognize stressors and take timeouts to manage their emotions, thoughts, and behaviors. For much of childhood, self-care is supported care. The most important factor in teaching them good self-care habits is the presence and practice of their caregivers. PACE yourself to show up with playfulness, acceptance, curiosity, and empathy.

CHAPTER 13

Back to Basics

Basic physical needs often underlie childhood emotional and behavioral meltdowns. Children and teens are particularly vulnerable to deficits in nutrition, hydration, and sleep. These impact their overall functioning as well as hamper their ability to regulate emotions and behaviors. Teaching children to take timeouts to meet these needs is the first step in developing good self-care habits.

Timeout for Nutrition

Hunger is frequently accompanied by low blood sugar, which can result in fatigue and irritability, commonly known as being hangry. The first questions to ask when your child or teen shows signs of stress are "When did you last eat?" and "What did you eat?" Foods with high sugar content or other simple carbohydrates provide a quick burst of energy; however, they burn off quickly and can leave a child with an empty fuel tank.

Implementing changes to a child's diet can be challenging. Let's face it—most children and teens (and adults, yeah, that's us) would rather have something salty, sweet, or laden with simple carbohydrates than a leafy green salad. Caregivers need to think outside the (snack) box when planning meals.

> **SHAUN SAYS:**
>
> I taught my granddaughter to enjoy almonds by singing the "Sometimes you feel like a nut" jingle from the old Almond Joy commercials. Almonds are packed full of nutrients and are a

good source of dietary fiber. They are naturally salt-free and low in sugar. And bonus—they fill you up fast. And yes, sometimes I feel like a nut!

You can lead a child to nutritional food, but you can't make them eat it. Saying: "Because I'm the parent," or "You're not leaving this table until . . .," falls short when teaching a child to appreciate a variety of healthy foods. The goal is to teach your kids to love what's good for them.

PRO TIP: ENCOURAGING HEALTHY FOOD CHOICES

Here are some tips for encouraging healthy food choices:

- **Make it fun.** People of all ages enjoy pleasurable experiences.
- **Involve the child.** Food always tastes better when you've shopped for ingredients and cooked it yourself. Allow children to participate in food selection and preparation.
- **Add variety.** Check your grocery store for exotic fruits and vegetables. What child is going to refuse trying something called dragon fruit?
- **Add color.** Children are particularly drawn to colorful foods. Many colorful fruits and vegetables have a high nutrient content. Choose the darkest green, the brightest orange, the deepest purple.
- **Don't force it.** Everyone in the family should give new foods a try, and it's okay if they don't like it. Children's taste palettes change rapidly, so revisit rejected foods in a few weeks or months.
- **Limit the amount of high-sugar/high-fat snack options.** We all need a treat from time to time. If you want your child to pick healthy options, replace sugary treats with grapes, blueberries, or other fruits.

Other helpful tips can be found at https://www.myplate.gov/.

Timeout for Hydration

We all need adequate water for overall health. Hydration is key for many important activities, including brain function. Dehydration results from lack of appropriate water intake and water loss due to physical activity or environmental temperature.

The body cools itself by the evaporation of sweat. Children are more vulnerable to dehydration than adults because they don't produce as much perspiration. Encourage your child to drink at least four ounces of fluid every fifteen to twenty minutes during high-intensity activities or when playing outside in warm temperatures.

> **PRO TIP: HEALTHY HYDRATION**
>
> Here are a few strategies to increase your child's water intake:
>
> - **Keep it close.** Keep water available throughout the day. Let your child pick out a special water bottle and set goals around how often it should be refilled.
> - **Keep it cool.** Fill your child's water bottle half full and put it in the freezer the night before school or sports activities.
> - **Keep it tasty.** Infuse a little healthy flavor by placing pieces of fruit in the water bottle.
> - **Keep it fun.** Children love colorful glasses and funky straws. Choose reusable cups and straws to encourage good stewardship of our environmental resources.
> - **Mix it up.** A wide variety of foods have high water content. Include them in your child's lunches and snacks. Yummy water-rich foods include soups, tomatoes, cucumbers, lettuce, melons, and other juicy fruits and vegetables.

> Early childhood is a good time to establish healthy habits. Avoid sugary beverages or those with substitute sweeteners. Growing up with a sweet tooth often leads to obesity, tooth decay, and a wide array of health problems. Give your child the gift of healthy tastes.

Timeout for Rest

Sleep is a basic need for every creature on the planet. All humans and animals need it to function and survive. Sleep is when the body restores itself. Heart vessels are repaired and the hormones that control the sensation of hunger are balanced. The brain sorts through the experiences of the day and files away important information. It also rehearses skills and thoughts to prepare for the next day.

Sleep deficiency makes it hard to think straight, and it has a negative impact on a child's ability to manage everyday stressors. Good quality sleep resets mental, emotional, and physical systems.

As children and adolescents grow, their need for sleep changes. See the chart on the next page to determine the amount of sleep your child needs.[1]

Sleep habits begin early. Just as the amount of needed sleep changes over time, the child's ability to fall asleep and stay asleep will vary throughout their life.

Caregivers play the primary role in helping young children establish good bedtime routines. Sleep habits become the child's responsibility as they demonstrate the maturity and skill to appropriately manage their needs. A wise caregiver keeps an eye out for times when the child may need a little support to stay on track.

The most important ways to help your child sleep better are to create a consistent pre-bedtime routine, monitor pre-bedtime content, and discontinue all screen activities before bedtime.

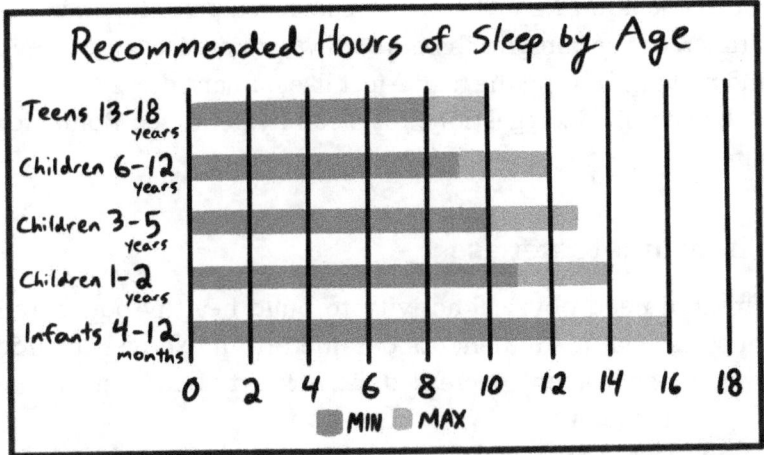

Each of these activities leads to decreased energy, a calm mood, and an expectation of sleep.

Good bedtime habits wire the brain to understand when it's time for sleep and we associate certain activities with winding down for the night. For some it's a light snack, reading a book, or cuddling with a family member. When a pre-bedtime routine is repeated consistently, it programs the brain to go to sleep more easily.

The world is full of inappropriate news events and entertainment options for children. Young minds are particularly sensitive to content they are unable to understand or control. When the human brain takes in violent or scary images, it often uses the sleeping hours to try to make sense of the information. This can result in poor sleep and nightmares.

Take time during the evening routine to plant seeds for pleasant dreams. Send your children to bed with stories of warm, delightful experiences or peaceful music to feed the calming part of their brain as they drift off to sleep.

Electronic devices increase stimulation. Discontinuing screen activities thirty to sixty minutes before bedtime decreases overstimulation. Some families create a charging station in the kitchen or the caregiver's bedroom where devices go to sleep and recharge during the night—just like humans do.

For detailed suggestions for sleep hygiene, see Bonus for Timeouts.

Timeout for Exercise

Children need physical activity to build healthy bones and muscles. The many benefits obtained from exercise include weight management, decreased risk of heart disease and diabetes, and longer life.

Physical activity contributes to a healthy brain. Children who engage in moderate to vigorous physical activity can think more clearly, focus better, and make more rational decisions. Exercise helps them feel happier and reduces worry.

Most young children don't need a structured exercise program because they play actively throughout the day. Older children and teens may need to be more intentional to counteract the sedentary lifestyle associated with longer school days and increased time spent on electronic devices. The goal for children ages six to seventeen is to spend at least sixty minutes a day in physical activity. Their exercise should include aerobic movement and activities that build bone and muscle strength.

There are easy ways to help children get enough physical activity.[2] Children of all ages enjoy games and activities like tag, soccer, or capture the flag. Exercise is more fun when the whole family participates. Whether it's a bike ride to the park or kayaking at the lake, your child will be more motivated to get moving if they're not on their own. It doesn't feel like work if everyone is laughing and encouraging one another.

And don't forget to include the animal family members. There are lots of ways to integrate pets into childhood fitness from a brisk walk with Rover to doing yoga with a goat. By including a family pet in your exercise routine, your child will learn responsibility and self-regulation, enjoy the unconditional love of a pet, and receive the benefit of physical activity.

Spending time in nature provides numerous opportunities for physical activity. Being in the natural light of the outdoors boosts your child's vitamin D level and produces a happier mood. A win, win, win!

◆ ◆ ◆

Effective supported care for children and adolescents starts with tending to the basics. Once nutrition, hydration, sleep, and recreation have been assessed and addressed, look at other stressors that impact overall well-being.

> **APPLYING A+ TO HEALTHY BASICS FOR CHILDREN AND ADOLESCENTS**
>
> Refer to the **A+ Model** discussed in Chapter 4: Your Basic Strategy and use it to ensure timeouts are being taken. Use the A+ worksheet provided in Bonus for Timeouts to facilitate this process.

CHAPTER 14

Don't Look Now, but I Might Be Freaking Out

There are two reasons to teach children and adolescents to take a timeout for emotional self-care: you want them to have the tools they need to feel better when they are overwhelmed by big emotions, and you want them to learn how to prevent becoming overwhelmed by life's stressors.[1]

Undesirable behaviors and out-of-control emotions indicate that a child or adolescent needs to take a timeout for self-care. An overwhelmed nervous system can lead to a tantrum, a meltdown, an explosion, crying, screaming, whining, hitting, pushing, defiance, lying, clinging, talking back, a negative attitude, a snarky tone of voice, or what many families call "the look." These are examples of tip-of-the-iceberg behaviors. Most often these expressions of distress are met with correction by caregivers without consideration for what lies beneath the surface emotion or behavior.

When a nervous system thermometer is reacting to stress by rising into the hot zone, the result is a hot zone coping strategy: fight, flight, or freeze. If we understand the underlying stressor, we can help our children use timeouts to bring their temperature back into the cool zone.

Beneath the Tip of the Iceberg

Let's look at a few examples of what lies beneath some common tip-of-the-iceberg behaviors. Remember, most children and adolescents use some form of each of these behaviors.

In American football there is a stiff-arm block. It's used by players to keep other players at an arm's distance and protect the football. In children, stiff-arm behavior is when your child

shuts you out or removes themselves from family interactions. This is common when children feel stressed and believe "nobody gets me or even wants to." This flight-or-freeze response of withdrawal is a self-protective attempt to create emotional and physical distance.

Another common distancing reaction is porcupine behavior, that is, when your child increases negative behaviors as a way of attaining increased attention. This prickly fight response may result in the child receiving more discipline and distance from caregivers. However, it's often a child's attempt to make caregivers prove they love them.

Every child (and adult) has experienced a meltdown or blow up. When your child exhibits increased emotional outbursts or physical aggression, recognize these are clues signaling they feel overwhelmed and need coregulation assistance.

You may not see perfectionism as beneath the tip-of-the-iceberg behavior, but trying to get things right all the time often leads to big emotions. If your child gets overly upset when they make a mistake or receive corrective feedback, you are seeing perfectionism behavior. This fight-response behavior communicates "I'll work hard to prove something or to earn love." The resulting tension almost always leads to negative emotional consequences.

Unless you are a die-hard Star Trek fan, you likely don't appreciate when your child is in "Kling-on" mode. Clinging behavior indicates anxiousness or fear of separation from you or other caregivers. This signals insecurity about losing the caregiver's presence and attention. This high anxiety is typically a freeze response but may also be flight.

Finally, we end our list of common beneath the tip-of-the-iceberg behaviors with whining. Whining can send a caregiver's nervous system into the hot zone as quickly as a meltdown or blow up. If you can view your child's complaining as a sign they're having difficulty expressing their need for caregiver care, it will be easier to respond with empathy and understanding. Whining is a fight response behavior that communicates "I'm not letting you off the hook until my needs are met."

Caregivers practicing **PACE** (introduced in Chapter 11), when faced with undesirable child-raising moments, can determine how best to respond to negative behaviors and high emotions. It's not easy. In fact, it's very hard to maintain a cool zone response because caregivers are human. A child's misbehaviors or mood swings can heat up the caregiver's thermometer, causing a reciprocal rise to the hot zone. If the caregiver has been mindful about taking their own timeouts for self-care, they have a better chance of exploring beneath the surface of the child's behavior. Real life often leaves caregivers near the end of their own resources, resulting in a vortex of reciprocal reactivity.

> **SHAUN SAYS:**
>
> Have you ever shouted to your child, "You are driving me crazy?" Yep, me too.
>
> I remember being on the bed next to my two-year-old daughter, crying, because I couldn't figure out how to make her do what I wanted. I don't recall what the task was, but I absolutely

remember the feeling of utter frustration and defeat. Now, a reality check reminds me that a twenty-pound two-year-old doesn't have the ability to control me. So, what happens in an adult brain when it gets caught up in a power struggle with a tiny tot? I'm sure if I'd known about **PACE** when she was a toddler, we both would have benefited.

My two-year-old didn't have an effective way to communicate what she needed, so she gave me the porcupine response. Instead of being curious about her behavior, I felt threatened. Below the surface of my behavior, I had plenty of parenting insecurity. The more I applied pressure for compliance, the more she resisted, and the angrier and more helpless I felt. She recovered more quickly than I did.

Thankfully, these days I share a special connection with my daughter. It's a joy to watch her navigate motherhood with more grace than I had.

Addressing Tip-of-the-Iceberg Behaviors

As a caregiver, you will have an emotional reaction to your child's behavior. When encountering tip-of-the-iceberg behaviors, you might feel disrespected, worried, frustrated, or embarrassed because of perceived judgment from others. This could be the looks you get from others when your toddler has a meltdown while grocery shopping or receiving well-intended—but misplaced—advice from a mother-in-law.

The first step is to take stock of your own emotions and calm your nervous system. Consider your own mini timeout so you can respond to your child with **PACE**. Shut out external distractions—the obvious side-eye stares in the grocery store—and focus on your child's experience. Consider the underlying source of their behavior. Could they be hungry, tired, or dehydrated? Is the situation too challenging for their developmental stage? Perhaps they're being asked to tackle something they don't understand or is beyond their ability. Maybe they're feeling lonely or need attention and connection. Are they overwhelmed, anxious, sad, afraid? Is the situation creating stress because it doesn't fit with your child's temperament?

Here's the beautiful thing: you don't have to figure it out on your own. In fact, you do your child a great service if you invite them to help identify the source. Younger children can start with how their physical body feels. Older children and teens are ready to consider a more complex view of their emotional experiences. You help your child develop increased autonomy for managing their emotions when you teach them to look below the surface of the iceberg. This aids development of self-awareness and self-regulation.

Once the underlying stressors, needs, and emotions are understood using **PACE**, you will be ready to respond with warmth and acceptance. A timeout to address basic physical needs may be just the ticket for addressing an emotional outburst. Perhaps your child needs a little time to focus on slowing their breath. Maybe physical touch or one-on-one time with you is the underlying need. The options are limitless when you can look below the surface.

> **SHAUN SAYS:**
>
> When I work with children, parents are often surprised to hear the first question I ask is, "What are you feeling in your body?" Even the youngest child can tell me her tummy feels funny or her head is going to explode, or her feet feel wiggly. The body is the gateway to early intervention and self-regulation. Teaching children about the connection between their emotions and their physical body is an excellent way to begin increasing their vocabulary so they can better identify and describe their emotional needs. Grownups could learn a lot if they paid attention to the signals their bodies send.

❖ ❖ ❖

Responding appropriately to a child's emotional state helps them to develop the self-regulation skills they'll use throughout their lifetime. You will be able to help children take the timeouts they need as you tune in to the true sources of their tip-of-the-iceberg behaviors. And while you're at it, give yourself the grace to develop your own skills using **PACE**. It takes time to build mastery of our own emotions, let alone teach our children the skills. Thankfully, the research that says meeting attachment needs 50-percent of the time tells us we have time and room for both successes and failures. Would right now be appropriate for a timeout for emotional self-care?

APPLYING A+ TO EMOTIONAL WELL-BEING FOR CHILDREN AND ADOLESCENTS

Refer to the **A+ Model** discussed in Chapter 4: Your Basic Strategy and use it to plan timeouts for emotional self-care. Use the A+ worksheet provided in Bonus for Timeouts to facilitate this process.

CHAPTER 15

Home Is Where the Heart Is

Home is where children learn about safety and security, relationships, values, and who they are in the context of a bigger world. It is also the training ground for learning how to manage their nervous system temperature in social relationships. Effective timeout skills will help them build confidence in their ability to regulate their emotions and behaviors when stress shows up within difficult situations.

By understanding the power of family relationships, you can discover which timeouts for relational care can help your child stay in the cool zone.

Relationships with Caregivers

Parents, stepparents, and others who care for children provide the foundation for all the relationships they will have throughout their lives. The caregiver-child relationship benefits from mutual respect and kindness. Let's examine some of the common elements in this relationship that impact the child's nervous system temperature.

Temperament

Personality and temperament traits often cause stress in the relationship between caregiver and child. They can also be a point of connection when recognized and valued. As you interact with your child, be mindful of their unique attributes—and yours.

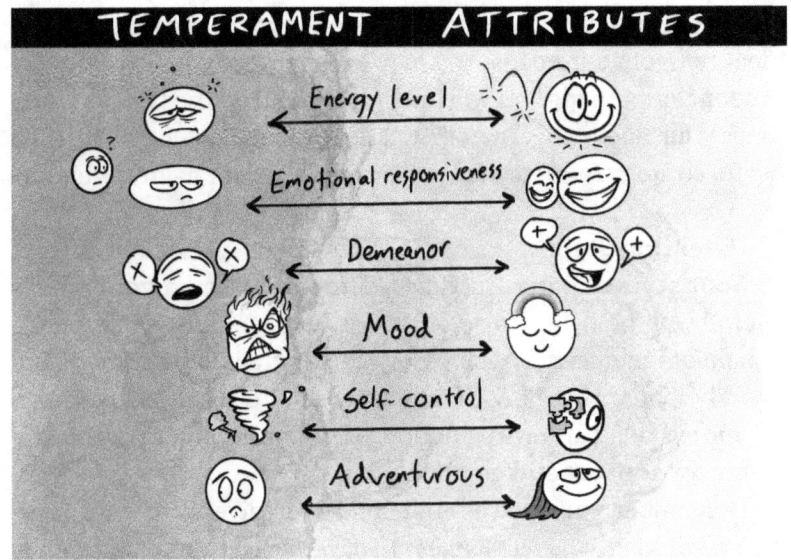

What works for one child or adolescent may be a complete flop for another, even when raised in the same household with the same caregivers.

Temperament includes a spectrum of attributes.[1] Whether the match (or mismatch) of temperament traits between you and your child brings connection and balance or stress in any situation depends on how you interpret the associated behaviors. For example, if you and your child share an adventurous spirit, both of you experience a positive benefit when you go rock climbing, skydiving, or dirt-bike riding together. The adventure itself is the timeout for relational care. On the other hand, your shared love of adventure might put you or your child in situations where one or both of you feel incredible stress. In this case, a quiet, relaxing timeout would be beneficial.

When temperament is ignored, caregivers and children become frustrated because they feel unseen, disrespected, or misunderstood. For example, you may be the cautious type and need quiet time to recover from activities. If your child knows no fear and has endless energy, you're likely to have frequent conflict. If you tune in to these differences, you can plan ways to meet both of your needs. You may each require your own type of timeout, or perhaps you will find a way to blend the timeouts and meet your needs together. **PACE** (introduced in Chapter 11) is a useful strategy for determining the best timeout in any situation.

Parenting Style

Your style of parenting has a direct impact on your child's overall well-being and also on yours. Young children are unable to regulate themselves well. They react to their environment and need help learning how to take timeouts to reset. Adolescents are more skilled at self-regulation while continuing to need caregivers for support and guidance.

Remember, your goal as your child's caregiver is to work yourself out of a job. The challenge is to pace the transfer of autonomy to match your child's developmental trajectory. At various times, the process will send everyone's temperature into the hot zone—that's normal. Timeouts help both of you reset your nervous system temperatures back to the cool zone.

Let's look at four common parenting styles and how they impact the interactions between you and your child. As you read the information, consider which style best reflects yours and what kind of timeouts will help you and your child.

"I'm the boss" (authoritarian)

Obedience is expected, and punishment is the primary form of correction. Expectations are high, and relational warmth takes a back seat to correct behaviors. A commonly used phrase is "Because I said so." Authoritarian parenting has a mixed impact. Children and caregivers may experience less stress because they both feel safe when everyone follows the rules. Children may feel heightened anxiety if rules are unclear, or they might become emotionally withdrawn if they feel their views are not considered by their caregivers.

"I'm the teacher and guide" (authoritative)

All behaviors are rewarded with warmth and nurture. When correction is needed the caregiver can say, "This didn't go well, so let's figure out what we can do differently next time." Children develop confidence, view themselves positively, and learn self-reliance and cooperation. This can be hard work for caregivers, like walking on a tightrope with no net. Caregivers need to have good strategies for regulating their own temperature so they can maintain a **PACE** approach. It takes a lot of practice to overcome episodes of failure.

"I'm your friend" (permissive)

A caregiver might say, "You have school tomorrow, but I guess a couple more hours of video games won't hurt." Permissive parenting has a mixed impact on both caregivers and children. Children feel a high level of self-assurance as they explore freely and develop creativity. It can be heartwarming for caregivers to watch their children discover their environments and talents. Children may feel high levels of stress in social situations where they must adjust to other people's expectations and needs, and caregivers can face disappointment and frustration when the child's free exploration has negative outcomes, such as poor grades or disrespectful behavior.

"You're on your own" (uninvolved)

This parenting style has the most detrimental impact on a child and is often the result when a caregiver has a difficult time regulating their own nervous system temperature. There are few rules and limited structure combined with minimal to no guidance from caregivers. In extreme cases, uninvolved parenting is considered child abuse by neglect. Children may experience some reduction of stress because caregivers are less likely to impose their own stressors on them. However, uninvolved parenting contributes to children having low self-esteem and low self-confidence. Children don't learn regulation and social skills, which can put them at risk of developing dangerous or inappropriate relationships.

Each parenting style has an impact on nervous system temperature regulation of both the caregiver and child. In fact, reaction to a parenting style can be the reason a timeout is needed. Parenting style may be part of a timeout strategy that helps reset a child's temperature to the cool zone.

Separation or Divorce

Approximately 20 percent of first marriages dissolve within the first five years and nearly half result in divorce by the twentieth year.[2] Most children adjust to a split household within two years, and the key to their adjustment is how their caregivers navigate the divorce. High conflict between spouses increases the children's risk of psychological, social, and behavioral problems.[3] Since this often leads to stress for all family members, professional help can be a beneficial resource.

Caregiver Reaction to Identity Exploration

Children and adolescents feel intense pressure to establish their identity. Social media often contributes to this pressure.

Caregivers need to be aware of the challenges their children face so they can respond with compassion and warmth as their children navigate this phase of life.

Many in older generations remember when asking "Who am I?" was about how you fit in the world and your purpose for existence. For children and teens today, that question is more than existential. They are expected to know who they are in a wide range of categories, including age, phase of life, race and ethnicity, gender, sexuality, socio-economic status, abilities and disabilities, gifts, and their online presence. They are expected to understand these parts of their identity at an age when they barely know what they want for lunch. And they must decide how they want to represent their identity to a global audience online. No pressure there, right?

It's normal to feel concern while your child navigates this phase of life. Perfectly sane caregivers may deny, avoid, or challenge the changes they witness as their children venture into new wardrobes, attitudes, peer groups, interests, or value systems that don't align with their concept of family or cultural norms. You love your children. You worry about their future, social well-being, and physical and emotional health. You want them to be accepted by family and friends. The stakes are high.

The unfortunate consequence of denial, avoidance, or taking a position of authority over your adolescent's identity exploration is a decrease in connectedness between the two of you. You can be part of your child's process by applying the **PACE** strategy.

> **PRO TIP: UNDERSTANDING IDENTITY**
>
> Identity, to your adolescent, likely means something different than it did during your teen years. Today's young people are talking about gender, sexuality, race, ethnicity, power, and privilege in ways unheard of a generation ago. If these are uncomfortable topics for you, do your homework and learn how to help your child navigate the messiness of today's identity formation.

Relationships with Siblings

Sibling conflict is as old as time itself. The Hebrew creation story recounts the conflict between the first siblings, Cain and Abel. It ended with the older brother murdering his younger brother. Putting extreme violence aside (a different topic altogether), bickering, disagreements, and fighting impact all family members, caregivers, friends, and pets. Sibling relationships are a key training ground for children to learn the skills they need to form broader social relationships and function well within them.

Sibling tension can be rooted in the children's desire to be special, unique, and attended to by their caregivers. Relationships are further strained by sibling comparisons or preferential treatment, whether the comparison or preferential treatment is enacted by caregivers or merely within the child's thoughts. Sibling conflict can create negative consequences and impact well-being for all. Conversely, it also provides an opportunity to learn conflict-resolution skills.

Caregivers can use timeouts to mitigate the stress of sibling conflict. These supported timeouts could involve separating siblings for some alone time, helping them change activities, or talking through the situation that led to the conflict. Options abound for helping each family member lower their nervous system temperature, and sibling conflict offers an opportunity for children to learn how to repair relationships after a blowup. Relationship repair requires family members to be in the cool zone.

Relationships with Extended Family

Relational care can include time spent with a warm, nurturing member of the extended family. Baking cookies with grandma, playing basketball with a cousin, or a quiet afternoon of reading with auntie are terrific opportunities for helping a child maintain a cool nervous system temperature.

Sometimes, extended family is the reason a timeout is needed. Grandpa Joe makes inappropriate comments. Cousin Lynn sneaks cigarettes behind the house. Aunt Jean drinks too much and gets overly emotional at every holiday celebration. Stress felt by children and adolescents connected to extended family interactions can be missed if caregivers experience their own challenges.

Whether it's that uncle who intentionally creates drama or the grandma who insists on hugging everyone, children don't always have the skill to advocate for their own needs. In some family situations, they aren't even allowed to.

View interactions with extended family as an opportunity to teach children about respect for others. Model respect for oneself by establishing appropriate boundaries (as discussed in Chapter 8), and give your children permission to do the same.

Consider how time spent with relatives will impact your child's nervous system. Then design an effective timeout for that situation.

> **PRO TIP: CHILDREN AND CONSENT**
>
> Teach the concept of consent early in your children's lives. Aunt Myrtle may be hurt if you don't make your child give her a kiss, but every child's body is their own. Except in cases of emergency, no one gets to touch them without permission. If your child only sees Aunt Myrtle once a year, how are they supposed to know she isn't a case of stranger danger? Give your child time to warm up and feel safe with relatives and let showing affection come as a natural extension of feelings. Aunt Myrtle will just have to be patient. And after all, patience is a virtue.
>
> How many times have you been threatened, bitten, or scratched by a pet that didn't want to be handled? A child's reaction may be more subtle. They may hide behind a parent or struggle to be released from a hug. What they may not say out loud is important and needs to be respected.

Relationships with Pets

Humans have an innate desire to connect with animals. And most children beg for a puppy, kitty, fishy, horsey, etc. Who hasn't seen a heartwarming image of a pet comforting a crying child? A pet offers a different kind of support than a parent, sibling, or human friend. Pet ownership provides opportunities for children to learn how to be responsible and show respect for another being.

As wonderful as pet interactions can be, they also come with risks for both the child and the pet. Matching your family needs with the right pet is crucial.

> **KELSEY SAYS:**
>
> From the moment I learned how to write, I added "puppy" to my Christmas list every year. My mom never caved. She knew the added responsibility would mostly fall on her shoulders. She reminded me throughout my adolescent years that she didn't want to be stuck with a dog after I left for college. At the time, I thought she was being incredibly unfair. Now that I'm in the life stage she was in when I was young, I understand her point of view.
>
> A pet may be seen as belonging to a child, but it's the responsibility of the parent. A young child cannot be expected to understand the nuances and needs of another sentient being. Since they're still developing their motor skills and learning the complex dynamics of social relationships, their behavior around animals can be inappropriate and dangerous for both the pet and the child. Parents must actively supervise when facilitating child-pet interactions to maintain respect and safety.
>
> To appease my constant demands for a puppy, my mom agreed to get a small pet when I was seven years old. She figured the time and financial commitment would be lower, and the shorter life span was an easier sell. I went to the pet store and

picked out my new companion: a rat I named Sunny. I was smitten. She was my partner in crime and my confidant. I learned the importance of healthy nutrition, appropriate habitats, regular cleaning and maintenance, and respectful handling. I also discovered that even a small animal was a huge responsibility. Sunny provided many life lessons—eventually lessons in death and letting go.

In early childhood, family is the primary influence on the formation of a child's view of self, others, and the world. Parents, siblings, extended family, and other adult caregivers play an important role. Learning to interact with a pet is an additional factor. Awareness of these influences enables caregivers to assist children in planning appropriate timeouts.

APPLYING A+ TO HOME IS WHERE THE HEART IS

Refer to the **A+ Model** discussed in Chapter 4: Your Basic Strategy and use it to work through stressors related to family relationships. Use the A+ worksheet provided in Bonus for Timeouts to facilitate this process.

CHAPTER 16

Peers and Priorities

Children's social skills grow as they progress through their developmental stages. By middle childhood, peers begin to hold increasing influence as friends start to contribute to a child's sense of identity and meet their social needs.

Each stage of development requires unique skills for taking a timeout for social self-care. Relational stressors can result in negative moods and behaviors. To support healthy social self-care, children and adolescents need both preventative and recovery timeouts. Preventative social self-care timeouts keep the nervous system temperature in the cool zone by fostering enjoyment in peer relationships, and recovery timeouts help when peer interactions send the nervous system temperature into the hot zone. This includes the challenges of living in a digital world.

Stages of Socialization

In Chapter 12 we talked about the developmental stages of childhood. Social relationships and skills also follow a developmental trajectory. As you provide supported care for your child's social well-being, it is important to understand the needs and stressors of each stage. Let's look at the impact of peer relationships during your child's different stages.[1]

Toddlerhood

Around eighteen months, children begin to enjoy having peers nearby. They are likely to play side by side, yet they are not yet skilled at cooperative play. Peer interactions are an important

part of the toddler's social development; be aware they can lead to overstimulation.

The stressors a toddler experiences in peer relationships are generally based on basic needs, such as hunger, rest, or safety. They need a trusted adult to negotiate relational conflict. Taking a timeout for supported care in this stage includes taking breaks for snacks, naps, and attention from a caregiver.

Common social situations where toddlers may need a timeout include the following:

- Spending time with another child for an extended period.
- Interacting with more than two other children at a time.
- Being cared for by someone other than a primary caregiver, such as a daycare worker or babysitter.
- Engaging in activities that evoke high arousal levels, such as a party, playing with a pet, or activities in new environments.

Early Childhood

Around three years old, children are learning to play *with* peers instead of merely alongside them. They are developing

144 TIMEOUTS FOR CHILDREN AND ADOLESCENTS

the ability to take turns and share joint goals, and their imaginative play expands to pretending games with other children. A three-year-old will do best with one or two playmates. By age five, they have developed enough social skills to accommodate a slightly larger playgroup. Preschool children are able to give praise to others and apologize for mistakes.

Making time for playdates is an important part of maintaining a cool zone nervous system temperature, because it meets their need for socialization and stimulation. A young child is easily stressed in social situations. Basic needs, power struggles, and safety, continue to be the primary reasons for a child's temperature to rise into the hot zone.

During this stage timeouts are still directed by caregivers. They need to teach children to pay attention to their bodies for clues that it's time to take a break.

Some common social situations that may require a timeout for relational care are as follows:

- Interacting with peer groups of more than four children.
- Participating in highly stimulating activities or environments.

- Times when they need to share prized possessions or want to play with other children's belongings.
- Situations that involve power sharing, for example, taking turns choosing a game or directing the sequence of imaginary play.
- Transitioning from one activity to another.

Middle Childhood

Peers are increasingly more important in the child's life. School expands their social skills, and they learn to function in a larger group. However, they want a best friend who shares their interests and affirms their sense of belonging.

During this stage, children tend to identify more closely with same-gender peers, but that changes gradually as they move closer to adolescence. Friendships help them ward off feelings of being in or out of peer groups and contribute to maintaining a cool zone nervous system temperature.

This time of life often feels like a scramble for acceptance in the innate comparison between self and others. Cliques, popularity, and bullying become ways of establishing a social identity. The need to belong to a peer group may conflict with basic needs and safety.

Children in this stage often must negotiate stressors on their own since a large part of their day is spent away from caregivers. Important social self-care skills include recognizing personal needs, setting appropriate boundaries with peers, and asking for help from a trusted adult, teacher, or playground monitor.

Common social situations where a timeout may be needed are as follows:

- After an extended time spent away from home, such as at school or a sleepover.
- Being the newcomer in an established peer group.
- Navigating conflict with close friends and other peers.
- Experiencing rejection from a friend.

- Being part of or rejected by a group that emphasizes exclusivity.
- Facing peer pressure to participate in activities that don't align with personal or family values.

Adolescence

Adolescents identify peers as the most important source of influence and acceptance. Whereas friendships contribute to rapid shifts into the hot zone, they can also help reset the nervous system temperature back to the cool zone. Time spent with a supportive friend can help offset an unpleasant interaction at home or school. At the same time, a social media post can send a teen spiraling into volcano mode. Peer influence creates a roller coaster of hot and cool zone moments.

Adolescents still need their caregivers for wisdom and guidance and to help them recover from stressful peer situations. Common questions during adolescence are "How do I measure up to my peers?" "Am I normal?" and "What's wrong with me?" These questions begin in early childhood and increase exponentially during adolescence as their bodies and brains undergo massive changes. The onset of puberty brings alterations in

height, weight, and muscle mass—not to mention hormonal fluctuation. Dips in confidence, dramatic shifts in likes and dislikes, and mood swings are common as they adjust to new social pressures and the rearrangement of friend groups.

Adolescents can assess their needs and decide to take appropriate timeouts for self-care. They continue to build on the skills begun in middle childhood, including communication, boundary setting, and knowing when to ask for help. A wise caregiver continues to use **PACE** (introduced in Chapter 11) to check in with their adolescent as they notice changes in behavior or mood.

The Challenge of Living in a Digital World

More than any previous generation, media and virtual sources impact the social life of children and adolescents, and it touches all stages of development. Like it or not, it is now part of every child's social development.

Think about how easy it is to sit a toddler in front of a TV show so you can get a few things done around the house. This strategy has been used since the inception of television. But now, there are plenty of apps, videos, and games for that same toddler if you put a digital tablet or cell phone in their hands. Parents have the difficult decision about the appropriate age to give these powerful devices to a child. For better or worse, technology in the form of hand-held devices is a fact of life.

In 2018, 75 percent of children ages thirteen through seventeen used social media.[2] In pre-pandemic 2020, children under that age were spending more than two hours a day on digital devices. Screen time expanded exponentially during the pandemic due to online learning and isolation from peers and extended family, but the screen time increase didn't stop there. More recent research shows almost half of toddlers now use a handheld device daily and many teens spend as much as nine hours a day online.[3] With the growing prevalence of AI, these numbers are sure to grow. Unfortunately, the content of children's screen time is overwhelmingly unmonitored by caregivers.[4]

The digital age brings both benefits and risks. The Internet provides access to unlimited amounts of useful information. It's a tremendous tool for writing research papers, learning algebra, and viewing works of art. And, as we learned during recent events, the Internet allows social interactions even when we can't be physically in the same place as our friends. For many children

and adolescents, the ability to chat with their friends online helps them feel more connected to their peers.

On the downside, the Internet subjects children and teens to content inappropriate for their stages of development. They can be overwhelmed with anxiety, fear, and shame when they view material they are not ready to effectively process.

Screen time and social media are often blamed for the rise in child and adolescent mental health problems. Research has failed to confirm this association because the Internet is just one factor contributing to young people's overall well-being. There is consensus that the digital world is one of those components.[5]

With rapid changes in technology, it's difficult for caregivers to provide safety guidelines. When we feel frightened about the impact on our children it might seem like the only way to keep children safe is to eliminate all access—but that's not possible.

Let's look at some of the benefits and risks associated with Internet access for children and adolescents.

Benefits and Opportunities

Keeping up with technology and knowing how to monitor your child's online presence can be challenging. However, it's important to recognize the powerful tools and opportunities the Internet offers for enhancing children's and adolescents' lives. Consider the following:

- **Education.** The digital world provides access to a broad range of educational games and videos, resources from academic institutions, and worldwide research in formats appropriate for every stage of childhood development.
- **Socialization.** Social media, texting, and instant messaging are common points of connection between friends and peers. For introverted children, these forms of communication reduce the pressure to think on their feet and allow them to create a positive social presence.
- **Creativity.** Numerous forums exist for music, dance, art, and other forms of creative expression where people can

share their passions, expand their skills, have their work viewed by others, and receive feedback.
- **Community.** Social media offers group and one-on-one interaction with others who share similar interests and viewpoints. Teens can find support systems during critical phases of life transitions, such as graduation, college, and emerging adulthood.
- **Caregiver engagement.** Technology provides unique opportunities for caregivers to understand their children's worlds. It can enhance relationships through shared interests and activities. It can also provide guidance and developmentally appropriate supervision that gradually transitions from close regulation to general oversight as your child matures. Invest the time and effort to achieve a basic understanding of technology, and you'll meet the challenge of stepping into your child's very real world.

Risks and Concerns

In addition to the danger of exposure to inappropriate content, here are some other risks the Internet poses for your kids:

- **24/7 access.** The digital world never sleeps. Children and adolescents often have difficulty regulating their screen time, which can lead to sleep deprivation and neglect of other parts of their lives. Constant online connection leads to fewer opportunities for children to practice independence and autonomy.
- **Privacy and misuse of data.** Children of all ages often forget the information they provide on the Internet is readily available to companies, savvy individuals, and predators. A photo texted to a friend can be modified and distributed to large groups of people. The demographic and psychographic information provided on a profile can be used for mass marketing purposes.
- **FOMO.** Fear of missing out is a real thing. Social media viewing can lead children and teens to believe everyone

else is having a spectacularly exciting life while they're stuck at home doing schoolwork.
- **Social record.** Although posted items seem to disappear, the information is never really gone. Many children have their entire lives documented on social media. This can lead to posts that impact their social, educational, or professional standing for years to come.
- **Cyberbullying.** Social media, chat rooms, and anonymous posting apps create environments where children and adolescents are vulnerable to ostracization and humiliation.
- **Cancel culture.** Children and teens may suffer serious consequences of impulsive, uninformed, or insensitive social media posts. Many young people experience the ultimate form of rejection: being "canceled," that is, unfriended, unfollowed, mocked, and publicly humiliated.
- **Pornography.** The Internet has made access to porn so easy that even toddlers are likely to stumble upon it. Studies have shown that 90 percent of teens have viewed online porn without the knowledge of their parents.[6] Sexually explicit content is also transmitted through texting, chatting, and social media. And that's not limited to teenagers. Reports show that 40 percent of children younger than thirteen have sent sexts.[7]

The digital world contains risks for children and adolescents, and they need to learn how to navigate those risks because it's not going away. It will only become increasingly complex, full of more benefits and risks. If caregivers don't enter their children's digital world, they will be shut out and left behind. You can only help your child build the skills they need to navigate the digital world safely if you accept this as part of their normal.

Digital World Timeout for Caregivers and Children
Weighing the benefits and challenges of the digital world against the risks is a challenge in itself—what a dilemma for

caregivers! The question lies in how you help your child navigate the complex world of technology. First, model the behaviors you want your child to embrace. Know when to put your own devices down and be present with your family members. This would be a terrific social self-care timeout to practice as a family. Second, create time with your child to reinforce safe guidelines for Internet use. Repeat these conversations and adjust for developmental stages. Finally, teach your child to take a break from screens and social media so they can evaluate how they feel after virtual interactions. This will help them learn how to transition from screen time to other activities when their nervous system needs a timeout.

Social self-care requires taking note of the types of activities that help or harm overall well-being whether those activities are in person or online.

> **PRO TIP: REDUCE TECHNOLOGY RISK**
>
> Caretakers may feel overwhelmed because the risks of the digital world are vast. There are many ways to help reduce the risks. New apps and software products are available to parents to monitor their children's online activities and enhance Internet safety. Practical applications of **PACE** parenting can help you play a meaningful role in your child's life as they develop their social identity.
>
> Here are a few strategies caregivers use to keep their children safe in the digital world:
>
> - **No devices allowed.** This is nearly impossible, and it places children at a disadvantage in peer relationships since many children and teens use texting and social media for communication outside of school. It also fails to prepare them for independence, higher education or the workforce. Even the Amish community, which has historically resisted technology of all types, has begun to

use computers and cell phones for business and personal communication.
- **Limit screen time and sites.** You can disconnect all devices at the point of access, such as unplugging routers and cable during specific hours of the day. Many routers and parental control apps give caretakers the ability to assign time and content restrictions to specific devices. Many of these apps allow parents to see messages, emails, and other forms of communication.
- **Limit locations of use.** Designate certain common areas of the house for device use rather than allowing isolated access in bedrooms. It's easier to monitor your child's content when you are physically present during their device time.
- **Regular checks and check-ins.** Conduct random inspections of your child's search history and device use. Better yet, have ongoing conversations with your child about their Internet use. Find out their interests, what they find helpful about certain platforms and apps, and who they interact with.

Bear in mind, determined children and adolescents will find a way to circumvent any safety feature you decide to install. Any kid can use a friend's phone or computer. A savvy one will find software that makes their Internet activities appear legitimate. The most powerful safety measures are your relationship with your child and your physical presence.

There is a lot to consider when trying to reduce the risks of the digital world. Take a moment to breathe. Parenting in today's world is no joke. Don't let fear make your parenting decisions, but rather guide your children from a place of love and positive intention. You've got this!

◆ ◆ ◆

As children move into adolescence, peer relationships have a greater impact on their sense of well-being and become a source of both positive and negative feedback. Both face-to-face and digital-world peer interactions are a training ground for adult relationships, making timeouts for social self-care more important than ever. Social self-care timeouts should include developmentally appropriate help from caregivers to set healthy boundaries and manage safe relationships. Caregivers can support this type of self-care by acknowledging that navigating peer relationships is tough and by being there to provide support and guidance. This is a time to celebrate the victories and be generous with hugs in the hard times.

> **APPLYING A+ TO STRESSORS WITH PEERS AND PRIORITIES**
>
> Refer to the **A+ Model** discussed in Chapter 4: Your Basic Strategy and apply it to relational care with peers. Use the A+ worksheet provided in Bonus for Timeouts to facilitate this process.

CHAPTER 17

Knowing Myself Inside and Out

Self-awareness is an important human endeavor. Understanding oneself is key to personal and spiritual development. The saying "An unexamined life is not worth living" is attributed to Greek philosopher Socrates, who also exhorted his followers to "Know thyself."

Developing self-awareness is a task children must learn over time. Children form ideas about their character, lovability, and value throughout childhood based on responses from their caregivers and other family members and later from interactions with peers. Self-awareness allows children to understand and communicate their thoughts, emotions, and needs.[1]

Self-awareness timeout strategies for children support their spiritual development.[2] We'll focus on three aspects of self-awareness: strengths and growing edges, values, and living with purpose. In each area, think about how you could implement intentional timeouts with your child to enhance their spiritual development.

How Do I Support My Child's Strengths?

Your child was born with unique strengths and the ability to learn and grow. Personal strengths are the knowledge, skills, abilities, and aptitudes your child possesses. They encompass your child's capacity for ways of thinking, feeling, and behaving—skills that come easily to your child along with their personal traits that help them succeed in certain situations and help define who they are. There will be tasks they are also not naturally good at, but they may be able to develop new competencies. These are their growing edges—the knowledge, skills, and abilities your child currently lacks, separate from the real limitations of their capabilities. Every human being has traits that make them a poor fit for specific activities. This can be hard for children and their caretakers to accept.

> **SHAUN SAYS:**
>
> I grew up with a mom who was my biggest cheerleader. She told me I could do anything I set my mind to. The upside is I never doubted my mother's love and support. I developed a can-do attitude that emboldened me to try a lot of different activities and adventures. This allowed me to start my own consulting business when my children were little and to complete a graduate degree after they grew up. It fueled multiple applications to the reality show *Survivor* because no matter how old I am, I still think I could win that game!
>
> The downside is I faced disappointments when my knowledge, skills, and aptitude were not good fits for my desires. I did not become an astronaut because it turns out claustrophobia is an undesirable trait when traveling into space. I would never make it as an Olympic gymnast no matter how much I trained because I don't have the body structure or courage for it.
>
> There are places in life where I learned to overlap my big ideas with the reality of my capabilities. I became an emotions doctor because my dislike for blood was not a match for being an MD. I travel internationally because travel to the stars isn't practical. Knowing what I can do, trying things that stretch me, and acknowledging what is not within my ability are all parts of knowing who I am.

Strengths and limitations don't have to limit your child's enjoyment of the world. In fact, in many cases running into the limit of their capabilities gives your child the opportunity to find new ways to incorporate their interests.

Encourage your children to develop their strengths to their full capacity, providing them with opportunities to participate in activities they enjoy. Help them to see their lesser-developed abilities as opportunities for growth. These could be areas where they reach out to others for support.

Learning to embrace growing edges is a lifelong pursuit and may cause a bit of stress in the process. Remember, we use the phrase growing edges rather than weaknesses because every human—and animal—is a work in progress. Weaknesses, to your child's ears, may suggest something is wrong with them. One's natural talents do not define the type of person they are. Any perceived lack of skill or ability is an opportunity to grow and develop, and reaching the limits of one's capabilities is part of being human—not a weakness—a good message for grown-ups as well.

SHAUN SAYS:

I love the confidence of early childhood where the sky is the limit and young children believe they can accomplish anything. I feel sad that life gradually erodes that feeling of unparalleled self-assurance.

My granddaughter was five years old when the COVID-19 quarantine hit our state. She enthusiastically told me she would find a cure for the coronavirus because she was "so good at science." I loved her enthusiasm, though her kindergarten curriculum didn't cover immunology. At age seven, she still loves science and looks forward to discovering new breakthroughs.

It's easy to chuckle at youthful ambition, but I encourage caregivers to respond with wonder and awe. After all, Madam Curie (known for discovering radium and polonium) was once a child. Instead of dismissing or patronizing my granddaughter, I celebrated her big goals. We worked on writing a book together titled *June Bug Cures COVID*.

Most children are happy to tell you what they're good at doing even when their perception of their strengths isn't exactly accurate. Family members often provide the first feedback on a child's view of their abilities. In early and middle childhood, peer input is incorporated. How they interpret this response varies widely depending on what they learn in their family system.

Caregivers can help children embrace both their strengths and their growing edges by emphasizing process over perfection and relationship over achievement. When caregivers provide space for family members to complement each other's skills and areas of improvement, they increase each family member's sense of belonging.[3] Children learn they are part of a team; they don't have to manage their world on their own. Other people's areas of expertise can help cover their own limitations. As author John Donne wrote, "No man is an island entire of itself; every man is a piece of the continent, a part of the main."[4]

> **PRO TIP: CELEBRATING STRENGTHS AND GROWING EDGES**
>
> Family is the first environment where children develop awareness about their personal strengths and weaknesses. Here are some strategies for encouraging healthy attitudes about talents and growing edges within the context of your family.
>
> *For Young Children*
> - **Create superhero art.** Each family member draws, paints, or colors a picture of their own superpowers (strengths) and their kryptonite (growing edges).
> - **Can-do/need-help lists.** Fold a piece of paper in half down the middle, and then open it back up. Title one half of the page "Things I'm Good At" and the other half "Things I Need Help With." Have your child create appropriate entries on each side and illustrate them.
>
> *For Older Children and Adolescents*
> - **View-of-self collages.** Provide card stock or poster board and a collection of images from magazines or printed from online sources. Each family member selects images that represent different parts of themselves. Encourage them to select representations of both strengths and

growing edges. Include words that describe characteristics, values, and aspirations.
- **Things I like about you.** Family members sit around a table. Each person has a piece of paper labeled with their name and the title "Things I Like about You." Pass the papers to the right. Each person writes an appropriate entry. Pass the papers again and continue the pattern until the papers have returned to their owners. This activity helps kiddos gain understanding about how others view them and also practice positive affirmation to others.
- **Stuck on a deserted island.** Family members work together to survive on an imaginary deserted island. Together you determine how to use your individual talents and skills to benefit the entire group. Who would collect and prepare food? Who would build shelter? Send rescue signals? Be creative and include some zany tasks for fun.

How Do I Give My Child the Gift of Values?

You demonstrate your values as you raise your children. Children usually accept their caregivers' values. As they approach adolescence, they begin to recognize ways in which their views align with or differ from their family's values. Adolescence is when things really start to change. They start defining their own set of values by asking questions or behaving in ways that make caregivers uncomfortable. A child's fundamental longing to be accepted by a peer group impacts their ability to live up to the standards their caregivers have tried to impart.[5] This

subconscious process is part of identity formation as talked about in Chapter 15 and is often a source of stress within families.

Teach children and adolescents to recognize and refine their personal value system. Life choices that align with their values reduce their spiritual stress and contribute to their overall well-being and satisfaction.[6]

> **CHARLENE SAYS:**
>
> My father valued punctuality. He set all the clocks in the house ahead by five minutes, so we'd never be late to an event. When leaving for activities, he'd sit in the car with the engine idling and wait for the rest of the family to climb in so we could go. He would speed to our destination to make sure we arrived on time, which was usually 10 to 15 minutes before others began to arrive.
>
> As a result, I rigidly adhered to arriving early to high school and college events. This frustrated my peers who figured they had a few more minutes before they had to arrive. And I felt frustrated waiting for them to show up. I was intolerant, accused them of being lazy and disorganized, and in turn they called me uptight and inflexible.
>
> Over time, I realized I could relax my values and reduce my anxiety at the same time. I learned that being on time or even fashionably late for some situations was socially acceptable. And I became more empathetic toward those who arrived a few minutes late.

Considering Values from Your Child's Perspective

Being connected to their family system makes it difficult for children and adolescents to identify their own values. They can become overwhelmed when separating out social, family, and personal expectations and goals from their guiding principles of life. This is normal. It's also why self-care timeouts for developing values is a supported care task.

Part of the caregiver's job is building the child's values vocabulary. There are hundreds of words used to describe values. In fact, an Internet search will reveal an endless number of values lists. Common values adopted by adolescents and younger children are independence, thrill-seeking, achievement, and public image, along with many other options to explore. Bonus for Timeouts includes a more extensive list of values and activities to help family members identify their core values.

Timeout to Help Your Child Identify Life Values
Making time to explore value systems is a meaningful way to help your children know themselves better. Approach these conversations with **PACE** (introduced in Chapter 11) to foster open communication. You could set aside one-on-one time with your child or use family time to broaden the conversation. Everyday interactions lay the foundation for values formation. Take a timeout with your child to explore their personal values too.

When discussing values, examine how your children's daily activities, behaviors, and attitudes align with their value system. Misalignment between these things is a contributor to chronic stress. Use the values clarification exercise provided in Bonus for Timeouts.

Any single value can have a positive or negative impact on your life. For example, the goal of parenting is to help children reach adulthood with the ability to develop their own ideas and behave in appropriate ways. However, an exaggerated emphasis on achieving independence can make it difficult for a teen to ask for help in situations where they want assistance. Adventure is a hallmark value of adolescence. On the flip side, it can lead to risk-taking behaviors that can be moderated in dialog with wise adults.

Certain combinations of values are likely to diminish a sense of well-being. For example, if a teen's top value priorities are pleasure, adventure, and power, they will likely have a lower sense of well-being than those who are oriented toward social tolerance, justice and equity, and caring for others.[7]

We all experience changes in our value systems as we go through different phases of life. Taking timeouts with your child to focus on values helps them identify the principles they want to live by. Then they will recognize how their values impact their overall well-being—an important self-care task.

Aligning Values with Lived Behaviors

Having a well-defined list of values supports a well-regulated nervous system. Help your child take note of ways in which their everyday activities either match up with their values or are in opposition to the principles they want to live by. The latter, cognitive dissonance in psychology-speak, is the "unpleasant psychological state resulting from inconsistency between two or more elements in a cognitive system."[8] When humans hold a specific value and still do things that don't support that value, they feel unhappy or dissatisfied with their lives.

SHAUN SAYS:

Education and meaningful occupation are two of the top values my husband and I hold. Based on our shared values, we assumed our three daughters would follow the same education and career paths we chose. That proved not to be the case.

Our oldest daughter holds family, education, and future planning as high priorities. She earned her master's degree in education and went on to teach high school mathematics. This path has provided her with a good income and summer breaks with her young children.

My middle daughter values creativity, lifelong learning, and caring for others. She is a licensed massage therapist with her own practice. She invests time and energy in a multitude of creative arts while massage provides the income she needs for independent living. Her clients literally put themselves in her hands for warmth and care.

My youngest daughter values relationships, intentionality, and loyalty, and chose to attend beauty school. She is a talented hair stylist who has built a solid clientele of individuals who trust her skills. Oftentimes she is an unofficial therapist for her long-term clients as she journeys through seasons of life with them.

I am extremely proud of all three of my girls. I had moments along the way when I wondered if I had failed them because their paths differed from my plans for them. If I had held on to that mindset, I would have pressured them to try to meet my goals instead of letting them live by their own values, and that would've been damaging to them and to our relationship.

Helping your children find their own values is an important part of raising them to be their best selves.

As you help your children identify their values, you'll learn a lot about them and yourself. Aligning their daily activities with those values will enable them to develop self-awareness, recognize their natural strengths, and find areas where they may need a little help or more practice.

HELPING ADOLESCENTS CLARIFY THEIR VALUES

Let's consider a hypothetical example of what the values alignment process could look like for an adolescent.

Jenna identifies friendships as a top priority, except she never seems to have time to spend with her friends. Her mother helps her evaluate her schedule. On weekdays, Jenna attends school and practices soccer. In the evenings, she does her homework and then spends a few hours on social media. On the weekends, Jenna works a part-time job and plays six hours of video games. While social media and video games provide an element of social interaction, they don't result in the same satisfaction as face-to-face activities with friends.

Jenna's mother suggests that she invite a friend to do homework together once a week. Additionally, Jenna decides to meet a group of friends at the park to shoot hoops on Saturday afternoons.

After a couple of weeks, Jenna and her mother reflect on

how the new plan is working. Jenna realizes that not only does she enjoy spending time with a friend after school, both she and her friend have improved their science grades. Jenna feels great after shooting hoops because she's exercising and laughing with a group of friends.

The changes Jenna made helped her live more in line with her value of friendships and provided added benefits she hadn't planned for. Win-win-win!

How Do I Help My Child Find Their Sense of Purpose?

When children and adolescents understand who they are and why their lives are important, they are more motivated to take good care of themselves. A sense of purpose contributes to spiritual, physical, and emotional health. Research shows it contributes to higher overall earning capacity.[9]

A child develops a sense of purpose in their early relationships. Positive relationships with caregivers, family members, and peers increase a young child's sense of hope and resilience. Negative relationships increase vulnerability to anxiety, depression, and other mental health issues. These relationships influence the child's overall well-being: physical, emotional, social, and spiritual.[10][11]

There is no magic way to help a child define their purpose. "Why am I here?" is an age-old question pondered by philosophers and poets alike. Perhaps the best gift you can give your children is to help them see themselves in the context of their family, friends, and community. Help them think about their purpose for living. In many ways, this is a spiritual pursuit.

In Part 1, we shared a quote from Brené Brown defining spirituality. Let's look at it again. "Spirituality is recognizing and celebrating that we are all inextricably connected to each other by a power greater than all of us, and that our connection to that power and to one another is grounded in love and compassion. Practicing spirituality brings a sense of perspective, meaning, and purpose to our lives."[12]

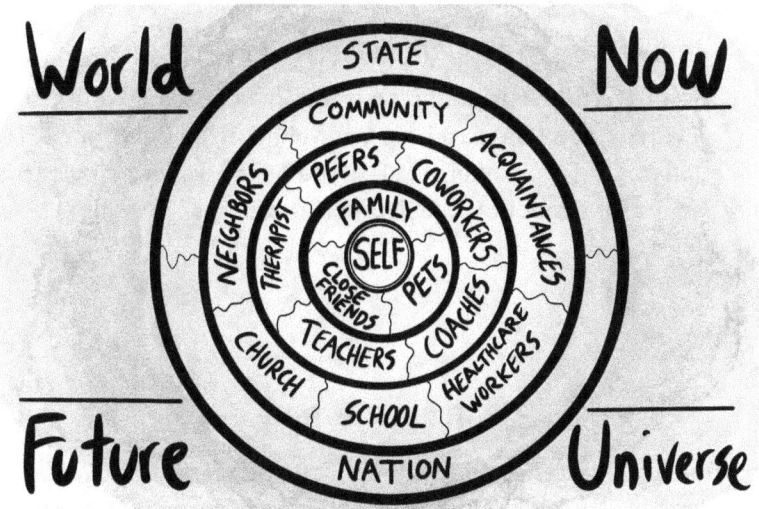

Your children are part of a broader world. Each interaction and experience impacts their view of themselves. The reverse is also true. They impact the people and situations around them. The "Circles of Context" image illustrates the ripples of relationships and environments most people experience. Children find their sense of purpose by living in connected families and communities grounded in love and compassion.

❖ ❖ ❖

Self-care timeouts to define values, build self-awareness, and develop a sense of purpose are all part of spiritual development. They add to the foundation of security provided by caregivers and allow children and adolescents to function in their world with confidence. Like all other aspects of your child's development—physical, social, and emotional—timeouts for spiritual self-care ensure that your child can reset their nervous system thermostat when they feel overwhelmed.

APPLYING A+ TO REDUCING SPIRITUAL STRESSORS

Refer to the **A+ Model** discussed in Chapter 4: Your Basic Strategy and use it to help your child or adolescent better understand their inner self. Use the A+ worksheet provided in Bonus for Timeouts to facilitate this process.

PART 3 WRAP-UP

Raising children is both challenging and rewarding. Guiding them through childhood, adolescence, and into early adulthood may stretch your skills and patience as a caregiver, but it's worth it! The strategies presented here in Part 3 will help keep your children's and adolescent's nervous systems temperatures in—or return them to—the cool zone. When you teach your child to honor their physical, emotional, social, and spiritual selves using effective timeouts, you prepare them to be a well-balanced adult who knows how to care for themselves and others. This life lesson is one of the most important ones you can pass on to future generations.

PART 4

Timeouts for Pets

As you spend time with your pets, consider the experience from their perspective. Like humans, a pet's nervous system temperature affects their mood and behavior. It can move from the cool zone to the hot zone in the blink of an eye. And, just like humans, pets benefit from timeouts that return them to the cool zone. Understanding when your pet's nervous system temperature may be rising will help you create a positive experience for all. Helping them reset their thermostats leads to a pet that behaves appropriately, a pet owner who is more relaxed, and a pet/person relationship that enhances the self-care needs of both parties.

The human side of the self-care conversation was presented in Part 2 – Timeouts for Adults and Part 3 – Timeouts for Children and Adolescents. Now it's time to focus on the animal side of the conversation in Part 4 – Timeouts for Pets.

CHAPTER 18

Perks and Perils of Pet Parenting

Those reading this chapter probably have or have had a pet, maybe a whole menagerie. The pet industry is booming and continues to grow as people seek interaction with animals while spending less time in nature. Even in times of crisis, many people dedicate significant portions of their dwindling budgets to support their pets. The COVID-19 pandemic was no exception. When people were initially told to shelter in their homes, pet adoptions skyrocketed, increasing 250 percent from the previous year.[1] Pets are not merely possessions, they're family.

Throughout this book, the terminology we use for pet owners includes parent, guardian, handler, and caregiver. We believe there is a higher level of responsibility when bringing a pet into your life than simple ownership. For better or worse, pet owners are tasked with the enormous job of providing for, caring for, protecting, nurturing, and guiding their pets throughout their lifetime. Navigating human lifestyles is challenging for pets and may result in nervous system temperature spikes for both the pet and the pet owner. It's the adult's responsibility to help the entire family take the necessary timeouts to come back into the cool zone. Part 4 will help you do that.

KELSEY SAYS:

My love of animals was apparent from my first word: dog! Growing up, we had various types of pets: dogs, cats, birds, fish, reptiles, livestock, and other small animals. My parents often found me sneaking off down the street and climbing fences into the pens of neighboring dogs and horses—not the safest childhood activity. Instead of dolls, I had bins of animal figurines and shelves full of animal plushies.

My fascination with pets continued as I got older. I raised puppies for Guide Dogs for the Blind, trained horses, and pursued animal breeding projects. I surrounded myself with books and videos featuring fictional animal characters and educational material on animal behavior and wellness. The dog and horse breed encyclopedias in my house had so many dog-eared pages the corners were beginning to fall off.

My passion came with a few setbacks. Some lessons I learned the hard way. Pet ownership came with feelings of guilt, sadness, frustration, anxiety, depression, panic, anger, fear, and even trauma. I suffered numerous pet-related injuries, some requiring hospitalization. Being an animal person came with financial stress and negative impacts on my social life and friendships. It often made me feel isolated and overwhelmed. I hadn't realized how challenging life with animals would be.

After the heartache, safety scares, incredible amounts of stress, and watching my pets drain my bank account month after month, I decided the perks of pet parenting still outweighed the struggles, and I began to view my mistakes as learning opportunities. Following my desire to dedicate my life to animals, I became a professional trainer and continued my education on how to cultivate positive, low-stress, healthy relationships between people and their pets.

How to Pick a Pet

Many of us feel intense societal pressure to have the perfect house with the perfect family and the perfect pets living in perfect harmony. "You should get a dog." "Why doesn't your kiddo have a pet?" "I can't believe you don't have any animals." "I love my cats. I couldn't imagine life without them." "You need to get a buddy for your pet. He's lonely." Sound familiar?

Friends and family members give unsolicited advice about which animals you should have, where to get them, and how to

PERKS AND PERILS OF PET PARENTING

raise them. Movies portray a wonderful, devoted relationship between pets and their people. Social media depicts animals being hugged and kissed by babies and toddlers with captions like "best friends" or "so sweet." These messages seem to say that adding a pet will be the answer to all your problems.

And then reality hits. Instead of "I'm so happy I did this," it's "Why on earth did I do this?"

Plenty of people are missing out on the self-care benefits of having pets while others are suffering because of a mismatch with their pets. Even if an animal is a great addition to the household, it adds extra work and worry to the lives of its human family.

Let's explore how to pick the right pet for your household and how to handle the pets you may already have.

Consider Your Lifestyle

First, consider if a pet is a good fit for your family, including your current pets. Discuss adding a pet with all members of the household (parents, kids, partner, roommate, or anyone who could be impacted by the new addition). Make sure everyone is in agreement before swinging by the pet store or animal shelter

on your way home from work. To quote Ben Franklin, "An ounce of prevention is worth a pound of cure." Bringing home a new pet can feel like bringing home a new baby. Be sure everyone is prepared to embark on this journey.

Bringing an animal into your home will create a lifetime relationship, and therefore, shouldn't be taken lightly. Think about all the things you want to experience with this animal, and then consider whether it would want to do those things with you.

Think about your values and envision the type of pet that will help you stay on track. Though your pets won't understand your values, the lifestyle needs of some pets will sync with yours while other pets will clash.

For example, if you're looking for an adventure cat that will go on walks and car rides with you, and you pick out an exceptionally nervous kitten, you probably won't realize that dream partnership. If your job requires extensive travel, or your family enjoys taking vacations that wouldn't be conducive to including a pet, you might not be successful with a new puppy that requires consistent routines and attention. Before bringing a new pet home, take a timeout to review the Values Checklist from Bonus for Timeouts. Finding a good match will allow for a smoother transition into pet parenting.

KELSEY SAYS:

We recently added chickens to our little farm, and we considered what type of flock protection animal would be the best suited for our lifestyle. Our current dogs wouldn't appreciate another dog on site, so a livestock guardian dog was not an option. Some people use donkeys or llamas to guard their poultry, but an animal of that size requires a large financial investment. Many homesteaders keep roosters around to watch the skies for aerial predators. I value a peaceful night's sleep, and I've had many experiences with roosters behaving aggressively toward humans, so that would not work for me. I also value companionship with all my animals.

I settled on guard geese. They are quite noisy when they detect a potential threat. I selected a breed that tends to be more human friendly. After I put in the upfront work of bonding with these birds, they became incredibly social. They run to greet me every day!

My values assessment paired me with ideal additions to our human-animal family.

Many pets don't flourish in today's modern environments. While you may be able to provide some luxuries for your pet, you are responsible for all their wellness needs. This can feel daunting for an animal caregiver, and it's important that your needs are also considered throughout the process. With the right pet in the right lifestyle, it is possible.

Consider Their L.E.G.S.®

How do you find the right pet? You may have heard "It's all in how you raise them." This slogan has gained traction as breed-specific legislation has gone into effect, banning some types of dogs in certain places. While it may be well-intentioned in raising awareness with responsible pet ownership, this slogan falls short and discourages proper research when choosing a pet.

Similarly, the Adopt, Don't Shop campaign, which promotes the importance of animal rescue, pushes adoption over education. There is no doubt that shopping through puppy mills (places where dogs are bred excessively with little to no regard for their welfare) is problematic. These facilities tend to produce puppies that are physically, mentally, and emotionally unwell. Pets worldwide are subjected to unethical, unregulated breeding practices by companies and organizations solely focused on the best interests of the business owners, stockholders, and board members—not the pet or pet owner. However, there are many ways to acquire an animal in addition to adopting from an agency or shopping through inhumane options.

These black-and-white mindsets imply that with the right product and practice, any pet can fit into any lifestyle. But that's not the case. Canine behavior consultant Kim Brophey[2] developed the **L.E.G.S. Model®**, an effective, succinct way to consider the various factors that work together to impact the behavior of your animal. She describes this system as a way to consider "the interaction of nature, nurture, and everything in between."[3]

Ultimately, you must look at all four **L.E.G.S.®** in order to best prepare for your future relationship with your pet. Paraphrased from Kim's book, *Meet Your Dog*, they are as follows:[4]

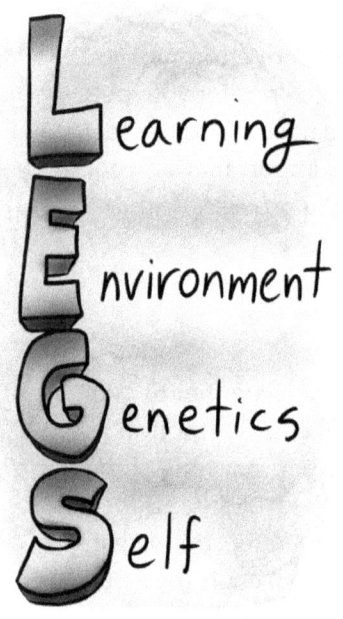

- **Learning.** What are your pet's experiences and education?
- **Environment.** What are the aspects of your pet's external world?
- **Genetics.** What is the DNA that designed your pet inside and out?
- **Self.** What is the unique interior world of your pet? Take into consideration their health, development, age, sex, and individuality.

Narrowing your view to one factor is unfair to the animal and will leave you both stuck in a challenging relationship with inappropriate expectations. The first step to building a successful relationship is recognizing the complexity of your pet.

Adopt or Shop?

Do you adopt or shop? It depends.

Adding a pet to your family comes with some level of risk, regardless of where you sourced the animal. It's like adding a new roommate. They could become your best friend, they could make your life miserable, or your relationship could land somewhere in between. The friction of a mismatched relationship has detrimental effects on the nervous system temperatures of those involved. All relationships take a bit of work to be truly successful. When considering all angles during this process, it makes sense to explore the value of timeouts.

CHARLENE SAYS:

When my daughter was in third grade, she told my husband and me that she wanted a cat. (She also went around the house pretending to be a cat, but that's a story for another type of book.) After some discussion, we began working with her to learn more about what it would mean to be responsible for a pet cat. We read books about cats. We talked to friends who had cats. After gathering the information we needed, we agreed to add a cat to our family.

We went to the pet store and purchased items to help the cat feel comfortable in our home. Our list of basics included food bowls and a litter box, catnip mice, and toys a cat could chase. We set everything up. Then it was time to add a cat.

On pet adoption day we returned to the pet store. I tried to steer the family's attention toward a gray-and-white kitty named Molly. She seemed calm and had been well cared for by her previous owners. While I was filling out the paperwork, my daughter and husband appeared at my side with an obviously distraught cat inside a kitty carrying case. "I want this one," my daughter announced. "His name is Chubby." So Molly's name was replaced with Chubby's on the adoption paperwork and we took him home.

Chubby was a beautiful tan tabby with a Maine Coon appearance. I could see why my daughter picked him out. In his history, we learned that he'd suffered a trauma as a kitten and had spent the last four months in a cage.

We were happy to offer Chubby a home, but we had to manage his neurotic behaviors throughout his lifetime. He eagerly played with my daughter, and he bonded with my husband, but he never became the cuddly cat we'd hoped to add to our family.

If your lifestyle can accommodate an animal who may have more complicated needs and you love the idea of rescuing your new buddy, absolutely check out rescue and adoption options. With a little patience, you're likely to find a great fit for your family.

If you have a lifestyle that requires a certain set of physical and behavioral traits for the animal to be successful, then going with a qualified, experienced breeder may be a better option for your household. There are many breeders out there who do a phenomenal job.

Do research and chat with certified—not self-appointed—experts so you can find the best match for you. Prepare to meet the needs of your new pet. Be honest about what you can provide financially, physically, emotionally, mentally, and socially for that animal. By taking timeouts for yourself, your family, and your future pets, you will be able to make the most informed choice possible to start your relationship with everyone's well-being in mind.

How to Make the Best of It

So far, we've focused on adding a new pet to your household, but what about the pet(s) you already have? Maybe your current one is causing you stress and you need to know what to do. Perhaps your pet is exhibiting symptoms of being in the hot zone and you wish they could take their own self-care timeout.

Millions of other pet parents are concerned about the same things. It's normal to experience these struggles in any relationship. There are actions you can take to create calm out of chaos, turn rowdy into relaxed, and shift stress to success. The remaining chapters in Part 4 will provide a comprehensive guide for addressing the needs of the animals in your home and enhancing your partnership with them.

How to Move On

If a pairing isn't right or the pet is not a good fit for you or your home, if the circumstances change or expectations aren't met, sometimes the best thing to do is move on.

It is okay to rehome a pet. It's also okay to euthanize a pet. A heavy stigma is sometimes associated with both options. But

there's nothing wrong with prioritizing quality of life (for the people and the pets) over judgment of others. Sanity and safety outweigh social stigma.

> **OPTIONS FOR LETTING GO**
>
> Losing Lulu[5] is a private Facebook group with a community of supportive, compassionate people who understand that sometimes the best option is the most challenging. If you're feeling overwhelmed, if you are concerned for the safety of your family, your pet, or the public, if you have worked with qualified experts on the mental and physical health of the pet, and behavioral euthanasia is an option on the table, please reach out to supportive, empathetic people in this group. They've been there too.

Guilt and shame are common when it is time to let a pet go. You may feel shame over your failures, shortcomings, and broken promises. You may feel guilty for having brought this animal into your home, for not being able to meet the animal's needs, or that family members have suffered because of this animal. Your emotions are valid. Consider the impacts for you, the other members of your family (human or animal), and the pet. Use the **Surf the Wave** strategy from Chapter 7 to help in processing this challenging situation. Sometimes the most appropriate, most beneficial, and most humane option is to let go.

> **KELSEY SAYS:**
>
> My husband and I met in dog training class, and we were smitten with each other's dogs from the start. Our dogs, however, weren't on the same page. It took a lot of controlled exposures and continued education on managing disgruntled dog relationships to finally get Bindi and Cairo to the point of tolerating each other. Then we added Evie.
>
> Evie was super cute, a love bug of a pit bull puppy. My

husband picked her up from the shelter when she was eight weeks old. She instantly bonded with Cairo—also a rescued pit bull. They were inseparable. As Evie grew up, we provided her with a great socialization plan and training program. She was often a demo dog in my training classes, and she loved making new friends. Her favorite thing to do was snuggle up with a warm blanket or her "brother" Cairo.

Evie's relationship to Bindi was quite different. Over the next eighteen months, they got into altercations that resulted in serious injury, putting Bindi through emergency surgery twice. Evie killed a kitten and attacked two other dogs. As a dog trainer, I was incredibly distressed by Evie's evolving aggression, and it became a major liability for my business. We brought in an expert in aggression cases, and after months of time, money, management, and tears, we decided Evie was no longer a good fit for our family.

This brief summation doesn't even touch the surface of the trauma and heartache involved in what felt like giving up on our dog and ourselves. Thankfully, a few amazing animal shelter workers helped us rehome her. Upon my request, the new owners were given my contact information, and we are still connected today. We loved seeing her updates, and they deeply appreciated the extensive behavior history we provided. Evie thrived with them, and we began to heal.

❖ ❖ ❖

Choosing a pet can be an exciting time for the family. Best results come with consideration of both the household's needs and the pet's needs. To keep everyone's nervous system in the cool zone, review the **L.E.G.S.® Model** to find the most compatible match for the entire family. Use the information in this chapter to ensure that you are set up to enjoy the perks of pet parenting and avoid the perils.

CHAPTER 19

Through the Ages and Stages

As your pet's primary caregiver, your relationship is the most important one they have. The moment you bring your new pet home, you begin creating the foundation for this relationship. Your role as pet parent is similar to that of a human parent, since your pet will mature and develop in your care. Knowing where your pet is in their development will guide you in your decisions for timeout strategies and set you up to have appropriate and reasonable expectations.

> **SHAUN SAYS:**
>
> I met coauthor Kelsey when my goldendoodle was a puppy. I quickly fell in love with her training methods, in part because she really understands the developmental stages of animals. I can't tell you how many times I observed similarities between Kelsey's instruction to pet owners and the advice I gave to parents regarding their children.
>
> As you read through this chapter, note the similarities between animal and human development and remember that the human-animal connection is mutually beneficial. I hope you will get as excited as I do about the commonalities among all living things.

Baby Animals

Many baby animals rely on their mothers to do most of the parenting, but that doesn't mean humans should be out of the picture. Depending on the species, baby animals could be quite functional, or they may be cute little eating and pooping blobs that can't hear or see their surroundings. In any case, brain development is happening.

By monitoring the stress levels of both mother and baby, you can influence their resilience and tolerance to stressors once they reach adulthood. The most important thing you can do at this stage is create timeouts to meet their basic survival needs for food, hydration, sleep, appropriate levels of contact, and temperature regulation.

Young Animals

Cuteness overload! A recent study showed that puppies reach maximum perceived cuteness at six to eight weeks, right at the time when they start looking to add humans to their social network, rather than always relying on their mothers.[1]

Young animals need guidance and focused parenting to help them become mature creatures able to navigate the challenges of adulthood. How weird it must be for an animal living in a human-centered environment. They arrive with only their natural instincts and that makes young animals quite challenging for humans to manage. At this stage, your pet's behavior, which you may find frustrating, could trigger your nervous system temperature to spike into the hot zone. Their thermometer is likely reading in the hot zone too.

A great strategy to support your young animals is the **PACE** approach (introduced in Chapter 11). Your pets are counting on you to support their learning in a compassionate and empathetic way. Being present during this stage helps them build trust in you, their two-legged caretaker. You have plenty of time to train your pets as they get older. Take timeouts now to appreciate the unique way a young animal views the world.

Adolescent Animals

Adolescence is a rough time for everyone, pets and people alike. Hormones are shifting, physical changes are happening, priorities

are adjusting, and the brain is still developing. Adolescent animals have a hard enough time dealing with their internal struggles. Add in external stressors for an overwhelming recipe. Because of the lack of nervous system regulation skills in adolescence, it's common to see animals in this stage get stuck in the hot zone and need extra assistance to reset their thermostat.

Pets in this age range need consistent boundaries that allow for as much agency as possible. This is easier said than done because they often make choices you will find challenging to support. However, if they're safe, it's important to allow adolescents the opportunity to express their independence as they learn and mature. Sound familiar?

KELSEY SAYS:

My clients can usually relate to their adolescent pet's struggles once I explain how their brain and body is changing. It's not that different from the phases of adolescence that humans go through.

Fortunately, raising an adolescent animal is much less complicated than raising a teenager. Your pet doesn't have

> thumbs—in most cases—so they are limited to the environment you provide for them. Though they may seem to be talking back, they can't say those hurtful phrases that often come out of a human teenager's mouth, and they won't invite all their friends over to throw a raging party in your absence. Plus, in most species, the animal adolescent stage is much shorter than the human adolescent one, so with time, grace, and patience—and maybe a little professional guidance—you will get through it.

Adult Animals

By the time a pet reaches adulthood, they have life pretty much figured out—or so they may think. They know which things are safe or dangerous. They recognize what behaviors are reinforcing and what behaviors help them avoid punishment. They have established neural pathways in their brains that help them navigate their day-to-day life efficiently. And like humans, neuroplasticity (introduced in Chapter 1) lasts forever. You can teach an old dog new tricks.

Though novice animals may not understand how to cope in environments they haven't been exposed to previously, they can

still learn many life skills and build resiliency. This is the time to enjoy your pet and appreciate the work it took to get to this point. Continue to meet their needs through appropriate physical, emotional, and social timeouts for the wonderful years ahead.

Senior Animals

Living with senior animals feels bittersweet. They need substantially less physical and mental stimulation to be satisfied, and they have developed deep bonds with their human and animal family members over the years spent together. However, observing your once-vibrant pet succumb to mental and physical ailments can be devastating, especially as their end-of-life transition approaches.

Senior animals aren't cheap. Vet visits can rack up serious bills, not counting medications, special diets, physical therapy, extra equipment, and other expenses. These struggle points often send pet owners into the hot zone as they try to navigate a new and unfamiliar territory of life with an aging pet.

It's important to remember to take time to meet your own needs as a caregiver of a dependent (as discussed in Chapter 10). Then spend time attending to the timeout needs of your senior pets. Just because they aren't as active as they once were, that doesn't mean they don't need physical attention to stay fit. They may not be pestering you for playtime, but they still need cognitive stimulation throughout the day. Treasure their golden years.

> **KELSEY SAYS:**
>
> Cairo, our rescue pit bull, aged quickly. At ten he was still acting like a normal adult, at eleven he started showing signs of aging, and before his twelfth birthday it was time to let him go. He became very needy during his last year: constantly whining for my attention, always underfoot, attached to me in what felt like a suffocating way, demanding his bed and meals prepared a certain way, unable to make it outside to go potty or get on

or off the furniture without assistance. We took him to physical therapy, which meant an ever-growing list of exercises, stretches, and treatments. His bucket of medications had to be delivered in new and inventive ways so he wouldn't refuse his doses. He became time consuming, financially taxing, and emotionally draining.

Having a senior dog was an emotional roller coaster. I often felt frustrated, followed by feelings of guilt. I should be appreciating every second I had with him. I should be able to drop everything and meet his needs since he wasn't able to take care of himself. I should be more supportive and attentive. Or so I told myself.

Since Cairo's passing, I have chosen to give myself a little grace. Cairo wasn't an easy dog at any stage, yet an amazing dog in his own way. I miss him, I appreciate him, and I am grateful for him. And now I'm preparing myself as our next senior dog enters her final season of life.

◆ ◆ ◆

Whether your pet is a baby, a senior, or somewhere in between, they depend on you to help them live a happy, healthy life. This time need not feel like a heavy weight on your shoulders. Focus on what they need at each developmental stage, and you can make the time you spend on timeouts efficient, effective, and enjoyable. Most pets have a much shorter lifespan than humans and they can transition through those stages in the blink of an eye. Take a timeout to appreciate who they are today.

CHAPTER 20
Balancing Body and Brain

Living as captive animals dependent on their bond with their caregivers is a blessing and a curse for pets. It's not natural for animals to be contained indoors or in enclosures all day, just like it's not natural for humans to sit and stare at screens all day. We all need opportunities to get up, move around, and engage in species-appropriate behavior, preferably out in nature. Indoor living conditions, veterinary treatments, and the consideration pets receive have improved greatly in recent years, but these alone cannot fulfill all their needs.

> **KELSEY SAYS:**
> During a recent winter, we had two major power outages at our house. One was during a record-setting ice storm and the other was in a record-setting heat wave. The extreme weather conditions prevented us from doing much outside, and public health concerns prevented us from engaging in social activities.
>
> I couldn't get much work done as I kept an eye on my dwindling phone and computer batteries, and recharging my devices in my car was not an option in freezing or sweltering conditions. So? I spent a lot of time in my house. With no entertainment. No work to do. No one to talk to. (My husband was traveling both times—how convenient for him.)
>
> I realized—this is how my animals live all the time. They are only given mental stimulation when I provide them with something to do. They can't read a book when they're feeling bored. They're hanging out, waiting for the next interesting thing to happen. No wonder my dog starts barking at squirrels after days of limited activity.

All pets have physiological and psychological needs. When we neglect these needs, we can see the symptoms of chronic stress and the associated physical and behavioral fallout.

It's common for pets with too little stimulation to become frustrated, anxious, and go a little stir crazy. They will find their own ways to drain their energy, which may not work well for the humans or other animals in the home. Those with too much stimulation or the incorrect type shut down, act out, and become overly reactive, even aggressive. Overstimulation can lead to injuries, both acute and chronic.

Timeouts for the general health of your pet involve recognizing the animal's needs and limitations and supporting their body and mind. The result is an enriched pet with a functional self-care plan.

Fostering enrichment for your pet encompasses "the process of providing captive animals with some form of stimulation to encourage natural behavior, which helps to improve or maintain their physical and mental health. The intent is to encourage natural behaviors, stimulate curiosity, and to give animals choice and control in their environment."[1]

There are a variety of ways to provide these opportunities for your pet. To ease the stress accrued with a captive lifestyle, allow your pet to realign with the natural world through exploratory enrichment options. Environment-based enrichment, which encourages investigation of new and interesting things, can be as simple as putting an unfamiliar object in the pet's living space for them to interact with or taking your pet out to experience a novel place. Scent-based enrichment allows your pet to use their olfactory system to process their surroundings and gather information, accomplished by letting your pet sniff an aromatic object or track smells on an outing.

SHAUN SAYS:

My goldendoodle, Bowlby (named after the Father of Attachment Theory), was a delightful puppy. We both enjoyed

> participating in Kelsey's training classes. One of the best things I learned is the recommendation to have some of Bowlby's outings be sniffy walks where he is allowed to stop and smell the roses—and every other thing he's interested in. It took pressure off our adventures because I didn't feel like we had to be in formal training mode every time we left the house. Good mental health for both of us.

Food-based enrichment, which enables your pet to rehearse their instinctual food acquisition behavior, is an area where many pets lack opportunities to meet their own needs. Animals living in their natural habitats will contribute large amounts of their physical and mental energy towards nourishing themselves. This opportunity to forage is lost on pets that have meals hand delivered to them. It may seem like you're spoiling your pet by making sure food is readily available. This may be activating their nervous system by blocking their ability to express natural behavior.

Though every individual animal comes with their set of complexities, with a little learning and awareness it can be simple to use timeouts to incorporate various types of enrichment into daily routines.

> **SUGGESTED READING**
>
> *Canine Enrichment for the Real World* by Allie Bender and Emily Strong[2] gives an in-depth description of various enrichment activities, why they work, and how to implement them. Even if you don't have a dog, this book has so many ideas, you're bound to find plenty of options that can be utilized for your species of pet.

From Wild Animal to Present Day Pet

Your pet may be tamed or domesticated, but after decades, centuries, or millennia of natural selection and genetic manipulation, they will still behave instinctively to meet their needs.

Consider how tigers acquire food in the wild. Their hunting skills, coat pattern, physical makeup, and temperament have developed to enhance their survival. In contrast, the way an elephant gets his meals in the wild is completely different. Responsible zookeepers utilize individual enrichment strategies for each animal to best support their self-care plans.

The pet in front of you is not that different from the wild animal in the zoo. It is experiencing a captive lifestyle that requires deliberate modifications to allow for natural behaviors to function. There are too many pet species to make a comprehensive food enrichment plan for each within the scope of this book, so check out the overviews in this chapter where we provide insight into the timeout activities for your pet. Have fun as you test out a variety of options.

> **KELSEY SAYS:**
>
> Implementing a food enrichment plan is one of the first things I recommend to clients when they begin a training program. It may not feel like training your pet when you swap the normal food dish out for a puzzle toy, but it's an easy way to tap into your pet's mental and physical energy without spending any extra time or effort. Many of my clients begin noticing a difference in their pet's behavior within a few days.

Food Enrichment

Here are some species-specific recommendations for food enrichment. Many of the examples provided can be used for other species as well.

Dogs

Some people think of canine pets as tamed wolves; however, dogs have evolved over thousands of years to coexist with humans, and they operate differently from their wild ancestors. They spend most of their day using problem-solving skills to navigate human environments. Even feral dogs, which account for about 80 percent of the world's dog population,[3] are dependent on humans in some ways, whether by rifling through trash, hanging around close enough to pick up scraps, or stealing from farms and restaurants.

For centuries, humans have been carefully breeding dogs for specific jobs, such as tracking and herding. Today, this genetically refined creature is brought into homes to lie around in confinement for hours. Many dogs have a hard time with this lifestyle and find ways to drain the energy previously reserved for those breed-specific tasks. When your dog chews the furniture, herds the children, and barks at strangers, they are acting out genetically hardwired drives.

Food enrichment is one of the easiest, most efficient ways to help dogs feel more satisfied in urban and suburban environments.

> **PRO TIP: SUPPORT YOUR DOG'S SCENT AND SCAVENGING INSTINCTS**
>
> Engage your dog's nose and scavenging instincts through hide-and-seek games by hiding meals and treats in the yard and around the house for your dog to find.

Cats

Cats in the wild will hunt, stalk, and kill their prey. They are more carnivorous than dogs, and when given the choice of eating kibble out of a food bowl or killing a mouse, many prefer the hunt. Dietary requirements for cats haven't been impacted through domestication nearly as much as dogs. Cats weren't brought to live exclusively indoors until the 1950s with the invention of cat litter. Until that time, cats consumed rodents, birds, and frogs as a primary food source, which is why cats continue to be used for pest control today.

Even with protein-rich diets and an array of toys to keep them busy, many cats are frustrated when hunting and exploration is limited to the confines of an apartment or house. A timeout for food enrichment allows your feline friend to rehearse their instinctual behaviors without releasing rodents into your living room.

> **PRO TIP: SUPPORT YOUR CAT'S PREDATORY INSTINCTS**
> Activate your cat's predatory instincts by providing puzzle toys that require chasing and capturing the goodies inside.

Birds

Many species of birds are kept as pets. Chickens, ducks, turkeys, and other poultry have been domesticated to make them easier to raise for agriculture. However, most pet birds are tamed, not domesticated. These bird species can be found living in the wild today. Though your pet bird may have been hatched in captivity, their natural tendencies remain.

Birds spend over half their waking hours foraging and eating. The rest of their time is divided between social interaction and feather maintenance. When acquiring food becomes boring, birds will often focus more on social engagement and feather preening, which can result in demanding behaviors that human's find annoying or lead to harmful feather destruction. Adding enrichment activities is a great way to keep captive birds happy and healthy.

> **PRO TIP: SUPPORT YOUR BIRD'S FORAGING BEHAVIORS**
> Tap into your bird's desire to forage with a variety of destructible food dispensers.

Horses and Herbivores

Horses, guinea pigs, rabbits, goats, sheep, and other herbivores are meant to spend most of their day grazing and browsing. Some species do best in vast pastures. Others enjoy a search through brush and shrubs to pick leaves, seeds, and fruits off the plants. These animals have digestive processes that require them to move constantly, eating small amounts as they go, rather than standing around and filling up on large sporadic meals. Horses, for example, are prone to stomach ulcers if they go more than a few hours without eating.

When herbivores meant to roam large spaces are confined to a cage, stall, or pen, they often develop stereotypic behaviors or become depressed. Providing consistent availability of forage and engaging ways to access it, helps these animals with both their physical and mental well-being.

> **PRO TIP: SUPPORT GRAZING FOR YOUR HORSES AND HERBIVORES**
>
> Keep your herbivore busy with a diet of varied foliage in slow feeder nets, bags, and bowls to encourage long bouts of regular grazing.

Reptiles, Amphibians, and Fish

Cold-blooded animals make wonderful companions. They need the same care and consideration. Some are predators and enjoy the hunt. Others are herbivores or omnivores and love a good plant to crunch on. Since every species has unique diet requirements, the enrichment options will vary from pet to pet. Simple shifts in how and what you feed can make all the difference in creating a diverse and engaging life for these terrestrial and aquatic friends.

> **PRO TIP: SUPPORT FOOD-FINDING INSTINCTS FOR YOUR REPTILES, AMPHIBIANS AND FISH**
>
> Tap into your pet's instincts by providing natural food sources in realistic habitats: inside their hidey-holes, under logs, or in their enclosure canopy.

Adding enrichment is both a proactive and reactive way to support the self-care of your pet. Use it as a preventative strategy to maintain cool zone temperatures or to help your pet regulate after a hot zone spike. When given their choice, many animals will strive to meet their own basic needs through instinctive behaviors, so it's on you to set them up with opportunities to do so. Without human intervention, they are limited in their ability to accomplish this in a modern captive lifestyle.

By channeling your pet's natural behaviors into a productive enrichment exercise, you give your pet a chance to impress you with their amazing skills rather than frustrate you with nuisance behaviors. Involve all members of the family in creating fun outlets for the pet. Children are excellent helpers at stuffing toys with goodies and hiding treats around the house. Provide enjoyable self-care opportunities for your pet to combat the chronic stress created by captivity, and you're on your way to a happy household.

Don't Forget Downtime

Supporting your pet's mind and body doesn't end with enrichment and exercise. This level of stimulation must be balanced with opportunities to relax and decompress. Taking a nap, settling on an outing, practicing calming behaviors, or spending time in a quiet, enclosed space are all useful tactics if excess stimulation is causing their nervous system temperature to rise.

Sleep Needs

Different species have different requirements for sleep, and pets living in busy home environments are often not getting their sleep needs met. Just like a toddler who skipped their nap, a sleep-deprived pet is not a pleasant creature to be around.

Consider the natural sleep cycle of your pet's species. Nocturnal animals, like the leopard gecko, do best when they get their shuteye during the day. Diurnal animals, like the parrot, wake up with the light and sleep when it's dark. Crepuscular animals, like the guinea pig, rabbit, dog, and cat, are active during the twilight periods of dawn and dusk and prefer to sleep at night and midday.

If you keep your pet awake during their natural sleep period, they'll start accruing a sleep deficit. Make sure your pet has quiet time at the appropriate time to meet their daily sleep requirements.

> **KELSEY SAYS:**
>
> Most of my clients' dogs do not get enough sleep. Dogs need more hours of sleep than humans—around fourteen to twenty hours per day, depending on the dog—and the quality of sleep must be considered. Creating a calm, quiet, safe place for the dog and building a nap routine into the daily schedule are often at the top of my suggestion list, regardless of the behavior concerns that prompted the need for training in the first place. Nobody is their best self when operating with a sleep deficit.

Space Needs

Everyone needs a timeout in their own space. Even extroverts require occasional moments to be by themselves to limit the constant flood of information from stimulating environments. Likewise, pets require moments of peace and quiet.

Not all animals are able to communicate this need. Many people have pets that constantly want human attention and are devastated if they must be alone for long periods of time. Putting the puppy in a pen or setting up the bird cage in a quiet part of the house, feels a bit strange when you expect the pet to be your constant companion. Distance makes the heart grow fonder, right? A little space gives both people and pets the necessary time to decompress and practice the skill of independence.

A timeout for seclusion doesn't mean you must imprison your pet or abandon them. If not practiced compassionately and correctly, forcing animals to be alone can create significant

distress. However, it is important for your pet to have a place that is theirs exclusively with no children or other animals present. The pet needs to know they can retreat to their comfort zone at any time and their space will be respected.

For some pets, this special space could be a bed, crate, cage, or pen, set in a less trafficked spot in the home, or far away from activity behind a closed door. This area will be comfortable for the pet and a convenient place for the pet parent to use for confinement or when a timeout is needed.

SEPARATION DISTRESS TO SEPARATION SUCCESS

Animals closely bonded to humans or other animals may be better off with their buddies more often to support their emotional wellness. The human's job is to prepare the pet for unexpected events, such as the person or animal they're attached to needing to stay overnight at the hospital or even passing away. Your pet may be used to you working from home, and then one day you take a job with a commute. Your pet may get injured and need to be confined for their own health and safety. The scenarios are endless.

> It is in the best interest of your pet to learn that separation isn't always tragic and may even be pleasant. Ask for help. Behavior experts can teach you how to turn separation distress into separation success.

Natural Outlets, Not Naughty Behaviors

When a child throws a tantrum, acts out, or behaves inappropriately, you can bet there are strong emotions beneath the surface. Similarly, when your pet seems to be naughty, consider why. It's not reasonable to expect an animal to act like their best self when their needs haven't been met. By providing timeouts for enrichment and downtime, you can channel perceived naughty behaviors into appropriate activities.

> **BENEFITS OF AN EXPERT OPINION**
>
> Mental illnesses, physical illnesses, pain, and nutrition can all have drastic effects on your pet's general wellness. If your pet is exhibiting symptoms or behaviors that seem extreme or confusing, discuss their physical and mental health with a veterinarian. Even if the pet appears physically healthy, an animal health professional or behavior expert may be able to provide a more comprehensive picture.

Balance is key when working toward wellness and implementing self-care for both humans and animals. We all need mental and physical exercise and rest to recharge. To keep your pet healthy, work the brain and the body through enrichment, engage with them, and let them sleep.

> **APPLYING A+ TO BALANCING BODY AND BRAIN**
>
> Refer to the **A+ Model** discussed in Chapter 4: Your Basic Strategy and use it to map out the various ways to build more balance into your pet's daily routines. Use the A+ worksheet provided in Bonus for Timeouts to facilitate this process.

◆ ◆ ◆

Supporting your pet's brain and body takes work to be successful and balanced and, when handled with care, need not create misery and stress among the family. Building self-care opportunities for your pet can be fun and engaging, fulfilling and satisfying, memorable and meaningful, as well as part of your routine. It can be exactly what you need when you and your pets need a timeout.

CHAPTER 21

Help! I Can't Speak Human!

Working with animals may feel more complicated than working with people. For one, obviously, animals can't use words to tell us what they need. Secondly, trying to understand what an animal is thinking or feeling by evaluating their behavior is confusing; physically they move differently based on their physiology and are covered in fur, scales, or feathers. Animal messaging can get lost in translation as inappropriate behaviors surface and nervous system temperatures climb. Interestingly though, if you know what to look for, reading animal body language can be simpler than you think.

Animals often behave like, well, animals. Most behavior issues are normal behavioral responses to a situation that serves a specific function for that species. When your dog growls at the neighbor, your cat marks the couch, your horse kicks, or your parrot attacks a family member, it's easy to understand why you believe your pet's actions are problematic.

KELSEY SAYS:

People call me for training services when they perceive they have a problem they can't fix. New client consultations often involve frustration, irritation, fear, and tears. I understand where these pet owners are coming from, and I have felt these emotions with my own pets. There is no training technique, perfect product, or magic wand that can instantly turn a stressful situation around. Pets aren't broken and in need of repair. They're doing the best they can with the resources available to them, much like their owners.

A holistic approach to addressing aspects of our pet's self-care needs is the most effective way to start making progress. Taking timeouts to take care of our pet's physical, emotional, and social well-being allows us to tackle problems at the root, not the behavioral symptoms. Owners can fall in love with their pets again as they appreciate the complex and unique personalities of their animals.

When your pet is acting out, they are likely experiencing physical or psychological distress, and that brings on stress for you. When you're stressed, it's easy to get upset or resort to reflexive punishment strategies. You may make matters worse by jumping into reaction mode by impulse or taking personal offense to the animal's instinctual response to their situation.

This is a great time to implement the **THRIVE** technique (introduced in Chapter 2). Practicing mindful breathing when you're dealing with an animal crisis might seem frivolous, but it is imperative that you deal with your own stress through a timeout strategy before you can address the behavior of your pet with a measure of rationality.

THE SOURCE OF UNHEALTHY BEHAVIOR

"When an animal is physically, behaviorally, or emotionally unhealthy, there will always be maladaptive behaviors."[1]

—Emily Strong, CDBC, SBA

What a Nuisance!

Let's be honest, there are pet behaviors that drive you crazy, right? But isn't the same thing true with any relationship? You aren't going to like everything another individual does, whether animal or human. Nuisance behaviors, if left unaddressed, can lead to major rifts in the relationship.

Most of your pet's nuisance behaviors are normal, species-appropriate behaviors. In a human household, they can be downright annoying. Pet vocalizations, for example, can be exceedingly stressful. The dog barking, the cat meowing, or the bird screeching can create quite the disturbance if you're trying to work from home, put the baby down for a nap, or heaven forbid, get a full night of sleep. Other behaviors, such as destructive chewing, marking or pottying indoors, food stealing, object eating, digging, or scratching can be a physical or financial burden if you repeatedly need to fix or replace furniture, landscaping, flooring, or other parts of your home. These behaviors can also be dangerous for your pet, resulting in emergency vet care, surgeries, or even the death of the animal.

People often rehome their pets when their partner, roommate, neighbor, child, or other important person in their life is fed up with the pet's behavior. Everyone's physical, emotional, and social health is important for keeping peace in the household. If you're struggling with your pet's undesirable behavior, this is a great time to seek professional support or training assistance.

> **KELSEY SAYS:**
>
> As I'm writing this section, my adolescent Labrador is barking his little heart out. Initially, I yelled, "Shut up!" This quieted him for all of fifteen seconds before he started back at it. My next responses consisted of yelling, "Dude, you're being annoying!" and then pleading, "Please be patient for just a few more minutes!" At that point, I recognized I was not only reacting impulsively from my own frustration, but my behavior was no different than his.
>
> We all have moments where we react without thinking. Every person has snapped at a loved one and then moments later realized that was a poor way to handle the situation.
>
> I finally said, "Go get your toy," not in the exasperated tones I was spewing before but in a peppy, engaging voice. The moment he did, I told him he was a good boy. I put down my laptop, and we went outside to play around for a bit. Honestly, it was a nice break from sitting at my computer for hours. I needed a minute to stretch my legs and switch gears. Back at my desk, he happily worked on a food-stuffed puzzle toy while I wrote a little more before wrapping up for the day.

Remember in Chapter 2 where we discussed the fidget and fool around response to a nervous system temperature warm up? Nuisance behaviors are signals, too. Your pet could display fussy or silly support-seeking behavior to help quell their stress response before they are overwhelmed by the physiological symptoms of the hot zone.

Be curious. Which need is not being met? Should you address their physical health or should you simply take a timeout to breathe and relax together? Use your pet's behavior as a diagnostic tool to determine the best way to bring them back to the cool zone. The more you observe without judgment, the more you will learn about your pet and their needs.

Why so Stressed?

Pets can experience stress, anxiety, trauma, and phobias similar to humans. You may wonder how an animal could possibly be stressed when they're living in a lovely home, eating premium food, and spending time with a caring family. Depending on their learning history, genetics, environment, and internal state—their **L.E.G.S.** ®—they may develop significant emotional responses to stressors in their daily lives.

When your pet is pacing, crying, hypervigilant, avoidant, disinterested in activities, or showing fear responses such as cowering, hiding, trembling, increased heart rate, rapid and shallow breathing, dilated pupils, or inability to eat, stop what you're doing and attend to them. Their nervous system thermometer is rising into the hot zone and their body is going into a flight or freeze response. It's time for a timeout.

It's easy to become frustrated with a fearful or anxious animal, and it isn't always an option for life to come to a complete halt whenever your pet is struggling. Try to help them feel more comfortable until there is an opportunity to fully address the need. A fantastic mantra to remember is: My pet is not giving me a hard time; they are having a hard time.

> **SHAUN SAYS:**
>
> My plan with Bowlby, my goldendoodle puppy, was to train him as a therapy dog to use in my clinic. And then COVID-19 hit. My daughter, Natalie, was unable to work because of the mandated closures, so Bowlby went to live with her. Natalie spent pretty

much all day every day in her apartment. She streamed hours of media, read several novels, and rarely left the confines of her home—a dramatic daily routine change for both daughter and pet.

About six months into the pandemic, we noticed Bowlby was no longer an easygoing pup. He showed signs of anxiety and stereotypic behaviors. He spun in circles, picked up Natalie's shoes at any sign of her leaving the house, and barked at every sound.

I took him to one of Kelsey's training sessions in the park to work on his behaviors. He spent the entire time panting and fidgeting, unable to complete the simplest tasks. His nervous system temperature was clearly in the hot zone. After a consultation with Kelsey, we worked on gradually increasing his socialization at a pace that worked best for him. We also talked to our veterinarian about adding an anti-anxiety medication.

Bowlby and his humans began to enjoy life together again. I'm not sure he will ever be my office partner, but he is an amazing emotional support animal for my daughter. The time we spent on recognizing and addressing his needs truly paid off.

Suzanne Clothier, renowned animal trainer, says, "Training should never be a version of *Fear Factor*."[2] Nothing good comes from forcing an animal to deal with their fear. This only results in more frustration for the human and more stress for the pet. Intentionally putting an animal in a stressful situation or trapping an animal so they can't escape will quickly deteriorate the animal's trust in the person responsible.

A timeout to assist an animal having a flight or freeze response may look more like providing social support. Acknowledge that your pet is struggling and offer comfort or take them away from the present stressor. Provide them with an opportunity to regulate their nervous system back to the cool zone. This reiterates to your pet that you are aware of their needs and can bring them back to a place of safety, building trust rather than tearing it down.

There are many strategies in Part 5 that can help you generate ideas for what timeouts in these instances could look like for your individual pet. When in doubt, contact a professional. Experienced trainers or veterinary behaviorists can help both you and your pet while keeping the relationship between you and your pet intact.

Are You Aggressive?

Aggression isn't a personality trait or a defining quality; it's a description of a behavior that occurs when the fight response is activated in the nervous system. In similar situations, humans may behave aggressively to protect themselves or the things and people they care about. That doesn't mean they're a bad person; it indicates they were put in a situation they were unable to handle in a different way.

What do you do when your pet displays aggressive behavior? First, take a timeout to give yourself permission to feel the emotions associated with their behavior. You are allowed to be afraid of your pet, or to experience shame, embarrassment, hopelessness, guilt, frustration, worry, despair, and anxiety. It's okay if you don't want to be around your pet and don't want others to be around them. Give yourself permission to feel all those emotions—and do it away from your pet. Reacting to their aggression with your own aggression won't get you the positive results you need.

ALWAYS CONSIDER YOUR PET'S EXPERIENCE

It used to be common practice to "Let a sleeping dog lie" or "Don't bother a dog with a bone." In recent years, the suggested methods changed to "Stick your hands in the dog's food bowl so they get used to you" or "Take the dog's toys away so they know you're in control." Understandably, this led to a major uptick in dog bites.

Many dogs will growl or bare their teeth when they're worried someone is going to invade their space or take away their resources. This guarding scenario is also seen in horses, birds, and other animals. When a person scolds their pet for behaving defensively, the animal has even more evidence that when people approach, bad things are likely to happen. Plus, if the animal is punished for communicating their stress—by growling, for example—they might skip that step the next time and escalate straight to a bite.

Be considerate of how your pet may feel in these scenarios. There's a reason for their behavior and extending a little compassion can often save the day.

Aggressive displays—growling, showing teeth, hissing, puffing up to look big, piloerection, pinning ears, vocalizing, or feigning bites toward the trigger—are good! These displays communicate the animal's distress without causing harm. Most animals practice this ritualized aggression with the intention to diffuse conflict instead of progressing to dangerous behavior.

If you shout at someone to back off when they invade your space, and they respond by leaving you alone, you don't need to escalate into violence to protect yourself. If your pet displays aggression to get the threatening thing, person, or animal, to go away, the best possible outcome would be for the threat to leave. This way the pet doesn't need to escalate their behavior to get their needs met.

After the pet's needs have been met, and they no longer feel the urge to display aggressive behavior, it's time to create a prevention plan—a timeout strategy to help reduce aggressive responses in the future. Talk through your options with a behavior professional. Because aggressive behavior in your pet creates so many strong emotions, it's ideal to work with someone outside the relationship who can help you navigate the process of moving forward.

Learning a New Language

You may be able to recognize the signals in your own body when you're in need of a timeout, but it may be challenging to notice when your pet is going through those physiological responses. Observing their body language and behavior is your best gauge for understanding your pet's emotional status.

There are many things to consider when reading body language. Think of each signal as a word. String together all the words to convey the full picture. Watch for dramatic as well as subtle signals to form the most accurate assessment of the animal. This takes practice, knowledge, patience, and a good eye.

The repertoire of communication signals in an animal's toolbox varies from species to species and pet to pet; however, most pet owners become familiar with their pet's communication style through simple observation in various contexts. For example, a cat may yawn to show stress, as well as when they wake up. In the morning, you can assume the cat is yawning normally, whereas in another context you could assume the yawning is an indication of a rising nervous system temperature. Look for abnormal behaviors, repeated behaviors, or excessive behaviors to identify whether a signal is due to a stressful state.

When you see these behaviors, take your cue to give your pet a timeout. Provide options they use naturally for self-soothing, such as a bone for chewing, or however your pet prefers, to get them licking, digging, drinking, moving, or sniffing. Your pet needs a break, and if you don't provide an option for them, they'll have to create one for themselves, one that may not be the most appropriate for your current situation.

Just like with humans, the most strategic time to implement a timeout is before the thermometer reaches the hot zone. Use your observation skills to improve your timing, and appropriately adjust your expectations so both you and your pet can be successful.

> **THE BEST SECOND LANGUAGE IS BODY LANGUAGE**
>
> Artist Lili Chin has a plethora of amazing animal body language resources ranging across multiple species. Her book *Doggie Language* makes it easy to become familiar with the subtleties of understanding canine communication signals, and her suggestions make for a fun and engaging pursuit for both adults and children.[3]

◆ ◆ ◆

Your pet can't speak human, but they can communicate with you—sometimes subtly, sometimes loudly and forcefully. Recognizing and attending to their signals goes a long way toward addressing their emotional well-being—and yours. A pet's emotional display may range from ferocious to fooling around. Regardless, you can learn their language and help moderate their behaviors, keeping everyone's temperature in the cool zone.

CHAPTER 22

Social Support Equals Social Success

Most pets flourish when they have strong, healthy bonds with other animals, especially those that belong to a species predisposed to living in flocks, herds, packs or other large social networks. Timeouts for play and social interaction provide mental and physical stimulation as well as the ability to practice communication and social skills. While many pets can easily form bonds across species lines, it is important for animals to have members of the same species in their life who speak their language. Pets who are isolated from social members often suffer from depression, boredom, and poor health.

Though playtime can be incredibly exciting and fun, social engagement doesn't need to be highly active. Pets must also learn how to spend time around other animals. Being calm when near other animals, passing other animals on outings, or watching other animals in public settings—like at the vet's office—are all essential to a healthy pet's social life. These moments of relaxation around social members can also serve as necessary timeouts to reset after stimulating interactions with others.

Overly Selective or Extra Social

Due to inherited genetics, limited or improper socialization, negative life experiences, and/or general social preferences, some pets are less comfortable around new animals or humans than others. Some prefer to only be around one individual or a small group. Some may be apprehensive and single out others for no apparent reason, such as men, children, people with hats, livestock, large dogs, cats, or some other defining quality.

Allow pets the autonomy to be selective in their relationships, just as humans are. If your pet is uncomfortable around certain people or animals, forced socialization is not beneficial. In fact, more exposure to stressful situations typically creates a stronger negative association with the stressor.

On the flip side, pets can become too excited in social situations. They may go bonkers when they meet a new friend. Behaviors at this end of the social spectrum are also indicative of a nervous system in the hot zone. Dogs may bark and lunge toward potential playmates across the street. Cats may weave the legs of that one guest who is not a cat person. The phrase "Don't worry, they're friendly," may not be reassuring for the target of your pet's excessive affection. Having a highly social animal requires extra attention on your part to make sure everyone has an enjoyable experience.

The DTR (Define the Relationship) Talk

Bringing multiple animals together presents the possibility of conflict. A pet that is mismatched with another pet is in a mismanaged environment can cause an interaction to go poorly. Relationships need to be balanced. Both parties must be willing participants in the interaction to have positive outcomes.

Pets who experience minimal stress while getting to know each other will likely build a strong, trusting relationship. At times when your pet or your pet's friend is not feeling friendly, letting the pets work out the conflict on their own often leads to a divided, distraught household. Utilizing safety tools such as gates, leads, and barriers can help everyone take things slowly and safely.

Every relationship has its ups and downs. If your pet gets into a fight with a friend or family member—animal or person—that doesn't necessarily mean they won't be able to thrive in their environment. It simply means there was an incident that needs your attention. Some pets easily move past social conflicts, while others need a more focused approach.

Don't forget the power of a timeout. Just like people, pets sometimes need a moment in a calm environment to take a breath.

> **RECOVERING FROM CONFLICTS**
>
> Being around an aggressive animal is incredibly stressful. Don't hesitate to reach out to a qualified professional to guide you through the steps involved in helping your pet recover from a fight. An unbiased, knowledgeable resource will help everyone address their emotional wellness and self-care.

Building relationships takes time. Sometimes you meet someone who becomes a fast friend where you feel like you've known each other forever. Otherwise, you slowly get to know someone over many small exposures and positive encounters. Consider this when choosing friends for your pet. Find activities both parties enjoy such as sniffing a new place, going on a walk, lying in a sunbeam, or playing a game, and then direct the focus there to remove unnecessary pressure on the social engagement.

Watching a movie on a first date is a great way to share an experience in a low-pressure scenario, and it gives you a topic of conversation for later. Think of your pet's version of going to the movies. These interactions can lay a solid foundation for a friendship and serve as a mutual timeout to help everyone's nervous system stay in the cool zone.

> **KNOW WHEN TO ASK FOR HELP**
>
> Pet professionals want to help you and your pet be successful. You're busy, right? Taking advantage of the skills, time, and expertise of a trainer, veterinarian, dog walker, pet sitter, groomer, or pet daycare provider can be a great way to make sure you meet everyone's needs—including your own.

Building a Better Bond

We often have high expectations for our pets to behave a certain way, particularly in social situations. Maybe you feel embarrassment when your pet is overly selective or extra social. On the other hand, you could feel scared if you don't have control of a situation when your pet is engaging with others.

To keep everyone's stress levels regulated during social interactions, make sure you keep your pet in situations they can handle successfully. Consider their **L.E.G.S.**® (introduced in Chapter 18) to determine how, when, and where your pet would prefer to socialize, and adjust your expectations to match. From there, you can begin building their social skills so they can maintain a cool zone temperature in a variety of social settings.

Talk It Through

We introduced the importance of learning your pet's language in Chapter 21. Through observation of your animal, you can begin recognizing where their nervous system temperature is at any given time. You will pick up on how comfortable or uncomfortable they are during a social interaction with you or another individual. Your pet has been observing you and learning your language in the same way.

Domesticated animals have been successfully responding to human body language and cues for thousands of years. Your dog, cat, cow, horse, or chicken gets to know your nervous system temperature and your intentions. While they may not comprehend your behavior, they are aware of it. Let's use our powers of clear communication to help our pets navigate challenging situations.

Using specific phrases and gestures is quite helpful when communicating to members of another species. Imagine trying to communicate with another human who doesn't speak your language. What's the first thing you'd try? You could gesture, use facial expressions, or even speak more loudly as if by doing that you'd be better understood. Being clear, concise, predictable, and consistent is the best way to get your point across. The same is true when communicating with pets.

> **KELSEY SAYS:**
>
> When we brought our feral mustang home, she had never been handled by a human. She didn't understand how to walk through gates or stick her nose into a bucket to find water. She didn't know how to respond to this strange bipedal primate in a cooperative way, and understandably, preferred the company of my other horses.
>
> To start building our relationship, I began narrating what I was doing. I said phrases like, "Here's your food," and "I'm just walking by." We worked up to "I'm going to touch you," and "Let's go for a walk." I felt a little silly at first. I figured she didn't understand me at all. Eventually, her behavior shifted. When I notified her about something I was doing first, she would noticeably relax and tolerate my actions. If I failed to notify her, she would startle or avoid me.
>
> Now I use this strategy with every animal interaction. I don't tell them my life story; I use short, repeatable phrases to explain my intentions. Whether they understand the actual words, or they simply find my tone reassuring, I'll never know. I like to chat, and it seems they like to listen.

Talk to your pets. Explain the ins and outs of what you're doing and what's happening around them. Let them know when you're going to interact with them or when another may try to interact. Clue them in on how things are going to work and what behaviors would be helpful in handling a particular situation. Connecting in this way will help your nervous systems co-regulate together and come to a place of understanding and harmony.

Lead by Example

Even if your pet doesn't respond well to your attempts at verbal communication, you are still giving them loads of information through your body language. Think of the phrase from psychologist Albert Mehrabian: "It's not what you say, it's how you say it." Recent studies show that humans can accurately determine if an interaction is positive or negative 80 percent of the time, even when the conversation is spoken in a different language. Robin Dunbar, anthropologist and evolutionary psychologist, says people often "invariably forget that the words we use are just the bricks that create conversations, and it is the conversations, not the words, that create the elegantly beautiful building of our relationships."[1]

Use this information to shape how you behave around your pets when you're attempting to communicate with them. If your nervous system temperature is rising and you scold, "Relax, give me a break!" at your pet, it's unlikely they will respond to the verbal cue and relax. Instead, practice **THRIVE** (introduced in Chapter 2). Calmly invite them to match your cooling nervous system temperature by saying "Let's relax," in a soothing voice. This is a much faster way to successfully reset the thermostat and supply everyone with the opportunity for a timeout.

Similarly, you can use your actions to model what you're hoping for from your pet. If you want them to move in a certain direction, move in that direction first. If you want to play with them, offer a silly behavior to invite them to join you. If you want them to ignore a distraction, show them how uninteresting it is and how little it bothers you. It's easy to get sucked into our pet's behavior and overreact. Instead, demonstrate your ideal behavior and lead by example. Set yourself up to be the one your pet relies on for social support.

Spend the Time

Taking timeouts with our pets helps both the human and animal nervous systems regulate to a relaxed place. It's an efficient way to provide self-care for multiple parties in the household. Whether you're taking a timeout for physical, emotional, social, or spiritual health reasons, practice with your pet and it will contribute to your mutually healthy relationship. As you continue to participate in timeouts together, you enhance the social health of both parties. This cycle of wellness grows and grows until it blooms into a truly special human and animal bond. This is when the pet becomes a member of your family. Remember to spend time appreciating your connection with your pet.

❖ ❖ ❖

Your pet has many social relationships and a need to maintain healthy social bonds. Schedule needed visits, playtime, and exposure with others, and make one-on-one time to nurture your relationship with your pets. Use appropriate expectations, clear communication, and effective leadership to support social wellness for both you and your pet. Your healthy relationship with your pet will bloom with more interaction, and it contributes to a successful self-care plan.

APPLYING A+ TO SUPPORTING YOUR PET'S SOCIAL HEALTH

Refer to the **A+ Model** discussed in Chapter 4: Your Basic Strategy and use it to map out the various ways you can provide social support for your pets. Use the A+ worksheet provided in Bonus for Timeouts to facilitate this process.

CHAPTER 23

From Ownership to Relationship

Discussing spiritual health for pets can seem a bit anthropomorphic, that is, "ascribing human characteristics to nonhuman things."[1] Until scientists find a way to create the fictional collar from the Disney PIXAR movie *Up*, used to translate the dog's thoughts into verbal language, we have no way of knowing what our pets find most important. We can only make assumptions based on their behaviors and measurable internal physiology. By evaluating strengths and growing edges, values, and sense of purpose through the lens of your relationship with your pet, we can still go a long way in creating a supported self-care plan.

Dr. Susan Friedman uses the term "cultural fog" to represent the ingrained societal beliefs about how and why animals behave the way they do.[2] Labeling pets as dominant, stubborn, aggressive, bad, crazy, lazy, etc., doesn't account for the reason behind their behavior. Viewing these sentient beings as unique and complex creatures can be incredibly helpful in creating a stronger understanding of our animal companions.

> **ADVICE FROM DR. FRIEDMAN**
>
> "I try to stay mindful of the need to extend compassion to one another. It's a lot to ask people to take the leap out of the cultural fog, away from practices they believe to be effective, toward new ways of understanding, predicting, and changing their world. I can't imagine a more amazing planet than this one, where animal life is at once so different and yet so similar. It is the similarities that intrigue me most, and learning principles are one great unifying feature across species."[3]

What Can I Do to Support My Pet's Strengths?

Think about your pet's favorite activity or anything at which they excel. It may be simple or goofy, such as "They are really good at eating breakfast," or maybe they have mastered a complex training skill. They may have a few fantastic personality attributes, or an amazing athletic ability. Regardless, your pet has many talents. Unfortunately, it's challenging to notice their list of achievements when the humans or animals in the family have a nervous system temperature in the hot zone.

Setting Up for Success

Limiting your pet's ability to make inappropriate choices and making it easy and rewarding for them to make the choices you want will help you support your pet's growing edges (introduced in Chapter 17). For example, you could put your dog behind a baby gate when guests come over to prevent over-exuberance at the doorway. Or set up climbing trees around the house so the cat always has easy access to an escape route when other household members run through the room at full speed.

If you live with a young child, you know you could spend all your waking hours being hyper-vigilant and teaching them not to stick their fingers or other items into the electrical outlets, or you could put covers on the outlets to manage the situation until this fascination passes. These simple environmental changes set up both the teacher—that's you—and the learner—that's your pet—for success. Be proactive to prevent the majority of conflicts in your relationship.

The more your pet can practice a new, appropriate behavior, the more likely they will engage in that behavior. Once a habit is formed, the brain doesn't distinguish between good and bad behavior; it simply repeats what is well rehearsed.

Your lifestyle doesn't have to be overly permissive or punitive, but it does need to be somewhat predictable. Clear, consistent boundaries will help your pet understand a world that could otherwise feel chaotic.

Building routines and structure into your daily life is a humane, ethical way to teach these boundaries while maintaining cool zone temperatures for the whole household. Dr. Scott Abraham Miller says, "Routines help almost everybody have a comfortable, familiar, efficient way of going about their day without experiencing stress or anxiety about everything you have to do and the choices you have to make."[4] Layering in this type of predictability will help your pet make beneficial choices for both their self-care needs and yours.

Your pet's learning environment makes a tremendous difference. If they are set up to make incorrect choices, how can they really be at fault? It's common for the struggles to be remembered over the strengths. Add a few tweaks to your daily routine and how you have things set up, and you'll be celebrating success in no time.

> **PRO TIP: REINFORCING CALM**
>
> One of the best tricks for creating more moments in the cool zone is to capture when your pet is displaying relaxed body language. Find something reinforcing for your pet—food typically works well—and give them a little bonus reward at times when they settle down, approach calmly, wait patiently, or offer other types of self-regulation. Often, when animals are relaxing, they are ignored. When they exhibit dramatic or stressful

behavior, they get feedback. Negative attention is still attention. Flip that around. Reinforce the successful, calm moments throughout the day. You may be surprised by how many there are.

What Values Contribute to a Healthy Life with My Pet?

Chapter 18 encourages value identification using the list in Bonus for Timeouts to help you determine which pet is the best fit for your household. Using the same list, you can choose the values that matter most in your current pet relationships. While we could guess that the average border collie values order and the average Anatolian shepherd values independence, we have no way of asking them. Here, we focus on a few values important to every pet species. By building autonomy, comfort, and cooperation into interactions with your pet, you will be able to evaluate what matters most to them and to your lives together.

Autonomy

The traditional cultural view of constant control over animals has created a truncated approach to meeting the needs of modern-day pets. Permitting them to make their own decisions and allowing them to create their own outcomes makes for a solid foundation when building a considerate animal-human relationship.

Giving your pet autonomy does not mean succumbing to their every whim. You can provide choices where there is no wrong answer. Parents of toddlers may recognize this strategy. Asking, "Which pair of shoes would you like to wear today?" versus "Put on your shoes!" gives the child a safe, low-stakes opportunity to control their outcome. Choice is equally important for our animals.

As you and your pet build your communication skills together, you will be able to ask more questions—and even be inspired by the answers. Ask your pet what they would prefer to do, which toy they like better, which direction they want to move. Ask where their favorite sleeping place is and how they like to be touched. All of this can be done through simple, non-judgmental observations of your animal in their environment. Bring your curious self to your interactions with your pet and give them the chance to incorporate autonomy into their daily experience with you. Respect the individual spark that your pet brings to your relationship and match it with awe and appreciation.

> **KELSEY SAYS:**
>
> When I started my animal training career over two decades ago, I would've scoffed at the notion of asking an animal if they wanted to participate in our session. If I told a dog to sit and they refused, that command was backed up with a quick jerk on the choke chain or by applying pressure on the dog's hips to force them to follow through. If I cued a horse to move faster and they refused, I kicked harder with my legs, used spurs, or smacked them with the tip of a whip to pressure them into picking up

> the pace. A noncompliant response from an animal was met with force or punishment because I believed it was imperative for them to obey.
>
> At the time, I never asked why the expectation was compliance. Is it because we said so? Is it about our ego? Is it about making the animal fit into the stigmatized mold of how a good pet should behave?
>
> In recent years, I have removed the "or else" component from working with animals. If I cue a behavior and the animal doesn't respond, I start with asking why. Why did the animal not respond? Was it a lack of understanding or a lack of motivation? Is the animal stressed or distracted? Have the animal's needs been met? If I can figure out the reason the animal said no, I can help them choose to say yes in the future.
>
> Asking "why" is a good place to start with humans, too. It helps to better understand behaviors and respond appropriately. Remember **PACE** from Chapter 11?

Decades of mislabeling an animal's stress signals as dominant behavior or disrespect has made humans believe they need to aggressively take charge. This is not the case. Your cat isn't trying to dominate you or the veterinarian when it struggles to get away. Your mare isn't being disrespectful when she pins her ears while being tacked up. Your dog is not going to become more disobedient if you comfort him when he's scared. When you force an animal to participate when they are clearly saying no, your pet will learn that you and/or the other humans in the area are not trustworthy during stressful procedures.

So, what are you supposed to do? Your pet has to be vaccinated, examined, groomed, handled, transported, etc. You need to meet the pet's health needs while also acknowledging their emotional needs of feeling safe and secure. The answer is simple. By giving your pet agency to make their own choices and by observing their body language to determine their nervous system temperature, you can build a relationship based on comfort and cooperation rather than compliance.

Comfort and Cooperation

When you give someone a hug, their body language tells you how comfortable they are with it. Did they dodge your arms with their body tense and stiff? Or did they mirror your behavior and lean into the embrace? If they have to voice, "Please let go of me," you missed some signals.

Animals are the same way. Your pet will let you know whether they are comfortable or not and if they want the interaction to continue or stop. For this to work, the animal needs to be able to opt in or opt out. Trapping an animal or restraining them on a tight lead voids the ability for consensual participation.

These consent-based practices apply to all types of interactions with pets. Your dog may not want to go for a walk, your horse may not want to have their halter put on, or your chicken may not want to be picked up. In many cases, these are avoidable stressors or actions that can take place later.

Taking a timeout for a values assessment in these instances is a way to respect your pet's voice and take a break, or it can turn into a teaching moment where you help your pet better understand and enjoy the activity. At these times, communication with your pet becomes a dialogue rather than a monologue.

ASKING FOR A PET'S CONSENT

You may have never thought of asking an animal for consent. Most people were never taught to do this. If you're unsure

> about how to incorporate more consent, reach out to a qualified professional to help you create a cooperative care plan.
> As Maya Angelou said in a moment of consoling Oprah Winfrey about mistakes made in her youth, "You did then what you knew how to do. Then when you knew better, you did better."[5] Explore the little steps you can take to do better moving forward. All self-care plans start somewhere.

Your pet won't always have an option, for example, when you face safety concerns or time restraints. Maybe you need to enforce a boundary for yourself or another family member that your pet is not allowed to cross. For the times you can't give your pet the opportunity to make their own choice, try to make the experience as low stress as possible. When you can't accept "no" as the answer to the consent question, don't ask.

Though sometimes you can't ask, try to set up as many comfortable and cooperative interactions as you can. Use the **A+ Model** to explore how to best communicate with your pet to make sure their voice is considered whenever possible. Being attuned to your animal's needs and preferences builds the trust needed for a wellness plan to thrive.

What are My Goals for a Purposeful Life with My Pet?

Relationships between a pet and their person are complicated, and expectations may not match reality. The goals you had when you brought your pet home may seem out of reach or are not attainable. What to do? Set new goals. Bring your pet's strengths and preferences, your growing edges, your pet's growing edges, and your values to the table and take time to weave the pieces together to create a new image of your shared future. Allow your self-care plan and your pet's self-care plan to complement each other as you set out on your purposeful life together.

KELSEY SAYS:

While volunteering for a rescue agency, I fostered a fearful puppy named Ember. Basically feral, she had never made any bonds with humans, had never been in a home, and had never been touched by a person other than when she was captured by animal control.

Taking on this puppy was more than I bargained for. Every day I was stressed, depressed, and overwhelmed by the amount of chaos she created. If I reached for her, she sprayed urine and feces everywhere. She escaped by jumping over, digging under, or chewing through every enclosure. She destroyed everything and even killed the neighbor's chickens.

To connect with this puppy, I had to respect her individuality. She was not a normal pet I could work with in the traditional way. She needed a more compassionate approach. I began to simply observe her choices and behavior. This shift in perspective changed everything.

One day, she decided I was safe and crawled right into my lap. From that point on, our relationship rapidly progressed, and I was able to find her a permanent home. This traumatized puppy blossomed into a loving family pet with a young boy as her best friend.

For a long time, I thought bringing Ember home was the worst decision I had ever made. In the end, I experienced a deep, powerful, and meaningful connection with this dog that had never experienced human kindness until she decided I was someone she could trust.

Take timeouts to create a deeper connection with your pet. This journey will contribute to your spiritual wellness and theirs too.

❖❖❖

Animals have incredibly rich emotional lives and experiences. By empowering your pet with a voice and a choice, you can bring confidence where there was confusion, security where there was concern. You can be a safe place in a sea of stressors for your pet simply by being aware of their needs and taking the necessary timeouts for their self-care. Bring curiosity and compassion into your relationship with your pet and experience the awe-inspiring connection this style of pet parenting brings to your life.

APPLYING A+ TO MOVE FROM OWNERSHIP TO RELATIONSHIP
Refer to the **A+ Model** discussed in Chapter 4: Your Basic Strategy and use it to map out the various strategies you can use to improve the relationship with your pets. Use the A+ worksheet provided in Bonus for Timeouts to facilitate this process.

PART 4 WRAP-UP

By implementing timeouts for your pets—and for yourself when around your pets—you can focus on everyone's self-care needs. **FOCUS** is a useful acronym for remembering the key points of animal wellness presented in Part 4.

- **Foster enrichment.** Enrichment is an easy way to channel your pet's energy into species-specific behavior, creating levels of satisfaction and contentment in the pet.
- **Observe body language.** Accurate observations of body language are imperative for your pet's wellness. Human-animal conversations shouldn't be one-sided. Listening to your pet through careful observation will help you adjust their self-care strategies.
- **Consider the context.** The surrounding environment and the emotional state of your pet will help you manage the situation appropriately. Setting your pet up for success from the start is an important self-care strategy that will have positive impacts on the entire household.
- **Understand your role.** As a pet owner, your role is about so much more than making a pet comply with your commands. By being an effective teacher and an empathetic pet parent, you can help your pet successfully navigate their world and build respectful, trusting relationships.
- **Support mind and body.** Mind and body are equally important. Many pets are unable to meet their physical, emotional, and social needs, and that hinders their ability to be their best selves.

Just like people, your pet's wants and needs will vary throughout the day and the years ahead. You can better understand their behavior by taking timeouts and refining your observation skills. Everyone's well-being will benefit.

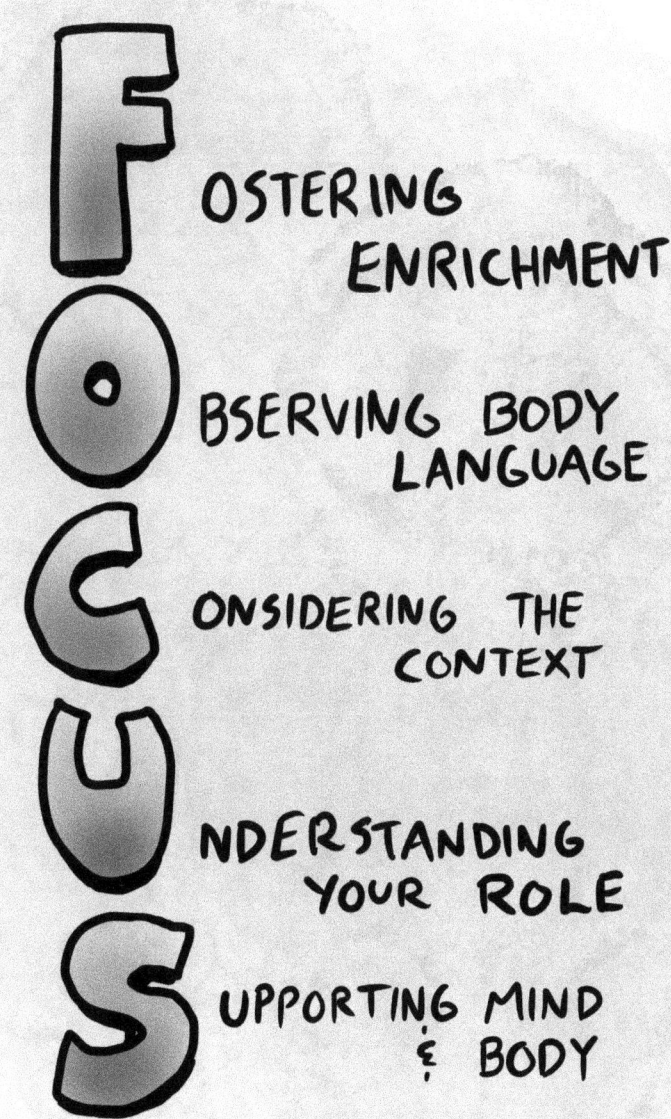

PART 5

Timeout Strategies Everyone Can Use

Up to this point we have focused on strategies for specific populations: adults, children, adolescents, and pets. Are you ready to dive into additional timeout practices everyone can use? When applying the **A+ Model**, you can slot them into the Assess Your Options step.

Part 5 begins by encouraging you to find your quiet place, followed by five powerful actions everyone can take: breathing, relaxing, focusing, affirming, and journaling. This part wraps up with tips for building positivity and activities for increasing joy, connection, and a sense of overall well-being.

Each chapter begins with basic steps, offers modifications for children and pets, and includes options for adding variety. You're sure to find something that works for you.

CHAPTER 24

Finding Your Quiet Place

Taking a beneficial timeout requires identifying your quiet place. It's hard to make time and space for quiet when life clamors for your attention. We're always thinking about what needs to be done and planning how to do it. Settling into a peaceful place away from life's busyness takes intention and a little skill. Each author has a different take on this. Here are their thoughts.

CHARLENE SAYS:

During my lifetime I've used many locations as quiet places. When I was a young girl, I liked to read in the apple tree behind our house and pretend I was Amy from the novel *Little Women*. In college, I took advantage of the study carrels in the library and enjoyed the view from the hill overlooking the campus. I've used the time waiting at red lights to still my mind by reciting a mantra.

Finding a quiet place is worth the effort, whether that's a physical location or a still place in your mind. Use your creativity to find a place that's right for you.

SHAUN SAYS:

I love picturing Charlene reading a book in the apple tree. One of my favorite Bible verses is Psalm 46:10, "Be still and know that I am God." My problem is I have a hard time being still and I'm not very good at creating a quiet space. Yes, there are times when the house is quiet, but my brain races. When I stop doing things, I don't stop thinking about new things to do. What can

I say? I'm an idea person and I work at implementing my ideas. Unfortunately, the way I'm wired doesn't leave much time for stillness.

One of the reasons I love the Oregon coast is that when I walk in the sand, hear the waves, and feel the moisture in the air, I feel more in touch with my body, mind, and soul. Just the thought of the sea puts me in a calmer place where I can breathe and feel refreshed. I inhale the salty air, exhale the day's stress, and then I'm ready to be quiet.

KELSEY SAYS:

I resonate with Shaun's description of being an idea person. As an entrepreneur, it's easy for me to spend my free time planning new business strategies and thinking about creative ways to address my never-ending to-do list.

My quiet place is with my animals. It's going on a stroll down a nature trail with my dog. Or pressing my face into my horse's mane and taking in the intoxicating smell—one of my favorites. Or sitting in the shade watching my chickens peck and scratch at the soil, looking for tasty treats. When I feel chaos swirl around me, being with animals and in nature slows me down and brings me into the present moment of observation and reflection, leaving chaos in the dust.

Timeout to Quiet Your Mind

Quieting your mind is easier when you're away from distractions. It can be done at any time, even during a busy workday or while driving from one activity to another. **Breathing in Calm** is an exercise you can practice in any situation for quieting your mind.

Start by slowing your breathing. Notice the rise and fall of your chest as you inhale and exhale. Say these phrases as you breathe in and out:

I am breathing in calm.
I am breathing out stress.
I am breathing in quietness.
I am breathing out restlessness.
I am breathing in relaxation.
I am breathing out tension.

Now that you've calmed your mind and body, you're ready to explore additional timeout practices. Some of these are simple and take only a few minutes. Others are more complex. Some apply to all ages and species, and some apply to specific groups: children, adults, or pets. All are based on principles verified by scientific research. Best of all, they're free and effective.

Developing New Practices

Any new practice starts with self-discipline and awareness. At first, you could use a strategy in response to stressors so you can feel a sense of calm and make rational decisions. You may notice the nervous system thermometer is rising in your child or pet and step in with a strategy to bring their temperature back down to a more appropriate level for the situation.

Continuous use of these strategies has preventive benefits. Developing the skills and practices as part of your normal routine reduces how often you and your loved ones feel overwhelmed and stressed. Give yourself the grace and time to develop new habits and incorporate them into your lifestyle. They will soon become part of who you are, and they will benefit you and those around you for the rest of your life.

> **CHARLENE SAYS:**
>
> I once worked for a company committed to employee injury prevention. Many of us sat at computers all day. To reduce sedentary activity, eyestrain, and the risk of repetitive motion injury, the company installed a program on each PC that reminded us to take a timeout every half hour.
>
> At each timeout, the program guided us through three minutes of exercises designed to reduce muscle and eye fatigue. It reminded us to stand, flex our fingers, and gaze into the distance. I also used it to remind myself to take a drink of water.
>
> Irritating as it was, the program worked. After I left that workplace, I set up my own reminder system that prompted me to do the same things. It became a habit I didn't want to break.

◆ ◆ ◆

Quieting your mind and focusing on breathing are foundational to most self-care practices. Keep this in mind as you read through the remainder of Part 5.

CHAPTER 25

Breathing

One of the easiest timeouts is simple: take a deep breath. Doctors and therapists recommend diaphragmatic breathing, a fancy way to say fill your lungs to the fullest. Use this as a first line of defense against physical symptoms of stress.[1] When you fill your lungs with slow, rhythmic breaths and relax your muscles, your heart rate calms, your adrenal system slows the flood of cortisol,[2] blood sugar stabilizes, digestive operations resume, and your prefrontal cortex gradually returns to full functioning.

Diaphragmatic breathing can shorten a stressful experience and decrease its associated health risks. It resets your nervous system thermostat. It even helps you sleep better. You can focus on your breathing at any time for any reason. The more you experience the positive benefits of deep breathing, the more appealing it becomes.

The Basics of Breathing

All breathing exercises involve sensory attention, slowing down, filling your lungs to the diaphragm, and slowly releasing your breath. Research shows that slowly exhaling activates the vagus nerve, which in turn slows your heart rate.[3] If you have a pulmonary condition or other breathing limitation, modify the depth of your inhale as needed and deepen as you're able. If you get dizzy or lightheaded, take a break and breathe normally until you're ready to start again.

Belly Breathing

Belly Breathing is an easy way to practice filling your lungs all the way to your diaphragm, which is located between your lungs and above your stomach.

1. Sit or stand comfortably.
2. Place your hand on your upper belly.
3. Slowly breathe in through your nose. If your belly expands during your inhale, you've filled your lungs to your diaphragm. Listen to the sound of the air coming in through your nose. Feel your hand move outward as your belly expands.
4. Pause for three seconds.
5. Slowly exhale through your mouth. To avoid hyperventilation and dizziness, exhale for twice as long as you inhaled. Your hand will sink down as you let all the air out of your lungs. You should hear a long, slow swoosh as you exhale.

Sensory attention includes noticing your hand rising and falling with your breaths and listening to the sounds of the inhale and exhale.

With repeated practice, **Belly Breathing** will become a natural way to bring your nervous system into the cool zone.

KELSEY SAYS:

Before writing this book, I was skeptical about the benefits of deep breathing in times of stress. However, as we were finalizing Part 5, I had a jarring plane ride that solidified the importance of breath work.

After multiple long flights jam-packed into a few days of travel, I sat on the plane for the last leg of my journey. Thirty minutes from our scheduled arrival time, the plane hit turbulence. I knew we were safe, but I felt my nervous system temperature rise anyway. For the next twenty-five minutes, the plane jumped and skipped, dropped quickly, and swerved suddenly in the worst turbulence I have ever experienced. Other passengers gasped, and I heard a few screams. The man next to me prayed while grasping the armrests.

Stress chemicals flowed through my system and my body tightened in response. I began to focus on my breath. I did the simple **Belly Breathing** exercise, and my body began shifting toward the cool zone. My stress subsided and my panic lessened with every breath.

I practiced this breathing exercise until the plane was safely on the ground. I know my breathing didn't impact the outcome of the flight, but it rerouted my personal experience. I walked off the plane calmly, unlike most of the other passengers.

Expand Your Breathing Skills

Once you've mastered the concept of basic diaphragmatic breathing, you can add some variety. We've included two different types of exercises for you to try. The first, **Square Breathing**, relies on the basics you learned with **Belly Breathing** and gives your mind something to work on at the same time. The second, **4-7-8 Breathing**, provides a more mindful approach taken from ancient Yoga practices. Take note how both examples incorporate the essential ingredients of diaphragmatic breathing. They work by activating your parasympathetic nervous system, and that helps return you to the cool zone.

Square Breathing

To practice **Square Breathing**, follow these steps:

1. Hold your pointer finger in front of your body. Imagine a square in front of you.
2. Slowly inhale through your nose for four seconds, moving your finger to the right to "draw" the top of the square. Listen to the sound of the air moving into your body.
3. Hold the breath for four seconds while drawing the right side of the square.
4. Slowly exhale for four seconds as you move your hand right to left to draw the bottom of the square. Listen for the soft swoosh as the air leaves your body.
5. Hold the breath for four seconds while you draw the left side of the square.
6. Repeat three times.

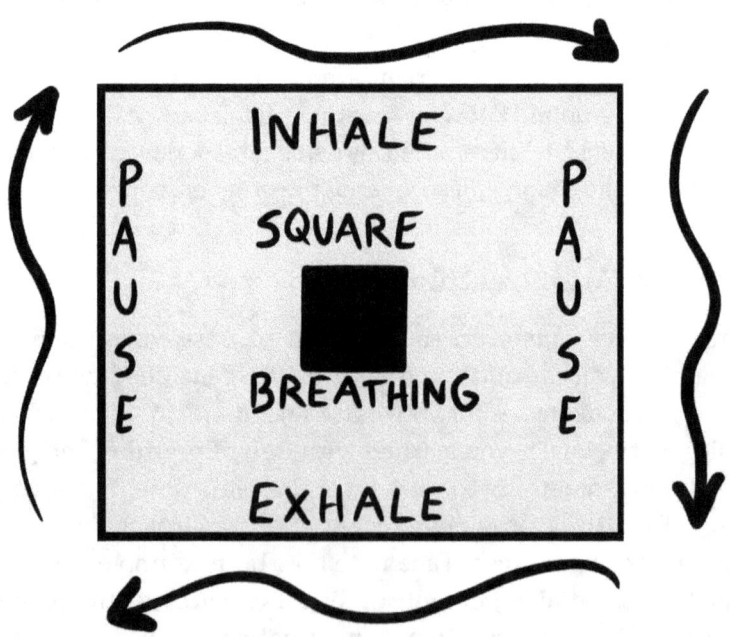

4-7-8 Breathing

Popularized by integrative medicine specialist Dr. Andrew Weil, the **4-7-8 Breathing** technique is frequently referred to as the relaxing breath.[4] It takes a little more focus to master and is worth the effort.

1. Stand, sit, or lie in a comfortable position. Keep your spine straight.
2. Rest your tongue against the ridge of tissue behind the back of your top front teeth. Keep it there for the entire exercise.
3. Empty your lungs by breathing out through your mouth.
4. Close your lips and breathe in through your nose for four counts. Take in enough air to allow you to hold your breath for seven counts.
5. Hold your breath for seven counts.
6. Exhale through your mouth by making a whooshing sound. Exhale slowly for eight counts.
7. Repeat for three more cycles.

Variation for Young Children

Children respond well to creative and fun breathing exercises. They may not be able to pronounce "diaphragmatic," but they can easily be taught to fill their lungs and breathe slowly.

Hot Cocoa Breaths

To practice **Hot Cocoa Breaths**, follow these steps:

1. Ask your child to hold their hands in front of them as if they're getting ready to sip from a cup of hot cocoa.
2. Have them take a slow, full inhale through their nose to fill their lungs. Listen to the sound of the air coming in. Imagine breathing in the aroma of the cocoa.
3. Tell them to hold their breath and count to three.
4. To exhale, have them blow across the top of their imaginary

cup of cocoa to cool it down. Breathe slowly so as not to slosh the yummy drink. Encourage them to listen to the soft, slow *shhh* sound as they empty their lungs. Instruct them to exhale twice as long as they inhaled.
5. Repeat several times.

With a little creativity, you can expand on **Hot Cocoa Breaths**. Consider activities that require slow breathing, such as cooling other hot substances, blowing bubbles through a wand, or making wishes with dandelions.

Variation for Pets

Animals often utilize diaphragmatic breathing. Dogs and horses are obvious with their dramatic deep breaths. You may notice them with your other pets too.

Bonus for Breaths

The more frequently your pet incorporates deep breathing into their day, the more they benefit from the physiological shifts in their brain and body. Just like us, our pets need practice and reinforcement to develop new habits. Since we can't explain to them why breathing exercises are beneficial, we may need to use rewards like food, praise, or petting to help facilitate behavior change.

Here is an easy way to encourage your pet to take timeouts for deep breathing:

1. Put some of your pet's favorite treats in your pocket.
2. During a time of relaxation with your pet (snuggling on the couch, grooming, hanging out outside together, etc.), gently place your hand on your pet's ribcage.
3. Feel the rib cage move as they inhale and exhale and note the frequency and depth of their breaths.
4. During a few moments of quiet coexistence, practice slow, relaxed breaths yourself.

5. When your pet takes a large breath that lasts for a few seconds, say yes and feed them a treat.
6. Go back to the relaxation you were doing before and repeat the process.

Many pets get excited when the food shows up. This is okay in the beginning. They eventually figure out that the treats show up when they take a deep breath, and they'll engage in long, calm breaths more often.

When your pet decides to do something else, that's fine. Some animals prefer to take timeouts by themselves. If you notice a nice deep breath from a distance, you can still say yes and toss them a treat, if that's helpful.

There are many breathing techniques you can try, and an Internet search will guide you to more. Start simple and do what works for you.

CHAPTER 26

Relaxing Your Muscles

Muscle relaxation helps calm your nervous system when you feel stressed out or overwhelmed by strong emotions. It reduces your body's stress response in two ways: you reverse the muscle tension caused by stress, and your brain's focus on the activity redirects it from the stressor. Research suggests that muscle relaxation provides the same benefits as deep breathing; however, the physiological and psychological benefits last longer.[1]

You can initiate muscle relaxation any time you begin to feel tense. It's an effective strategy for returning to the cool zone when your nervous system temperature heats up.

The Basics of Muscle Relaxation

Some muscle relaxation exercises focus on a single part of the body where stress typically collects, such as your shoulders or neck. Others aim to help relax your entire body. All the techniques include body mindfulness (paying close attention to the parts of your body) and slow breathing. Most include tensing and then releasing your muscles.

Be kind to your body as you do these exercises. Don't clench your muscles so tightly you feel pain. A gentle tension before releasing will accomplish the goal of full muscle relaxation.

Time your breathing so you inhale as you tense your muscles. Then exhale as you release the tension.

Shoulder Shrug and Neck Stretches

Like bookends, stretches can begin and end formal exercise sessions. Use them anytime the mood strikes. They're quite beneficial for interrupting long periods of desk or computer-focused work.

To practice **Shoulder Shrug** and **Neck Stretches**, follow these steps:

1. Take in a nice, slow breath. Exhale twice as slowly as you inhaled.
2. Shrug your shoulders, pulling them up close to your ears and then release, causing them to drop. Repeat the **Shoulder Shrug** three times. Keep a slow pace and breathe in and out with each shrug.
3. While inhaling, lower your chin to your chest. Feel the stretch in the back of your neck. Exhale.
4. While inhaling, look up at the ceiling. Feel the stretch in the front of your neck. Exhale.
5. While inhaling, lean your head to the right, feel the stretch on the left side of your neck, and bring your right ear toward your right shoulder. Exhale.
6. Do the same while leaning your head to the left. Exhale.
7. Inhale while dropping your chin to your chest and rolling your head in a clockwise motion until your chin is back to your chest. Exhale.
8. Do the same while rolling your head in a counterclockwise motion. Exhale.

This muscle relaxation exercise targets one specific area of your body. Consider how you could modify this technique for other tense muscle groups. For example, if you lift heavy objects, you may want to focus on your lower back. If you do extensive computer work, regular wrist and lower arm stretches will lower your risk of carpal tunnel pain from using your mouse and keyboard for extended periods of time. Engage in muscle relaxation exercises several times a day as part of your regular routine.

Progressive Muscle Relaxation

The goal of **Progressive Muscle Relaxation (PMR)** is to relax each muscle group in your body. This exercise can focus on only the larger regions of the body or work each side of your body separately.

It may look like there are a lot of steps here, but once you've done this a couple of times, you won't need the prompts. Simply work your way from your toes to the top of your head. Do this after you've climbed into bed for the night and get a good start on a restful sleep.

To practice **PMR**, follow these steps:

1. Lie down on your back in a quiet place. Close your eyes and keep them closed throughout the exercise.
2. Take in a relaxing breath. Picture the air filling your lungs. Hold your breath for three seconds. Exhale slowly. Imagine the tension leaving your body with your breath.
3. As you go through the next steps, inhale as you tighten your muscles and exhale as you relax them. Notice how each body part feels when under tension and when relaxed.
4. Curl your toes and arch your feet. Hold for three seconds. Release the tension in your feet.
5. Tense your calf muscles. Hold them tightly for three seconds. Release the tension in your calves.
6. Tightly squeeze your thighs together. Hold for three seconds. Release the tension in your thighs.
7. Tense your pelvis and glutes. Hold for three seconds. Release the tension in your pelvis and glutes.
8. Suck in your stomach and squeeze to hold the tension for three seconds. Release the tension in your stomach.
9. Tense your back by bringing your shoulders together behind you. Hold for three seconds. Release your shoulders.
10. Make a fist in both hands and hold tight for three seconds. Release the tension in your hands.
11. Squeeze your arms tight to your sides for three seconds. Release the tension in your arms and shoulders.
12. Scrunch your face for three seconds. Release the tension in your neck and face.

13. Tense your entire body tightly and hold for three seconds. Release the tension and allow your body to go limp.
14. Breathe in slowly. Exhale twice as slowly.
15. Gently wake your body up by slowly moving your muscles. Notice how your body feels.
16. Stretch, breathe deeply, and open your eyes.

Expand Your Muscle Relaxation Skills

The **Body Scan** technique is a nice follow-up to **PMR** or can be used independently to help you develop awareness of where your body is holding tension, stress, pain, or other discomfort. A **Body Scan** is commonly used to treat chronic pain.[2] Research shows that both **PMR** and **Body Scan** help improve sleep and reduce stress and anxiety. The **Body Scan** can also alleviate a depressed mood.[3]

Like **PMR**, you can use **Body Scan** to focus on individual body parts or broad regions. Doing shortened **Body Scans** throughout your day can reduce the toll of daily stressors.

Body Scan

Follow these steps for a full **Body Scan**. If your attention wanders at any point, which is normal, return your attention to your body.

1. Sit comfortably in a chair or lie down on your back in a quiet place. Close your eyes and keep them closed throughout the exercise. Maintain slow, rhythmic breathing.
2. Notice the weight of your body in the chair or on the floor or bed. Focus on how your body feels.
3. Take two to three slow, deep breaths.
4. Shift your attention to your feet and then progress upward through your body. At each spot, notice any tension, pain, tingling, or numbness.
5. If you don't experience any strong sensations in a part of your body, move on. If you come upon an unpleasant

sensation, take a moment to breathe into that spot to soothe the area. Try a gentle movement to help muscles relax.
6. Notice your body as a whole. Breathe gently, and slowly return your attention to the environment around you.

Variation for Young Children

Most children are unaware of how their muscles tense during episodes of high emotion. One of the best ways to help your child learn mood and behavioral regulation is to teach them to connect what they feel in their body to what they feel emotionally.

Tin Soldier/Rag Doll

Tin Soldier/Rag Doll is a simple way for children to practice tightening their muscles and then relaxing them, a good tool for body awareness.[4]

As you instruct your child to complete these steps, do the exercises with them:

1. Stand tall with your feet together and your arms by your sides, like a tin soldier.
2. Take in a long, slow breath. As you breathe in, keep your body rigid, and tighten all your muscles as much as you can.
3. Hold your breath and keep your muscles tight for three seconds.
4. Breathe out slowly. As you exhale, let your upper body flop over at your waist like a rag doll. Let your legs relax and get bendy. Dangle your arms toward the ground and sway back and forth.
5. Repeat.

> **SHAUN SAYS:**
>
> Dr. Elizabeth Hamilton, one of my clinical mentors, taught me this technique. Every time I use it in my practice, I remember the classroom full of doctoral students marching around like tin soldiers and then flopping over like rag dolls. These movements relax the muscles. They also improve your mood because who can flop over without bursting into laughter?

The keys for teaching children good muscle relaxation skills are creativity and fun. Modify **Tin Soldier/Rag Doll** for variety. Perhaps use trees as your theme: a strong, tall oak and a floppy weeping willow swaying in the breeze. Or use animals: a tiny turtle all balled up in his shell curled up small and tight paired with a butterfly flitting above the earth, loose, light and floaty. Every time you play these games with your child, you are increasing their body awareness and teaching them how muscle relaxation can help them stay in the cool zone.

Variation for Pets

You have seen those quiet moments when your pet falls into a deep slumber, unaware of small outside distractions and completely at rest. You can also teach your pet how to incorporate muscle relaxation into their daily routines.

Say Please

Caregivers often teach children to ask politely and calmly when they want something. Hearing an expression of good manners is much more pleasant than listening to their screams, having them pull at your clothing, or watching them snatch the desired object from you. It encourages them to bring awareness to their behavior and their body. Wouldn't it be nice if you could teach your pets how to say please too? Yes, you can.

1. Hold something your pet would like to access—their meal or a favorite toy—and look at your pet expectantly. Don't tease or lure them with it, just calmly hold it out of reach.
2. Wait patiently while your pet tries various behaviors to gain access to what's in your hand. Breathe deeply, relax your shoulders, and stay tuned in to your pet's behavior. If necessary, place a barrier between you and your pet, a baby gate, for example, so both of you are safe throughout the exercise.
3. The moment your pet relaxes any of their muscles, say yes and give your pet access to the item. A body language shift that indicates relaxation may be subtle. If their bouncy body becomes still, or they switch to a more comfortable position, reinforce that change.
4. The next time you practice this exercise, wait until the pet engages in a slightly more relaxed behavior. Eventually, when you grab the desired item, your pet will take a moment to compose themself and wait patiently for you to give them access to it.

KELSEY SAYS:

I live and work with many different pet species, so I had to find a **Say Please** behavior that made sense for each of them. For my dogs, I look for a sit behavior. For my cat, it's standing still with a loose upright tail. For my horses, I wait for still feet, a slightly lowered head, and ears pricked forward. These body language signals let me know when their bodies are relaxing and their nervous systems are regulating.

As you notice your pet's signs of relaxation and show appreciation for them, moments of stillness will be added to your daily routine. By using your pet's behavior as a cue for both of you to take a timeout, you can incorporate more self-care for yourself and other members of your family.

◆ ◆ ◆

Muscle tension is sneaky. Frequently, you won't notice it until you contract a headache or experience pain in your neck and shoulders. Your body is talking to you. Respond to it by practicing some of the relaxation techniques suggested in this chapter.

CHAPTER 27

Focusing Your Mind

In this busy world, we can become preoccupied, distracted, and restless, making it hard to physically relax or mentally focus. This is where mindfulness helps provide the ideal timeout.

The Basics of Mindfulness

A simple definition of mindfulness is paying attention to what's happening inside and outside your body with acceptance, patience, and kindness. Some professionals consider it "the basic human ability to be fully present, aware of where we are and what we're doing, and not overly reactive or overwhelmed by what's going on around us."[1] Research shows that mindfulness practices help reduce stress, depression, and anxiety. They also increase the functioning of the prefrontal cortex, the part of your brain used for impulse control, attention, focus, decision-making, and emotional regulation.[2]

Mindfulness practices are often categorized into three groups: informal, formal, and intensive.[3] Informal practices, like taking a walk and noticing what's around you, lingering over a hot beverage, or using **THRIVE** (introduced in Chapter 2), can be worked into your daily routine. Formal practices require you to set aside a specific time and place. Intensive practices involve working with a mentor or attending a retreat. In this chapter, we'll limit our discussion to informal and formal practices.

STOP

STOP is a strategy derived from the work of Dr. Marsha Linehan, creator of Dialectical Behavior Therapy (DBT),[4] which trains you to be purposeful when dealing with difficult situations.

- **Stop.** When strong emotions seem to force you into acting without thinking, recognize the trigger and refuse to react.
- **Take a step back.** Give yourself permission to take the time you need to determine your most effective response. When others are involved, you can say, "Let me think about it," or "Let's plan to discuss this later. What would work for you?"
- **Observe.** Examine the situation and those involved. Evaluate the options for action.
- **Proceed mindfully.** Engage your prefrontal cortex to determine an effective course of action. Move forward with positive intention.

Some therapists add a second **P** for **Practice what works**.

As you become proficient with **STOP**, you'll identify which strategies work well for you. With continued practice, you'll gain emotional resilience and improve your overall well-being.

Five Senses Mindfulness

When learning mindfulness skills, you will use your five senses. They help you turn your attention to something specific happening in the present moment. Try this **Five Senses Mindfulness** activity:

1. **Sit in a quiet place where you won't be disturbed.** Relax into your chair and tune in to your sensory system. As you respond to the following prompts, notice objects with specificity and list their subtle aspects. For example, if you're seeing the electrical outlet by a sink, you could describe the small black and red GFI buttons. Stretch your senses to identify details that could be missed when you're operating on autopilot.

2. **Name five things you can see.** Describe them in great detail in your mind or softly if you prefer, noting the shape, color, texture, and any other element you detect.
3. **Name five things you can hear.** Close your eyes. Listen for the little creaks that indicate your pet is near, the sound of the wind outside your window, the murmur of someone talking in another room. Describe the quiet.
4. **Name five things you can feel on your skin.** Notice the seam in the toe of your sock, the feeling of your chair beneath you, the brush of a breeze from an open window or ventilation system.
5. **Name five things you can smell.** Close your eyes. Tune in to the smells that accompany hair products, laundry soap, or scents that drift in from outside. Note aromas associated with food preparation. Identify both pleasant and unpleasant smells.
6. **Name five things you can taste.** This may be imaginary or an actual food item in your mouth. Use common sense here. Don't put things in your mouth that aren't meant to be tasted.

Mindful Eating

Mindful Eating is a version of **Five Senses Mindfulness**. Use it to slow down automatic eating behaviors. Sit somewhere comfortable and quiet. Place a small treat on a tray or table before you and get ready to tune in to your five senses.

1. Close your eyes and take a slow, deep breath.
2. Open your eyes and look at the treat. Describe it in detail in your mind or aloud. Does it look soft or hard? Smooth or bumpy? Big or small? Round or square? What color is it? Look at the treat as you've never done before.
3. Pick up the treat. Describe how it feels. Does your sense of touch match with what you see?
4. Hold the treat close to your ear and give it a little shake. Does it make any sound? What if you tap it? Is it solid or hollow? Describe any sensation your ear picks up.

5. Hold the treat up to your nose. How does it smell? Is it pleasant? Does it evoke a memory? Does the aroma predict what it will taste like? Describe the smell in detail.
6. Place the treat in your mouth, but don't chew just yet. Describe the taste and texture of the treat on your tongue.
7. Slowly chew the treat. Describe the experience. What does it taste like? How does it feel in your mouth?
8. Swallow the treat. Describe the experience in detail. How does it feel as it goes down your throat? Is there any aftertaste or remaining texture?
9. Finish with a slow, deep breath.

Expand Your Mindfulness Skills

The **Five Senses Mindfulness** exercise shows how simple, everyday activities can be slowed down to increase your attention and focus. Consider how you can modify the exercise for other routine activities, such as brushing your teeth, walking barefoot, sitting in your office chair, or enjoying a meal.

Once you feel comfortable paying attention to your body, you're ready to expand your skills to your inner world—your thoughts and emotions. Mindful reflection on negative thoughts and overwhelming feelings gives you a chance to release the power they hold over you.

Leaves on a Stream

Leaves on a Stream[5] helps you see your thoughts and feelings as passing sensations instead of dangers or facts.

1. Sit in a comfortable position. Close your eyes or let them rest gently on a fixed spot.
2. Visualize yourself sitting beside a gently flowing stream with leaves floating along the surface. Enjoy the sensation for ten seconds.
3. For the next few minutes, take each thought that enters your mind—pleasurable, painful, or neutral—and place it

on an imaginary leaf. Pause for twenty seconds and let it float by.
4. If your thoughts stop, continue to watch the stream until they start up again.
5. Allow the stream to flow naturally. Don't try to speed it up or rush the leaves along. Don't rush your thoughts along either. You're not trying to get rid of them. You're allowing them to come and go at their own pace.
6. If your mind tells you, *This is dumb, I'm bored,* or *I'm not doing this right*, place those thoughts on leaves and let them pass.
7. If a leaf gets stuck, allow it to hang around until it's ready to float by. If the thought comes up again, watch it float by a second time.
8. If a difficult or painful feeling arises, acknowledge it. Notice the emotion. Then place it on a leaf and allow it to float along.
9. From time to time, your day-to-day thoughts may distract you from being fully present in this exercise. As soon as you realize that you've become sidetracked, bring your attention back to the visualization exercise.

> **SHAUN SAYS:**
>
> I use many versions of **Leaves on a Stream** with my patients. One of my favorites is **Watching Clouds in the Sky**. In this exercise, you lie on your back and imagine you're on a warm hillside on a sunny summer day with fluffy white clouds floating across the blue sky. Breathe easily and relax. Place your thoughts and feelings on the clouds and allow them to drift off into the distance. If needed, gently blow the clouds on their way. This is a popular option where I live; Oregon winters can be brutally gray.
>
> What other modifications can you come up with for your family? Be creative!

Variation for Young Children

Children live in the present. Ask your child how long it's been since they last had a meltdown, and they'll likely respond, "A long time ago," even if it was only an hour ago. Children's perception of time is very different from our own. If it's not happening right now, it was a long time ago.

This is both a benefit and a challenge. A young child may leave a brief disappointment in the past (yay!), but they have a limited ability to associate rewards and consequences to events of the past or into a projected future.

Children benefit from mindfulness and meditation practices because these activities help them better understand their present behaviors and emotions. Using **What Do I Feel** is a good place to start.

What Do I Feel?

The **What Do I Feel** game helps young children tune in to their bodies and focus on the moment. This is equally effective for people of any age. It's designed to be a little silly, so have fun with it.

1. Sit or stand in a comfortable position and close your eyes.
2. Breathe in and out in a slow, comfortable rhythm.

260 TIMEOUT STRATEGIES EVERYONE CAN USE

3. What is your big toe feeling right now? Can you feel the inside of your sock or shoe? Is it comfortable or squished? What would your big toe say if it could talk right now?
4. What does the tip of your nose feel like right now? Is it warm or cold? What do you smell? Is it a happy aroma?
5. What is your belly button feeling right now? Is it talking to your tummy? Can you touch it with your fingertip? Does it have fuzzies inside it? What does it feel like when you giggle?
6. Continue with other body parts. Ask questions that help your child think outside the box so they really tune in to their physical body.
7. Take in a relaxing breath and exhale slowly. Open your eyes and smile.

Variation for Pets

Have you ever walked into a professional office and noticed a fish tank on display? The soothing trickle of water, the humming of hundreds of tiny air bubbles, the plants swaying with the flow of the current, and the fish gliding through their underwater world

make most people feel a little more at ease. The tranquility of a fish tank can help take your mind off the impending appointment or the frustrations of the day.

Reptile, amphibian, and aquatic animal owners often feel the same response when their pets are interacting with the rocks, logs, plants, and water features in their enclosures. Simply observing animals and nature is an easy way to incorporate moments of mindfulness into your day.

Top Ten

Tricia Case, founder of Trailblazing Tails, a company devoted to making dogs' lives better, says, "Dogs talk with their bodies. Listen!"[6] Recognizing the shifts in a pet's behavior, posture, vocalizations, and other notable changes in body language enables children and adults to hone their observation skills with any pet.

Use the **Top Ten** activity explained here to practice this type of mindfulness with your pet. Sit or stand and take a few deep breaths to ground yourself. If playing this game with a child, encourage them to breathe deeply as well.

1. Name ten observable things about your pet. These shouldn't be guesses, like "I think my pet feels happy." They should be things someone else can observe, such as "The cat has brown fur." They could be visual observations or something that uses other senses, like "I feel a tickle when the bunny sniffs me."
2. Each time you play this game, try to name ten different things. Perhaps your pet is in a different position or engaging in a different activity. Do your best to stretch your powers of observation.

Just Checking In

Many pet-related struggles occur when the animal is unable to pay attention to their human. While you're trying to control your dog on a walk, soothe your spooky horse, catch your flighty bird, or persuade your disinterested cat, you'll have much better success if your pet can focus their mind on you.

Animals get distracted. They see, smell, and hear things in their environment that humans don't always perceive. Once they notice the distraction, let them process it and disengage from it naturally rather than becoming fixated or overly concerned with it. This helps teach your pet to soothe their nervous system using the same mindfulness strategies previously discussed for humans. You can help your pet with this simple **Just Checking In** exercise:

1. Find a place where you and your pet can watch distractions from a distance. Sitting together at your front window to watch passersby or finding a quiet place off the beaten path to observe passing traffic are two great options. You can also set up little distractions in your home.
2. Once your pet notices the distraction, silently count the seconds they watch it. If they move toward or away from it, you're too close. Find a place where your pet can process without moving around too much.
3. When your pet glances in your direction, say yes and offer them a treat. Then go back to calmly watching the distraction.
4. When your pet looks at the distraction again, count the seconds and repeat the process. As your pet becomes more comfortable, they will likely remain distracted for shorter periods of time.
5. Practice this in different contexts to see which distractions your pet watches for longer or shorter durations.

This process helps your pet recognize distractions without responding to them in an overly reactive way. It also helps you develop your awareness of the various environments you venture into with your pet. Your pet will become more mindful of their surroundings and more in tune with you and your calming behavior.

Training your brain to focus is an important aspect of self-care. It puts you in touch with both body and mind. It can still the noise of life, bring calm, and restore optimism. Try a few practices today to see which ones work best for you.

CHAPTER 28

Reciting Mantras and Practicing Meditation

Many people think of mantras and meditations as faith-based practices, a way of reducing stress by connecting to a higher power. While mantras and meditations can be beneficial for spiritual health, there are also evidence-based practices that contribute to physical and emotional health.

Research shows that even novice meditators experience reduced stress, increased attention, better focus, improved working memory, and empathy for others. They also have a lower concentration of the inflammatory markers that lead to illnesses such as diabetes and cardiovascular disease. Practicing meditation for an extended period results in lower levels of the stress hormone cortisol,[1] improved compassion to the point of taking action to help others, stronger selective attention, better immunity, and decreased reactivity to daily stressors.[2]

To begin, we'll examine the simplest form of meditation, creating and using mantras. Then we'll move on to more complex forms of meditation.

The Basics of Mantras and Meditation

There is a popular misunderstanding that meditation means making one's mind go blank. (Your mind cannot go blank unless you're unconscious or deceased.) The truth is that meditation is an advanced form of mindfulness. The key ingredients of meditation are breathing, releasing negative thoughts and emotions, bringing in positive thoughts and emotions, and relaxing mind and body. It's not emptying your mind; it's turning your attention to what is in your mind and actively letting go of whatever is causing damage to your physical, mental, and spiritual well-being.

For our discussion, we define a mantra as a short phrase or sentence you repeat to yourself for a specific purpose. The goal is to lower your nervous system temperature, help you focus, and encourage you. A good example is the phrase: "Just keep swimming," repeated by the blue tang fish Dory in the Disney PIXAR movie *Finding Nemo*. That may be a fish's version of "Keep putting one foot in front of the other."

Positive Self-Talk

Positive Self-Talk is an example of using a mantra when you need a little encouragement or are caught in a loop of self-judgment. Consider posting a mantra phrase on your bathroom mirror and speak it out loud to yourself every morning if you're alone. When you're in a public place, repeat the phrase in your mind.

To practice **Positive Self-Talk,** follow these steps:

1. Take a moment to slow your breathing.
2. Notice what thoughts and emotions are present in your mind.
3. Choose an encouraging phrase to repeat slowly and rhythmically. If possible, speak the words out loud to reinforce

the positive message. If you have difficulty thinking of a phrase, try one of these:
- I'm doing my best, and that is enough.
- I am loved.
- I am enough.
- I have the skills I need to deal with this situation.
- In this moment, I have everything I need.

CHARLENE SAYS:

Using a mantra proved to be helpful when dealing with the events that occurred after my husband was unexpectedly laid off from his job in the fall of 2007. Though stunned, we remained optimistic that he would quickly find a similar job. Then the recession of 2008 hit and opportunities in his field dried up. We drew on our savings to pay for living expenses. To complicate things further, our daughter was applying for college, and we worried how we would pay for it. Our predictable life suddenly felt out of control, and our carefully planned future became uncertain.

To deal with the chaos, I wrote a mantra affirming that our lives were guided by the Divine, that our daily needs were met, and that a good job offer would present itself at the right time. I acknowledged in that moment, I had everything I needed. I carried the mantra around in my pocket and recited it multiple times a day when anxieties bubbled to the surface. Eventually, I felt a sense of peace from merely touching the piece of paper; I no longer had to take it out and read it.

Three and a half years later—yes, it took that long for everything to work out—my husband found a comparable professional position. I transitioned from being self-employed to working a traditional job with benefits, and our daughter went to college on an honors scholarship.

My mantra wasn't magic. Saying it didn't make all those good things happen. But it did keep me in the frame of mind

I needed to be present with my family, to be positive during trying times, and to take advantage of options as they presented themselves.

I Choose to Believe

I Choose to Believe is a mantra based on the research of Brené Brown. We suggest the following:

1. Take a moment to slow your breathing.
2. Notice what thoughts and emotions are present in your mind.
3. Read the following statement slowly and consider each phrase as it applies to you: "I choose to believe that each and every person, including me, is doing the best they can with the tools they have available to them at this moment."[3]
4. Repeat as needed.

BREAKING DOWN "I CHOOSE TO BELIEVE"

Dr. Christopher Pachel, DVM, DACVB, CABC, practicing in Portland, Oregon, says, "When I'm struggling in any way, I quickly break **I Choose to Believe** down into the individual components and it almost always helps to get me back into a frame of mind more functional than where I was immediately prior."[4] For him, it works like this:

- "I choose . . . " This is a choice, which makes it active rather than passive.
- "to believe . . . " Even when the "facts" of the situation suggest otherwise.
- "each and every person . . . " I don't get to draw lines as to who belongs where in an "us versus them" dichotomy.
- "including me . . . " This was a hard addition, as I tend to look outward rather than inward.
- "doing the best they can . . . " It may not be perfect, and

> their best may not be moving them in a direction that is in alignment with my goals or intentions, but that doesn't negate the belief.
> - "with the tools they have..." This pulls in learning history unique to the individual.
> - "available to them in that moment." This factors in emotional reactions and the knowledge that even when tools exist, they aren't uniformly accessible across all situations or experiences.

Expand Your Mantra and Meditation Skills

More advanced meditation combines mindfulness and mantras with a few significant differences. Advanced meditation requires a quiet, comfortable place free from distractions. It uses a longer text than a mantra. Many meditations last about five minutes, and many yoga classes end with a short meditation. Meditations may be self-directed or guided by a facilitator or meditation app. They may be done in a group or individually. They may include soft music, scents, and mild movement. Because of the focus required, it can be helpful to set aside a specific time of day to meditate, commonly first thing in the morning or right before bedtime. Many find the **Loving Kindness Meditation** a good place to start.

Loving Kindness Meditation

The **Loving Kindness Meditation** is designed to embrace loving kindness for oneself and then extend it to others.[5]

1. Sit in a comfortable position.
2. Breathe in and out in a slow, comfortable rhythm. Close your eyes.
3. Hold your hand over your heart and say to yourself, "May I find joy. May I feel peace. May I be kind. May I love and be loved."

4. Think of a friend or family member. Say to them, "May you find joy. May you feel peace. May you be kind. May you love and be loved."
5. Think of someone in your community, like a teacher, a leader, or a cashier at the grocery store. Say to them in your mind, "May you find joy. May you feel peace. May you be kind. May you love and be loved."
6. Direct your thoughts to the whole world and say, "May all people and all beings find joy. May we all feel peace. May we all be kind. May everyone love and be loved."
7. Finish with a deep breath.

The **Loving Kindness Meditation** is a beautiful example of how meditation can bring peace to your day as well as extend kind thoughts to your loved ones, community, and the world. As you build your comfort with scripted meditations, you may want to try adapting words from a poem, song, or other meaningful quote. You may wish to create your own personal meditation from scratch.

> **CHARLENE SAYS:**
> When I was seventeen, I attended a youth conference where a speaker explained meditation. He gave us examples and told us that by meditating regularly we would become better students, better athletes, and be more successful in life. (I'm sure his observations were anecdotal, since the research on evidence-based practices wasn't published until years later.[6]) I bought into the idea of meditation and started practicing with the examples we were given at the conference.
>
> I have no way of knowing what my life would've been like without this calming coping technique. I can only attest that it's been very helpful to me when releasing my worries at the end of a busy day and by staying positive and hopeful during difficult times.

Variation for Young Children

Young children are typically more ready to adapt simple meditation practices than adults. They already live in the present. Meditation skills naturally develop as children practice mantras and mindfulness activities.

Breathe in Calm for Children

The **Breathe in Calm** exercise (introduced in Chapter 24) is a terrific way to teach children a simple meditation. Be creative as you modify the exercise to work with children. They love it when you add something silly to the mantra.

1. Start by instructing your child to slow their breathing. Guide them to notice the rise and fall of their belly as they inhale and exhale.
2. Ask them to repeat the following phrases as they breathe in and out:
    a. Breathe in sunshine, breathe out rain clouds.
    b. Breathe in happy, breathe out sad.
    c. Breathe in warm snuggles, breathe out bedtime scaries.
    d. Breathe in marshmallows, breathe out broccoli. (Just kidding—a lot of kids love broccoli.)
3. Finish with a deep breath.

There are endless possibilities. Use ideas relevant to your child in the moment: heroes and villains from games and videos, thoughts and emotions, or physical experiences.

Variations for Pets

Incorporating your pet into your mantra and meditation practice can help you recognize that they too are doing their best with the tools they have available. Though we encourage you to create your own personalized mantras, here are some examples you may choose to include in your meditation practice:

- My pet brings me joy and gratitude.
- Today I will appreciate my pet's individuality and spirit.
- I will bring energy, intelligence, imagination, and love to my relationship with my pet.
- Today I choose kinship with my pet. Today I choose to understand my pet. Today I choose happiness with my pet.

Lazy Training

This is a great technique to practice when you want to encourage your pet to bring their brain and body down to a peaceful state. Though we refer to it as **Lazy Training,** this exercise is a proactive strategy used to help everyone's nervous systems reach the cool zone. The setup may be different depending on the pet's species, but the concept works for a variety of animals, particularly the ones who watch you for social cues.

1. Find a low-distraction, pet-safe, comfortable area for your pet, and sit down where your pet can see you but can't reach you.
2. Take a few deep breaths using one of the previously mentioned techniques, and feel your body begin to relax. You can also work on the **Shoulder Shrug** and **Neck Stretches** while you're demonstrating a relaxed state.
3. Watch your pet out of the corner of your eye so as not to stare at them.
4. Wait for your pet and focus on your breathing.
5. When your pet repositions into a restful posture, calmly praise and place a treat where they can reach it without moving. A restful posture for your pet could be lying down, lowering their head, resting their foot, or even doing a big stretch. The point is to reward the pet's ability to settle, and with repetition, you'll soon see your pet offer these relaxed behaviors more and more frequently.

No one likes to be commanded to relax, which could create frustration instead. The same goes for pets. In the **Lazy Training** technique, your relaxation prompts the opportunity for your pet to relax with you. They don't have to. If they choose to, they will be rewarded for their efforts.

Many people involve their pets in their timeout practices because it feels good. By including them in your mantra and meditation practice, you'll teach your pets how to take timeouts by example.

◆ ◆ ◆

Mantras are a type of self-talk that can help you view situations in new and different ways. Meditations may be valuable in retraining your thinking. Both are powerful tools for coping with life's stressors and promoting well-being. With a little practice, you can add them to your self-care strategies. You will benefit and so will those around you, including your pets.

CHAPTER 29

Putting Pen to Paper

Many self-care professionals advocate journaling to process events or to set aside one's worries so the mind is freed to look at life with a fresh perspective.

In an era where texting and blogging are common forms of communication and expressions can be communicated with emojis, writing longhand may seem old-fashioned or unnecessary. Research shows that your brain works differently when you handwrite things instead of typing them.[1] Experts who advocate handwriting do so because writing in any form has benefits, including telling one's story on social media, writing a blog post, or keeping a personal journal on a computer.[2] However you do it, writing can help you achieve goals, track progress and growth, gain self-confidence, improve communication skills, reduce stress and anxiety, find inspiration, and strengthen memory.[3]

CHARLENE SAYS:

Some time ago I attended a series of lectures on soul care. When the speaker talked about meditation, there was a murmur of assent. When he mentioned prayer, heads nodded. The topic of fasting received a positive response. But when he introduced the practice of journaling, the audience burst into spontaneous you've-got-to-be-kidding-me laughter. Apparently, very few in the group enjoyed writing or were willing to consider it as a form of soul care.

Perhaps you're skeptical of the idea of journaling. Watching a TV program, eating a snack, or enjoying a beverage may seem like better timeout options. Journaling seems to appeal to those with a specific temperament; however, I encourage you to try it. Be open to discovering the benefits before deciding whether it's for you.

The Basics of Journaling

You may be wondering what kind of journal you should try. Popular suggestions include a gratitude journal, a food journal, a fitness journal, or simply a stream of consciousness journal. The only right way to journal is whatever is most helpful to you. Experts say, "the simple act of taking the time to get in touch with your mind, body, and spirit is what's truly important."[4]

Journaling can be done at any time. Those who enjoy it usually set aside a routine time of day—typically early morning or end of evening. Choose a time when you can spend three to five minutes in your quiet place reflecting and writing.

To begin, choose a method and media that appeal to you. It may be pen and paper, colored pencils and a sketchbook, or a coloring book with pictures that allow you to portray your thoughts and feelings.

Don't be concerned with spelling or grammar. You're the only one who's going to see these entries unless you choose to share them.

Simple Reflection

Recording, drawing, or coloring simple reflections is a good place to start. Consider the following ideas:

- In the morning, evaluate your emotional state. Do you feel happy, sad, mad, or glad about the day ahead? Why?
- In the evening, record and/or sketch images of the day's high point and low point.
- Write five adjectives that describe your day. Be honest and specific. For example, "apathetic" is better than "meh."
- List five things you're grateful for. This can include the basics: food, shelter, and safety.

- Identify whatever is on your mind at the moment. This could be upcoming activities, worries about work, family, money, etc. Fold up the piece of paper and place it in a jar, vase, or bowl and say, "I have the skills and abilities to take care of these things." When they come to mind again later, affirm you are handling them.

Expand Your Journaling Skills

A quick online search will pull up dozens of preprinted journals for persons of all ages with daily writing prompts, beautiful artwork, and inspirational sayings. You don't need a store-bought journal. A spiral-bound notebook works just as well and allows you to add your own drawings or poems.

CHARLENE SAYS:

Here's an example of how poetry works for me as a journaling activity. Writing "Sitting Still" helped me clarify my feelings and anticipate a new direction in life as I looked forward to retirement.

Sitting Still
This act of sitting still
Causes such chaos.
This hot cup of tea, poured to clear the mind,
Clutters it.
Apparitions rise with the steam.
"Be an artist, be a singer, be a poet," they scream.
Haunting specters of youthful ambitions
That dissipate as they rise into the cool air.
The teacup becomes a seething caldron,
Its contents a potion of early expectations,
Aspirations not yet realized.
I sip it slowly.
There's no talisman
Against these ghosts from the past.

Busyness can stifle their voices.
Amid the din of family life, they scuttle from the room.
In these few minutes of silence,
While I'm sitting with a cup of tea,
They come creeping back,
Clamoring for attention,
Begging for resurrection.
I drink the potion,
Longing for a magical transformation
Into the person
Of my girlhood dreams.

Move from recording details to personal reflection. Dive beneath surface emotions and behaviors and examine the depths of your inner world as you write about how life events impact your present thoughts and feelings. This kind of journaling fosters personal growth, so allow more time for your writing. You may benefit from looking over previous entries to see how your thoughts have developed and note which things you worried about that never happened.

Consider switching from one type of journaling to another, for example, transitioning from stream of consciousness to gratitude journaling or reflective writing.

Gratitude Journal

A basic **Gratitude Journal** records things you're thankful for. This may include the people and pets in your life, financial blessings, possessions, accomplishments, or personal abilities.

Worry Journal

This activity allows your mind to put away your worried thoughts. Here are the steps for creating a **Worry Journal**:

1. Find a notebook or journal. It can be fancy or have a plain cover you can decorate.
2. Take a moment to identify your worry-related thoughts.
3. Write each thought in your journal.
4. Put the journal in a drawer or other safe place. Tell yourself that you're putting your worries away.
5. Add entries to your journal as new worry thoughts show up, and then put it back when you're done.

Expressive Writing

Expressive Writing is helpful for processing emotional traumas, large and small. In twenty to thirty minutes of continuous writing, explore your deep thoughts and feelings about upsetting experiences.[5] This often brings up sadness or stronger emotions, but they typically pass quickly as you keep writing.

Here are some benefits of **Expressive Writing**:[6]

- Helps you make sense of your life.
- Adds perspective.
- Enables you to develop a more coherent narrative as your stories become simpler and more understandable.
- Frees up working memory since you're no longer spending mental energy to continually process the experience.
- Reduces long-term stress and the symptoms that accompany it, such as sleeplessness.
- Results in more time to spend in quality relationships with others.

> **PRO TIP: SEEKING PROFESSIONAL ASSISTANCE FOR PROCESSING TRAUMA**
>
> If you suffer from significant mood destabilization, flashbacks, nightmares, or other frightening post-trauma symptoms, don't try to navigate these on your own. Seek a qualified therapist to help you process the past in a safe and healing way.

Private or Public?

Recording your private thoughts has great value. What would happen if someone else read them? If that concerns you, plan to keep your journal hidden. If you're tempted to invade a family member's privacy, choose to respect their confidentiality.

Variation for Young Children

With younger children, the goal of journaling is to build skills and a loving curiosity for reflecting on their inner world. Make it fun.

Consider your child's likes and dislikes, personality and temperament, developmental stage, and age-related attention span. Simple activities like **Color Your Feelings** or **Worry Monsters** provide creative options to identify and decrease worries and negative thoughts.

Color Your Feelings

This activity is a good opportunity to engage in your child's process. Narrate what you see them doing. For example, "Ooh, you're using a lot of yellow there," or, "Hmm, I see how you completely filled in that corner." As you use curiosity to guide your child through the following steps:

1. Sit at a table with a blank piece of paper and crayons or colorful markers.
2. Close your eyes and take a moment to look inside yourself. What are you feeling?
3. Fill the entire page with different colors that represent your feelings.
4. When you're done, talk through your colors with someone close to you.

Remember, this activity is about the process rather than the end result. If your child fills the page with black crayon, don't immediately go into problem-solving or correction mode. Ask gentle questions, empathize, and comfort your child until they're ready to talk through their feelings.

Worry Monsters

This activity helps children move worries out of their thoughts and put them on paper. After the worry has been drawn, the child turns it into a silly monster to defuse the power of the thought.

Before starting this exercise, accept, validate, and express empathy for your child's every worry and fear. Give them a big hug. Then guide them through these steps:

1. Sit at a table with a blank piece of paper and crayons and/or colorful markers.
2. Ask your child to take a moment to think about what worries or fears are bothering them.
3. Help your child give the worry a name. For example, if they feel afraid at bedtime, they could call it the Big Bad Bedtime Monster.
4. Ask your child to draw their monster on the paper. Make it colorful and scary.
5. Have your child write the monster's name on their drawing. (Or help them write the name.)
6. Now have some fun. Help your child add goofy decorations to their monster, like butterfly wings, a rainbow tail, or big googly eyes. Have them turn it into the silliest monster they've ever seen.
7. Ask your child to give the monster a new name. Their Big Bad Bedtime Monster could become the Big Bubble Bedtime Monster.
8. Post the silly monster picture somewhere your child can see it whenever they feel worried. You could put their Big Bubble Bedtime Monster on the ceiling over their bed so they'll remember that the bedtime monster is pretty goofy!

> **SHAUN SAYS:**
>
> I've used the **Worry Monster** activity many times and am always amazed at how much it helps children overcome some of their biggest concerns. We use the monster's silly name throughout therapy, especially whenever the worry comes up. I've shared lots of giggles with my young patients when a scary monster gets a rainbow unicorn horn.

There are numerous ways to use journaling to explore emotions and thoughts with your child. You could have them select popular emojis or use a feelings chart to talk about their day. Feelings charts take many forms and typically ask a child to identify feelings by providing cartoon-style facial expressions.[7] The key is to be nonjudgmental throughout the process.

Variation for Pets

Can journaling work for pets? Sure! No, we're not suggesting you buy your pet a notebook and fancy pen. You can write in a journal set aside specifically for your pet. What a great idea!

Because you spend time with your pet on a regular basis, it's challenging to notice changes in their behavior. Imagine your pet had an extreme emotional response to a particular trigger. After months of working on it together, you will have made notes about how their response became manageable. Documentation will help you appreciate the progress as well as provide clues and reminders about any future issues that may arise.

Pet Progress Report

In your pet journal, write down what you love about your pet. What do they do that makes you smile? Record data like how much your pet eats and what they weigh. Journal about your pet's favorite toy, game, or activity, and how they respond when certain situations arise. Write about what you'd like to work on with your pet. Include a topic that drives you absolutely crazy about your pet or an improvement in their behavior or care practices. Which timeout strategies have you tried or would like to try with your pet?

Keep up with this practice on a regular basis (weekly, monthly, quarterly), and you'll start to notice trends. You will feel moments of joy, gratitude, and motivation as you reflect on changes and compare entries. If you don't track your **Pet Progress Report**, you may never notice the improvements or regressions your pet may experience.

Journaling provides a unique opportunity to get things off your mind so you can relax and stop worrying about them. It can be as simple as drawing an stick figure cartoon in your daily planner or writing out a few paragraphs either longhand or with a word processor. Any way you choose to do it, it has positive benefits to your overall well-being.

CHAPTER 30

Ending on a Positive Note

This final chapter describes practical activities that contribute to an overall sense of well-being for you and your family members as you plant seeds of joy and foster connection between you and the others in your life—both human and animal. By taking these actions regularly, you will create new healthy habits.

The Basics of Building Positivity

Our world isn't an easy place in which to live. We all carry responsibilities, challenges, and burdens. Even on good days we can have moments when we feel cloaked in weariness. Taking a timeout for self-care sounds beautiful, and it's comforting to know that joy is within our grasp. Each of the exercises in this chapter has one important requirement: it should be pleasurable for you.

We'll start with the simplest technique and then provide more enjoyable activities scientifically proven to be beneficial.

Smile

Research shows that both genuine and fake smiles have many benefits.[1] Among them are reduced stress, a more positive mood, and a calmed body. The physical act of smiling releases serotonin and dopamine, hormones essential to emotional well-being. And smiling is contagious. Next time you're in a social setting, spread positivity by smiling. Taking a timeout doesn't get any easier than this.

Enjoyable Activities

One of the most prescribed strategies for relieving depression is engaging in pleasurable activities. Doing things that make you feel good lowers cortisol levels, improves sleep, reduces stress, and contributes to positive relationships.[2]

Set aside time each week to do at least one activity that slows you down and makes you happy. You could take a warm bath or watch a comedy that makes you laugh out loud. Bonus for Timeouts has a helpful list of activities to try.

Your choice doesn't have to be anything fancy. While you could go on an international excursion or spend a whole day at the spa, the simplest activities often bring the greatest moments of joy.

> **SHAUN SAYS:**
>
> My mother's favorite movie was *North Avenue Irregulars*, a 1979 Disney film. She used to laugh so hard, we would end up with happy tears rolling down our cheeks. My siblings and I watched it with our children after Mom's memorial service and it still brought laughs. Anytime I'm feeling a little down, I call up a memory of watching this movie with my mom and I smile. Laughter really is the best medicine.

Expand Your Positivity Skills

To improve your mood and your physical health, take your joy-making skills up a notch with activities that pull from the part of your brain that loves beauty. Include art and music in your individual timeouts. Foster connection by inviting other family members to join you.

Art and Creativity

Using the creative part of your brain turns your thoughts away from worries and stressors. It also changes your perspective about yourself and others.³ Art is both abstract and hands-on; it challenges your brain and demands attention. It calms your mind and promotes a positive perspective.

Here are a few suggestions to get you started. Get involved in whatever stretches your artistic side. Throw out your inner critic and get creative about your creativity.

- **Color.** No one is too old to get out a coloring book and crayons, markers, colored pencils, or gel pens.
- **Painting.** Break out the oil paints or watercolors and some inexpensive canvas. Use abstract art to represent your inner world.
- **Collage.** On a piece of poster board, create a collage that represents your interests, activities, characteristics, thoughts, and emotions. Include who you are in the context of your family, friends, peers, and colleagues.

Music

Hans Christian Anderson said, "Where words fail, music speaks."⁴ Music communicates in ways that cannot otherwise be expressed. You don't have to be a virtuoso to use music as part of your timeout strategies. Here are a few ideas to get you started:

- **Create music.** Play the instruments you have. Or use household items to make joyful sounds.
- **Listen to soothing music.** Select music that matches your current mood. Then try changing your mood with a different style of music. Pay attention to your body's reaction to the calming sounds. Do you notice your heart rate slowing down as you listen? The emphasis here is on instrumental music. When you listen to songs with lyrics, your mind focuses on the words. When you listen to instrumental music, your mind and body respond to the emotion communicated through the sounds.

Variation for Young Children

Every idea presented in this chapter is a terrific way to help your child return to the cool zone when their nervous system temperature rises. The **Smile** technique produces laughter and joy when family members do it together. Children are quick to invite you to participate in their favorite activity. Put a crayon in a child's hand and they'll excitedly produce art. Sing "If You're Happy and You Know it," and soon everyone is clapping their hands and stomping their feet.

> **Imaginative Bedtime Stories**
> **Imaginative Bedtime Stories** is another way to incorporate the magic of creativity in a child's timeouts. It brings mindfulness, meditation, and imagination together in a way that teaches children to relax their bodies and calm their busy minds.
>
> 1. Lie beside your child on their bed or the floor.
> 2. Ask them to close their eyes and take a slow breath.

3. Using a soft, gentle voice, begin telling or reading a story that takes them to a beautiful, fun, magical, or colorful place. You may decide to include pets or favorite stuffed animals in the journey.
4. At various points in the story, draw your child's attention to how each part of their body is feeling and which emotions they experience.
5. When the story is over, take a moment to breathe slowly, and then wrap up with an expression of affection.

Remember to have developmentally appropriate expectations as you try out any of these techniques. A two-year-old is likely to get wiggly after a few minutes. Start with short moments of art, music, or storytelling, and expand as your child develops greater capacity for creative practices.

> **SHAUN SAYS:**
>
> My children loved my husband's bedtime stories. He created fantastic journeys that took three little girls and their horses, dogs, and unicorns to distant magical places. Close friends and other family members often made cameo appearances in the stories. Each character was a modification of the person's real name. Heather became Heather the Feather. Natalie was Nat the Gnat Bug, and Danielle was Little Bo-PeePee Danielle. (This was supposed to be a play on "Little Bo-Peep," but somehow it went sideways.) These stories remained favorites into their adult years.
>
> Now, as Mema and PopPop, we continue the tradition by telling stories to our grandchildren in which they have amazing adventures featuring them. I'm sure Baby Luke will get some starring roles soon.
>
> These moments not only help the kiddos wind down after an exciting day, but they also create wonderful lifelong memories.

Variation for Pets

Play encompasses many aspects of physical and emotional regulation, and animals engage in play all the time. Animal behavior experts Gordon Burghardt and Marc Bekoff determined that, "Something counts as play for animals if they do it voluntarily over and over again, only when they're not stressed, and it's somehow different than a more serious version of that behavior."[5] Additionally, they found that, "Play is important for social, physical, and cognitive development, but it also prepares animals for the unexpected." Playing serves as a natural timeout practice and helps build coping skills for future stressful situations.

Have fun with your pets. Enjoying their joy is a great way to provide you and them with necessary self-care.

Can you tell when your animal is playing? Tail wags from dogs, batting behavior from cats, lofty trots from horses, bouncing in rabbits and guinea pigs. Many animals have a "play face," and some even smile and laugh when they're feeling exceptionally jovial.

We all need more joy in our lives. You don't have to engage in a formal, structured, extensive play session. In fact, many people feel better by simply walking through the door at the end of a long day and observing their pet's silliness upon their arrival. Watching your pet batting a random object around or tossing it in the air can be enough to make you laugh.

> **KELSEY SAYS:**
>
> My pets make me smile every day. I giggle when they race around getting their wiggles out, and I enjoy a full belly laugh when they do something ludicrous. Sometimes it's a forced laugh as I remind myself to find the humor in their shenanigans. In any case, it helps me retain my positive outlook.
>
> Recently, my husband and I were sitting on the couch with a small gap between us. Our dog couldn't quite reach that desirable spot, so she jumped onto the coffee table—all 101 pounds of her! At that moment, I could have scolded her for breaking our "no dogs on tables" policy or switched into "teacher mode" to redirect her behavior. Instead, I took a picture of this ginormous, generally well-behaved dog standing on the coffee table.
>
> Afterward, she gingerly tiptoed to the couch spot she wanted all along and flopped down between us, looking mighty pleased with herself.
>
> I could've made a big deal about her "bad" choice, but I didn't want to go through the frustration/anger/shame/guilt spiral that often follows an impulsive, reflexive punishment. Laughing about it was better for my self-care and for my relationship with her. I still get a kick out of sending my husband that picture with the caption, "Look how naughty your dog is!" She's his dog when she's naughty, of course.

Animals often mirror our emotional state. When you're sad, your pet may slow down and offer comfort or give you space. If you're tense, you'll see tension in your pet, too. When you're angry, your pet may offer appeasement signals to diffuse the intensity of the moment. And if you're playful and light, your pet may reflect that energy right back.

When you laugh, smile, dance, or play with a toy, see if your pet reciprocates with silliness. If they seem confused, you may be holding on to a bit of residual stress. Or maybe they don't know how to play games with you yet. When your pet has fun and feels happy, incorporate playful activities into your normal routine. You'll be enjoying each other's joy in no time.

❖ ❖ ❖

A positive outlook on life is one of the best aspects of self-care. You can demonstrate this to others by smiling and to yourself by engaging in pleasurable activities. Doing things you enjoy relaxes both body and mind and keeps your nervous system temperature in the cool zone.

PART 5 WRAP-UP

In Part 5, we provided short and simple activities as well as some that require more time and effort. We recognize how life often dictates the need for brief moments of self-care, and we want you to have lots of options when you work through the **A+ Model** to formulate timeouts for you and your family members.

Consider selecting one self-care practice to use this week (or month or year). You'll be more successful if you don't try to do too much at once. Find your favorites and dive in—one strategy at a time.

Bonus for Timeouts

The authors have assembled these additional resources to assist you in planning your timeouts. They include the following:

- An **A+** worksheet to guide you in working with physical, emotional, social, and spiritual stressors.
- A decision tree to help you determine when a timeout is needed and which strategy could be most beneficial.
- Tips for restful sleep.
- A core values list and instructions for a values clarification exercise.
- Suggestions for self-care activities that promote a sense of well-being.

A+ Worksheet

Now that you know more about the stressors that impact the physical, emotional, social, and spiritual aspects of life, apply the **A+ Model** to return your nervous system temperature to the cool zone. See Chapter 4: Your Basic Strategy for guidance.

A+ WORKSHEET

AWARENESS OF INTERNAL STATE

What physiological symptoms do you experience when your nervous system temperature rises?

_____
_____
_____
_____

What behaviors do you observe in yourself, your family members, your pets?

_____
_____
_____
_____

ACQUIRE INFORMATION

What could be the cause of a rise in nervous system temperature?

_____
_____
_____
_____

What lies beneath the surface of the behaviors you are observing?

_____
_____
_____
_____

ASSESS YOUR OPTIONS

Which strategies discussed in the book could be helpful to you in lowering your nervous system temperature?

_____

_____

_____

ACT NOW

Choose an option and begin using it now. Try it out for several weeks or a month.

_____

_____

_____

APPRAISE RESULTS AND ADJUST IF NECESSARY

How well did the selected option work for you?

_____

_____

_____

Were you able to recognize changes in your internal state and hit the reset button more often?

_____

_____

_____

Would you choose a different strategy next time? Why or why not?

_____

_____

_____

Recognize When a Timeout Is Needed

Children in all age groups will benefit from learning how to select appropriate timeouts when they run into challenges or feel their nervous system temperature rise. Here is an example of how you can walk through a decision tree for choosing an effective timeout for self-care. Remember, children will need caregiver assistance to work through the decision tree. Children will benefit by learning to ask the question, "Do I need help?" and then working through the options presented.

Do I Need Help?

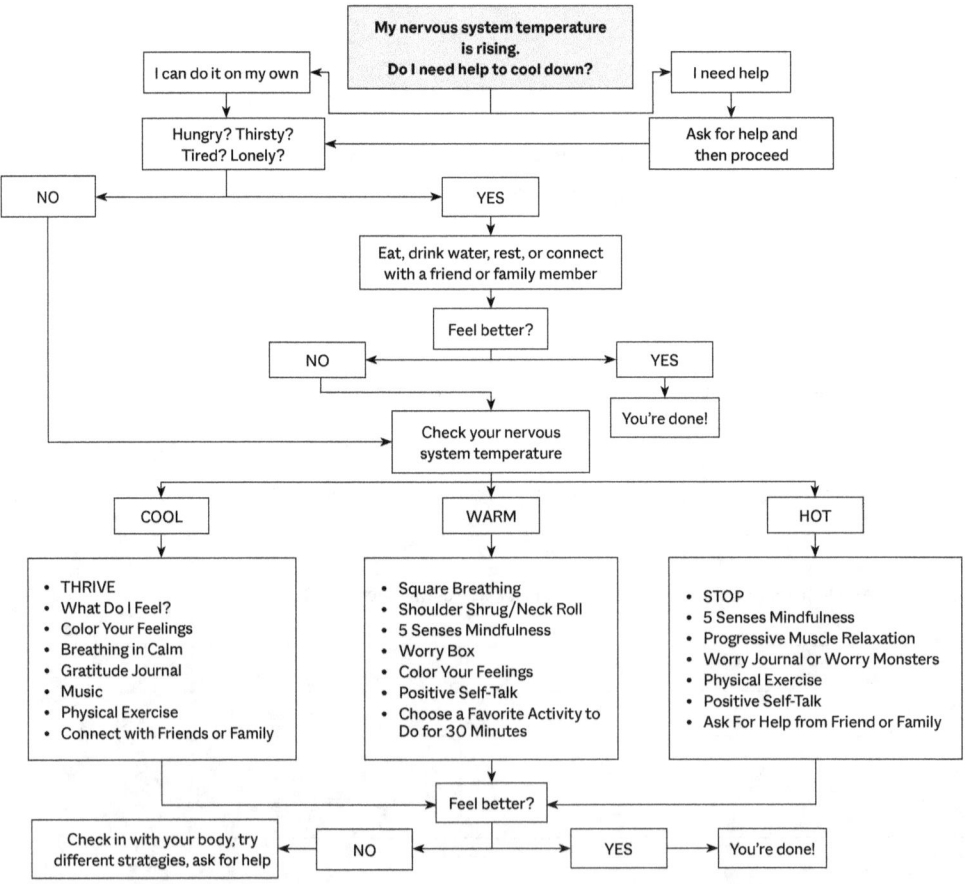

Sleep Hygiene

Many people struggle with sleep issues from lack of sleep, interrupted sleep, or both. Use these suggestions to set up an optimal environment for restful sleep, good for adults and children. Here are a few habits that scientists believe promote healthy sleep:[1]

General Tips
- Get plenty of sunshine during the day.
- Get plenty of physical activity each day.
- Follow your physician's advice about daytime napping.
- Include quiet, calm, and relaxing activities leading up to bedtime.
- Maintain a predictable bedtime routine.
- Maintain the same sleep and wake-up routine even on weekends.
- Use bed for sleep, sick, and sex—nothing else.
- Dim your lights as bedtime approaches.
- Avoid caffeine for at least 6 hours prior to bedtime.
- Limit alcohol consumption, especially later in the evening.
- Discontinue device time at least 30 minutes before bedtime.
- Allow at least an hour between dinner and bedtime.
- Limit fluid intake between dinner and bedtime.
- Make your alarm clock less visible to avoid watching the time.
- Keep the bedroom cool, quiet, and comfortable.
- Keep pets out of your bed.
- Get into bed when drowsy.
- Get out of bed if not asleep within 20 minutes and return when drowsy.

Child-Specific Bedtime Tips
- Have a light snack and glass of water before getting in bed.
- Go to the bathroom before climbing into bed.
- Cuddle with a soft toy or blanket.

- Don't watch scary or stimulating stories or videos before bedtime (or really, ever!).
- Parents: Keep bedtime checkups short and sweet.

Core Values Selection and Exercise

Core Values

This list of 83 core values was created at the University of New Mexico.[2] It can be used as a stand-alone checklist or with the following **Values Clarification** activity. Values clarification benefits both adults and children.

ACCEPTANCE: to be accepted as I am
ACCURACY: to be accurate in my opinions and beliefs
ACHIEVEMENT: to have important accomplishments
ADVENTURE: to have new and exciting experiences
ATTRACTIVENESS: to be physically attractive
AUTHORITY: to oversee and be responsible for others
AUTONOMY: to be self-determined and independent
BEAUTY: to appreciate beauty around me
CARING: to take care of others
CHALLENGE: to take on difficult tasks and problems
CHANGE: to have a life full of change and variety
COMFORT: to have a pleasant and comfortable life
COMMITMENT: to make enduring, meaningful commitments
COMPASSION: to feel and act on concern for others
CONTRIBUTION: to make a lasting contribution in the world
COOPERATION: to work collaboratively with others
COURTESY: to be considerate and polite toward others
CREATIVITY: to have new and original ideas
DEPENDABILITY: to be reliable and trustworthy
DUTY: to carry out my duties and obligations
ECOLOGY: to live in harmony with the environment
EXCITEMENT: to have a life full of thrills and stimulation
FAITHFULNESS: to be loyal and true in relationships
FAME: to be known and recognized

FAMILY: to have a happy, loving family
FITNESS: to be physically fit and strong
FLEXIBILITY: to adjust to new circumstances easily
FORGIVENESS: to be forgiving of others
FRIENDSHIP: to have close, supportive friends
FUN: to play and have fun
GENEROSITY: to give what I have to others
GENUINENESS: to act in a manner that is true to who I am
GOD'S WILL: to seek and obey the will of God
GROWTH: to keep changing and growing
HEALTH: to be physically well and healthy
HELPFULNESS: to be helpful to others
HONESTY: to be honest and truthful
HOPE: to maintain a positive and optimistic outlook
HUMILITY: to be modest and unassuming
HUMOR: to see the humorous side of myself and the world
INDEPENDENCE: to be free from dependence on others
INDUSTRY: to work hard and well at my life tasks
INNER PEACE: to experience personal peace
INTIMACY: to share my innermost experiences with others
JUSTICE: to promote fair and equal treatment for all
KNOWLEDGE: to learn and contribute valuable knowledge
LEISURE: to take time to relax and enjoy
LOVED: to be loved by those close to me
LOVING: to give love to others
MASTERY: to be competent in my everyday activities
MINDFULNESS: to live conscious and mindful of the present moment
MODERATION: to avoid excesses and find a middle ground
MONOGAMY: to have one close, loving relationship
NON-CONFORMITY: to question and challenge authority and norms
NURTURANCE: to take care of and nurture others
OPENNESS: to be open to new experiences, ideas, and options
ORDER: to have a life that is well-ordered and organized

PASSION: to have deep feelings about ideas, activities, or people
PLEASURE: to feel good
POPULARITY: to be well-liked by many people
POWER: to have control over others
PURPOSE: to have meaning and direction in my life
RATIONALITY: to be guided by reason and logic
REALISM: to see and act realistically and practically
RESPONSIBILITY: to make and carry out responsible decisions
RISK: to take risks and chances
ROMANCE: to have intense, exciting love in my life
SAFETY: to be safe and secure
SELF-ACCEPTANCE: to accept myself as I am
SELF-CONTROL: to be disciplined in my own actions
SELF-ESTEEM: to feel good about myself
SELF-KNOWLEDGE: to have a deep and honest understanding of myself
SERVICE: to be of service to others
SEXUALITY: to have an active and satisfying sex life
SIMPLICITY: to live life simply with minimal needs
SOLITUDE: to have time and space where I can be apart from others
SPIRITUALITY: to grow and mature spiritually
STABILITY: to have a life that stays fairly consistent
TOLERANCE: to accept and respect those who differ from me
TRADITION: to follow respected patterns of the past
VIRTUE: to live a morally pure and excellent life
WEALTH: to have plenty of money
WORLD PEACE: to work to promote peace in the world

Values Clarification Exercise

These instructions are written for an individual's use. It can be used to help your child identify their core values with slight modifications. If you use it with your child or teen, remember to adjust for their developmental capabilities.

1. Review the list above. Add other values important to you if not already on the list.
2. As you read through the list, put a check mark beside any of the values that feel important. Remember, this is not a judgment about good or bad values. It is not about what should be important or what is important to anyone else. It is about what is important to you.
3. Now, go through your check marked words and circle any values important to you.
4. Narrow your circled items to your top five values.
5. Finally, rank them from 1 to 5 in order of importance, with number 1 being your most important value.
6. Wrap up the timeout with reflection on the values you identified. What makes these specific values important to you? What does it mean to you? How do you see these values play out in your life?

A few salient questions can help you look for mismatches between your behaviors and values:

- Do your daily life activities match with your top values?
- Do your top values match with how you see yourself?
- Do your activities match with how you want others to see you?

If the answer to any of these questions is no, you are likely to feel stress or unhappiness. Be realistic. Nobody lives up to their values 100 percent of the time, but when we don't, we don't feel like our best selves. Explore how to align your daily life, behaviors, and relationships with your values. Of course, this will come with some pitfalls. If you value travel and leisure time while lacking a stable source of income, you will either have to get creative or you may not be able to engage in activities that align with your value system.

Children face this type of dilemma all the time. For example, if play and friendships are among your child's top priorities, they may want to reduce school hours to make more room for fun. This is a good time to talk about the phases of life, including the educational phase expected throughout youth. The key is to consider how their values could be worked into required activities.

Self-Care Activities

Listed below are activities that some find calming. Self-care activities are usually pleasurable, inexpensive, and take only a few minutes. The goal is to give yourself, a child, or a pet a bit of time to recharge and reset the nervous system thermostat. Select the ones that may be useful to the members of your household. Many of these suggestions will also work for your pets. Discuss the options below with your veterinarian before trying them with your pets at home to avoid inadvertent harm. Here are some ideas to get you started.

Activities Alone
- Sit in the sunshine.
- Watch a sunset.
- Watch a sunrise.
- Gaze at the stars.
- Take your pet for a walk.
- Spend time relaxing with your pet.
- Write a letter or send a card.
- Take a bubble bath.
- Get a massage.
- Take a nap.
- Doodle.
- Work on a puzzle or play sudoku.
- Read a new book.
- Read the comics.
- Take the scenic route home from work.
- Practice Yoga.
- Do nothing!

Activities with Others
- Have a picnic.
- Call a friend.
- Invite a friend to coffee or over for tea.
- Give a friend a hug.
- Visit an older person.
- Work on puzzles or play games with residents of a retirement home.
- Send a funny meme to a friend.
- Tell a dad joke.
- Go bowling.
- Have an impromptu dance party.
- Join an exercise group.

Activities in Nature
- Go for a walk barefoot.
- Go birdwatching.
- Visit an aquarium.
- Pick wildflowers and make a bouquet.
- Add a new plant to your garden.
- Go for a bike ride.
- Go on a hike.

Beverages
- Drink soothing warm beverages in cold weather.
- Prepare cold beverages during warm weather.

Crafts
- Make a gift for a friend.
- Make an origami crane.
- Color in a coloring book.
- Paint a nature scene.
- Take pictures of something beautiful or goofy.
- Make a photo album out of moments with your pet.
- Try a new craft.

- Teach someone how to do one of your hobbies.
- Develop a collection: coins, shells, etc.

Foods
- Eat foods high in antioxidants.
- Try a new recipe.
- Experiment with other cuisines.
- Try out plant-based meal options.

Music
- Listen to music with a slow beat and a simple melody, preferably instrumental to avoid the brain processing words;[3] choose good audio quality. (Poor audio quality increases stress.)
- Listen to soundscapes.
- Listen to music that includes nature sounds such as ocean waves or songbirds.
- Listen to classical music. (It is enjoyable for both humans and animals.[4])
- Create music using sound-producing items near you.
- Learn to play an instrument.

Scents
- Light a candle.
- Diffuse essential oils.

Home Decor
- Use relaxing room colors: blue, violet, pink, green, gray, tan, white, yellow.
- Create wall art and photography of nature scenes.
- Purchase fresh flower arrangements.
- Nurture green houseplants. (Easy-care flowering plants such as African violets and peace lilies soothe both mind and spirit.)

Notes

Why This Book?
1. Cindy Veldhuis et al, "Addressing the critical need for long-term mental health data during the COVID-19 pandemic: Changes in mental health from April to September 2020," *Preventive Medicine*, February 2021, 146 no. 4: 106465, DOI:10.1016/j.ypmed.2021.106465.

Introduction to Timeouts
1. For a detailed description of the original intent of timeouts, its uses and effectiveness, see "Time-Out Interventions and Strategies: A Brief Review and Recommendations," *International Journal of Special Education* 21, no. 3 (2006): 22–29.
2. Susan Callaghan et al., "Still Feeling Good: The US Wellness Market Continues to Boom," McKinsey & Company, September 19, 2022, https://www.mckinsey.com/industries/consumer-packaged-goods/our-insights/still-feeling-good-the-us-wellness-market-continues-to-boom.
3. Throughout the book we spell timeout as one word following the convention of the sporting world. In sports, calling a timeout refers to an official pause in the action.
4. David J. Disabato et al., "Self-Care Behaviors and Affect during the Early Stages of the COVID-19 Pandemic," *Health Psychology* 41, no. 11 (2022): 839.
5. Elizabeth A. Bayliss et al., "Descriptions of Barriers to Self-care by Persons with Comorbid Chronic Diseases," *Annals of Family Medicine* 1, no. 1 (2003): 19.
6. Mary S. Himmelstein and Diana T. Sanchez, "Masculinity Impediments: Internalized Masculinity Contributes to Healthcare Avoidance in Men and Women," *Journal of Health Psychology* 21, no. 7 (2016): 1289.
7. Maryam Sina, Jonathan Graffy, and David Simmons., "Associations between Barriers to Self-care and Diabetes Complications among Patients with Type 2 Diabetes," *Diabetes Research and Clinical Practice* 141, (2018): 128–129.

Chapter 1. In Your Brain

1. Hans Selye, "Stress and the General Adaptation Syndrome," *British Medical Journal* 1, no. 4667 (June 17, 1950): 1383.
2. Micky A. Akinrodoye and Froshing Lui, "Neuroanatomy, Somatic Nervous System," *StatPearls*, StatPearls Publishing, November 7, 2022, https://pubmed.ncbi.nlm.nih.gov/32310487/.
3. Joshua A. Waxenbaum, Vamsi Reddy, and Matthew Varacallo, "Anatomy, Autonomic Nervous System," *StatPearls*, StatPearls Publishing, July 24, 2023, https://pubmed.ncbi.nlm.nih.gov/30969667/.
4. Jacob Tindle and Prasanna Tadi, "Neuroanatomy, Parasympathetic Nervous System," *StatPearls*, StatPearls Publishing, October 22, 2023, https://pubmed.ncbi.nlm.nih.gov/31985934/.

Chapter 3. In Your Life

1. "Key Findings from the Global Religious Futures Project," Pew Research Center, December 21, 2022, https://www.pewresearch.org/religion/2022/12/21/key-findings-from-the-global-religious-futures-project/.
2. George L. Engel, "The Need for a New Medical Model: A Challenge for Biomedicine," *Psychodynamic Psychiatry* 40, no. 3 (September 2012): 386–387, https://doi.org/10.1521/pdps.2012.40.3.377.
3. Dana E. King, *Faith, Spirituality and Medicine: Toward the Making of a Healing Practitioner* (Binghamton, NY: Haworth Pastoral Press, 2000), 9–11.
4. "A Changing World: Global Views on Diversity, Gender Equality, Family Life and the Importance of Religion," Pew Research Center, April 22, 2019, https://www.pewresearch.org/global/2019/04/22/a-changing-world-global-views-on-diversity-gender-equality-family-life-and-the-importance-of-religion/.
5. Brené Brown, *The Gifts of Imperfection, 10th Anniversary Edition* (New York: Random House, 2020), 86.

Chapter 4. Your Basic Strategy

1. Created by Charlene A. Derby, M.A. All rights reserved. Used by permission.

Chapter 5. But I'm an Adult, Right?

1. The concepts of psychosocial development referenced for each stage of life in this chapter are taken from the work of psychologist Erik Erikson. Erikson was one of the first to discuss identity development across the human lifespan instead of focusing only on childhood. See Erik H. Erikson, *Childhood and Society* (New York: W. W. Norton & Company, 1963), 261–273.

2. Peter McGraw, "If You Desperately Want Taylor Swift to Marry Travis Kelce, This is for You," HuffPost Personal, December 20, 2023. (Via Apple News)
3. For further elaboration on this perspective, see Peter McGraw's podcast *Solo: The Single Person's Guide to a Remarkable Life*, and his upcoming book published by Diversion Books, *Solo: Building a Remarkable Life of Your Own*.
4. McGraw, "If You Desperately."
5. Jean Guerreo, "I'm not ashamed of being childless in my 30s, not at Christmas or any time of year," *The Los Angeles Times*, December 18, 2023, A11.
6. Susan Siman, "The Rise of the Only Child: What's behind the rising number of single-child families," Channel 3000 News, Madison, Wisconsin, February 24, 2020, https://www.channel3000.com/the-rise-of-the-only-child-whats-behind-the-rising-number-of-single-child-families/.
7. "Cognitive Health and Older Adults," National Institute on Aging, October 1, 2020, https://www.nia.nih.gov/health/cognitive-health-and-older-adults.
8. "Growing Older in America: The Health & Retirement Study," ed. Freddi Karp, National Institute on Aging, March 2007, 20–23, https://www.nia.nih.gov/sites/default/files/2017-06/health_and_retirement_study_0.pdf.
9. "Growing Older," 20.

Chapter 6. Building a Healthy Foundation

1. "Benefits of Healthy Eating," Centers for Disease Control and Prevention, May 16, 2021. https://www.cdc.gov/nutrition/resources-publications/benefits-of-healthy-eating.html.
2. "Learn How to Eat Healthy with MyPlate," U.S. Department of Agriculture, https://www.myplate.gov/, accessed May 7, 2024.
3. Matthew Walker, *Why We Sleep: Unlocking the Power of Sleep and Dreams* (New York: Scribner, 2017), 3.
4. "Healthy Living: Get Enough Sleep," U.S. Department of Health and Human Services, August 4, 2023, https://health.gov/myhealthfinder/topics/everyday-healthy-living/mental-health-and-relationships/get-enough-sleep#panel-1.
5. Daniel Lieberman, "Just Move: Scientist Author Debunks Myths About Exercise and Sleep," interview by Terry Gross, *Fresh Air*, NPR, January 21, 2021, audio 36, https://www.npr.org/sections/health-shots/2021/01/21/959140732/just-move-scientist-author-debunks-myths-about-exercise-and-sleep.
6. Lieberman, interview.
7. Kelly Brogan, *A Mind of Your Own* (New York: Harper Wave, 2016), 188–189.

8. Mike Marino, *Anxiety and Depression Boot Camp: Get Your Life Back—Now!* (Jasper Media LLC., 2009), 113.
9. "9 Benefits of Yoga," Johns Hopkins Medicine, accessed May 7, 2024, https://www.hopkinsmedicine.org/health/wellness-and-prevention/9-benefits-of-yoga.
10. Kristen Weir, "Nurtured by Nature," *American Psychological Association* 51, no. 3 (April 1, 2020): 50. https://www.apa.org/monitor/2020/04/nurtured-nature.

Chapter 7. Keeping My Cool

1. "Emotional Wellness Toolkit," National Institutes of Health, August 8, 2022. https://www.nih.gov/health-information/emotional-wellness-toolkit.
2. "Emotional Wellness," University of New Hampshire, accessed May 7, 2024. https://www.unh.edu/health/emotional-wellness.
3. Katrina McCoy, "Calling Emotions by Name," *Psychology Today*, (October 10, 2023). https://www.psychologytoday.com/us/blog/finding-the-right-words/202310/calling-emotions-by-name.
4. Paul Ekman, "Universal Emotions," Paul Ekman Group, LLC (2024) https://www.paulekman.com/universal-emotions/.
5. Understanding the range of emotions may be an interesting study. For examples, conduct an Internet search using the key words, "range of emotions" or "emotional classifications."
6. McCoy, "Calling Emotions."
7. McCoy.
8. Elizabeth Scott, "What to Know If You're Concerned About a Toxic Relationship," Verywell Mind, November 3, 2023, https://www.verywellmind.com/toxic-relationships-4174665.
9. Johannes Odendaal, "Animal-Assisted Therapy—Magic or Medicine?" *Journal of Psychosomatic Research* 49, no. 4 (October 2000): 279, https://doi.org/10.1016/S0022-3999(00)00183-5.

Chapter 8. Enjoying Others

1. Matthew D. Lieberman, *Social: Why Our Brains Are Wired to Connect*, (New York: Crown Publishers, 2013), 42.
2. Roy F. Baumeister and Mark R. Leary, "The Need to Belong: Desire for Interpersonal Attachments as a Fundamental Human Motivation," *Psychological Bulletin*, 117, no. 3 (1995): 497-529, https://doi.org/10.1037/0033-2909.117.3.497.
3. Created by Shaun Davis, PsyD. All rights reserved. Used by permission.
4. Julianne Holt-Lunstad, "Loneliness and Social Isolation as Risk Factors: The Power of Social Connection in Prevention," *American Journal of Lifestyle Medicine* 15, no. 5 (2021): 568, https://doi.org/10.1177/15598276211009454.

5. Henry Cloud and John Townsend, *Boundaries* (Grand Rapids, Michigan: 2017), 30.
6. Sheri Jacobson, "Connecting with People: What It Is and Isn't, and Why You Might Find It Hard," *Harley Therapy Counseling* (blog), March 14, 2023, https://www.harleytherapy.co.uk/counselling/connecting-with-people.htm.
7. Emma Seppala, "Connectedness & Health: the Science of Social Connection," The Center for Compassion and Altruism Research and Education, Stanford Medicine, May 8, 2014, http://ccare.stanford.edu/uncategorized/connectedness-health-the-science-of-social-connection-infographic/.
8. "What Is Active Listening?" Center for Creative Leadership, February 14, 2024, https://www.ccl.org/articles/leading-effectively-articles/coaching-others-use-active-listening-skills/.
9. Julia Cameron, *The Listening Path: The Creative Art of Attention* (New York: St. Martin's Essentials, 2021), 100.

Chapter 9. Fostering Connection
1. Tom Rath, *StrengthsFinder 2.0* (New York: Gallup Press, 2007), 5.
2. Rath, 9.
3. Shalom H. Schwartz, "An Overview of the Schwartz Theory of Basic Values," *Online Readings in Psychology and Culture* 2, no. 1 (December 2012): 3, https://doi.org/10.9707/2307-0919.1116.
4. *Young America Sings*, ed. Dennis Hartman (Los Angeles: National High School Poetry Press, 1969), 94.
5. Kristen Weir, "Nurtured by Nature," *American Psychological Association* 51, no. 3, (April 1, 2020): 50. https://www.apa.org/monitor/2020/04/nurtured-nature.
6. "Improve Your Health by Connecting with Nature," Forest Service: U.S. Department of Agriculture, April 27, 2020. https://www.fs.usda.gov/inside-fs/delivering-mission/deliver/improve-your-health-connecting-nature.
7. Lee Ann Womack "I Hope You Dance," Lee Ann Womack and Sons of the Desert, from the album "I Hope You Dance," 2000.
8. Eleanor Morgan, "Oh wow! How getting more awe can improve your life—and even make you a nicer person," *The Guardian*, September 23, 2022. https://www.theguardian.com/lifeandstyle/2022/sep/23/how-getting-more-awe-can-improve-your-life-and-even-make-you-a-nicer-person.
9. Michael Easter, "The '20-5-3' Rule Prescribes How Much Time to Spend Outside," *Men's Health*, June 4, 2021, https://www.menshealth.com/fitness/a36547849/how-much-time-should-i-spend-outside/.

Chapter 10. When Others Depend on Me

1. "Caregiving in the United States 2020," AARP, National Alliance for Caregiving, Washington, DC, May 14, 2020, https://doi.org/10.26419/ppi.00103.001.
2. Jane L. Givens et al., "Depressive Symptoms among Dementia Caregivers: Role of Mediating Factors," *The American Journal of Geriatric Psychiatry* 22, no. 5 (2014): 487–488.
3. Corinna E. Löckenhoff et al., "Five-Factor Personality Traits and Subjective Health among Caregivers: The Role of Caregiver Strain and Self-efficacy," *Psychology and Aging* 26, no. 3 (2011): 592.

Chapter 11. Laying the Foundation

1. Susan S. Woodhouse et al, "Secure Base Provision: A New Approach," *Child Development* 91, no. 1 (February 11, 2019): e249–e265. https://srcd.onlinelibrary.wiley.com/doi/10.1111/cdev.13224.
2. Daniel Hughes, *Attachment-Focused Family Therapy Workbook* (New York: W.W. Norton & Company Inc., 2011), 93–128.
3. Hughes, 95.

Chapter 12. The Developing Human

1. Mariam Arain et al., "Maturation of the Adolescent Brain," *Neuropsychiatric Disease and Treatment* no. 2013-9, (April 3, 2013): 451, https://doi.org/10.2147/NDT.S39776.
2. Susan M. Sawyer et al., "The Age of Adolescence," *The Lancet Child & Adolescent Health* (January 17, 2018): 227, https://www.thelancet.com/journals/lanchi/article/PIIS2352-4642(18)30022-1/fulltext.
3. Kaspar Sørenson et al., "Recent Secular Trends in Pubertal Timing: Implications for Evaluation and Diagnosis of Precocious Puberty," *Hormone Research in Pediatrics* 77, no. 3 (2012): 143.

Chapter 13. Back to Basics

1. "How Much Sleep Do I Need?" Centers for Disease Control and Prevention, September 14, 2022, https://www.cdc.gov/sleep/about_sleep/how_much_sleep.html.
2. "Benefits of Physical Activity," Centers for Disease Control and Prevention, August 1, 2023, https://www.cdc.gov/physicalactivity/basics/pa-health/index.htm.

Chapter 14. Don't Look Now, but I Might Be Freaking Out

1. A good resource for helping children understand and manage emotions and feelings are the books by author and illustrator Trace Moroney. For more information, visit her website, https://www.tracemoroney.com/home.

Chapter 15. Home Is Where the Heart Is
1. "Temperament," American Psychological Association, *APA Dictionary of Psychology*, 2022, https://dictionary.apa.org/temperament.
2. "Key Statistics from the National Survey of Family Growth—D Listing," Centers for Disease Control and Prevention, accessed May 7, 2024, https://www.cdc.gov/nchs/nsfg/key_statistics/d.htm#divorce.
3. "Healthy Divorce: How to Make Your Split as Smooth as Possible," *American Psychological Association*, 2013, http://www.apa.org/topics/divorce-child-custody/healthy.

Chapter 16. Peers and Priorities
1. Fatima Malik and Raman Marwaha, *Developmental Stages of Social Emotional Development in Children, StatPearls*, StatPearls Publishing, September 18, 2022, https://www.ncbi.nlm.nih.gov/books/NBK534819/.
2. "Social Media and Teens," *American Academy of Child and Adolescent Psychiatry*, no. 100, (March 2018), https://www.aacap.org/AACAP/Families_and_Youth/Facts_for_Families/FFF-Guide/Social-Media-and-Teens-100.aspx.
3. Simon Kemp, "Digital 2022: Time Spent with Connected Tech Continues to Rise," January 26, 2022, https://datareportal.com/reports/digital-2022-time-spent-with-connected-tech.
4. Victoria Rideout and Michael Robb, "The Common Sense Census: Media Use by Kids Age Zero to Eight, 2020," *Common Sense Media* (2020): 41.
5. Candice Odgers and Michael Robb, "Tweens, Teens, Tech, and Mental Health: Coming of Age in an Increasingly Digital, Uncertain, and Unequal World," *Common Sense Media* (July 29, 2020).
6. "Do Parents Really Know How Many Teens Watch Online Porn?" *Hartford HealthCare*, October 26, 2020, https://hartfordhealthcare.org/about-us/news-press/news-detail?articleId=29384&publicid=469.
7. Daniella Genovese, "Sexting Study Shows Kids Starting Before They Even Turn 13," *FOX Business*, December 18, 2019, https://www.foxbusiness.com/lifestyle/sexting-children-study.

Chapter 17. Knowing Myself Inside and Out
1. Heidi Flavian, "Towards Teaching and Beyond: Strengthening Education by Understanding Students' Self-awareness Development," *Power and Education* 8, no. 1 (2016): 98–99, https://journals.sagepub.com/doi/10.1177/1757743815624118.
2. Kelly Richards et al., "Self-care and Well-being in Mental Health Professionals: The Mediating Effects of Self-awareness and Mindfulness," *Journal of Mental Health Counseling* 32, no. 3 (2010): 258–260, https://doi.org/10.17744/mehc.32.3.0n31v88304423806.

3. Krista Soria and Robin Stubblefield, "Knowing Me, Knowing You," *Journal of College Student Retention: Research, Theory, and Practice* 17, no. 3 (2015): 365–367.
4. John Donne, "No Man Is an Island," *All Poetry*, 2022, https://allpoetry.com/No-man-is-an-island.
5. Roy Baumeister and Mark R. Leary, "The Need to Belong," *Psychological Bulletin* 117, no. 3 (1995): 520–521.
6. Agnieszka Bojanowska and Konrad Piotrowski, "Is Person-Group Value Congruence Always a Good Thing? Values and Well-being Among Maladjusted Teens and Their Peers," *Frontiers in Psychology* 11, no. 2035 (2020).
7. Bojanowska, "Is Person-Group Value," 8–9.
8. "Cognitive Dissonance," *APA Dictionary of Psychology*, accessed May 7, 2024, https://dictionary.apa.org/cognitive-dissonance.
9. Gemma A. Baugh et al., "Fifty States of Purpose: Examining Sense of Purpose Across the United States," *The Journal of Positive Psychology* 16, no. 3 (2021): 43–44.
10. Anna Gorrese, "Peer Attachment and Youth Internalizing Problems: A Meta-Analysis," *Child and Youth Care Forum* 45, no. 2 (2016): 197.
11. Xu Jiang, E. Scott Huber, and Kimberly J. Hills, "Parent Attachment and Early Adolescents Life Satisfaction: The Mediating Effect of Hope," *Psychology in the Schools* 50, no. 4 (2013): 347–349.
12. Brown, *Gifts*, 86.

Chapter 18. Perks and Perils of Pet Parenting
1. Jeffery Ho, Sabir Hussain, and Oliver Sparagano, "Did the COVID-19 Pandemic Spark a Public Interest in Pet Adoption?" *Frontiers in Veterinary Science* 8, no. 2021 (May 7, 2021), https://doi.org/10.3389/fvets.2021.647308.
2. Kim Brophey is an Applied Ethologist with FDM, CDBC, CPDT-KA certifications. She is the developer of the LEGS® Model and Founder of the Family Dog Mediation Education Center.
3. Kim Brophey, "Talking Cases with Kim Brophey," *Cog-Dog Radio*, April 6, 2021, (time 2:20), https://www.listennotes.com/podcasts/cog-dog-radio/talking-cases-with-kim-brophey-itpRDNASEPY/.
4. Kim Brophey, *Meet Your Dog: The Game-Changing Guide to Understanding Your Dog's Behavior* (San Francisco: Chronicle Books, 2018), 19–23.
5. See https://www.facebook.com/groups/losinglulu.

Chapter 19. Through the Ages and Stage
1. Nadine Chersini, Nathan J. Hall, and Clive D. L. Wynne, "Dog Pups' Attractiveness to Humans Peaks at Weaning Age," *Anthrozoos* 31, no. 3 (May 3, 2018): 309–318, https://doi.org/10.1080/08927936.2018.1455454.

Chapter 20. Balancing Body and Brain
1. Kirstynn Joseph, "The Stimulating Science of Animal Enrichment," *Untamed Science*, May 2019, https://untamedscience.com/biology/ecology/ecology-articles/the-stimulating-science-of-animal-enrichment/.
2. Allie Bender and Emily Strong, *Canine Enrichment for the Real World* (Wenatchee, Washington: Dogwise Publishing, 2019).
3. Monika Martyn, "How Many Dogs Are in the World and What the Canine Population Means to Humans," *World Animal Foundation*, September 12, 2023, https://worldanimalfoundation.org/dogs/how-many-dogs-are-in-the-world/.

Chapter 21. Help! I Can't Speak Human!
1. Marissa Martino, "Episode #17: The Importance of Enrichment with Emily Strong and Allie Bender," *Paws & Reward Podcast*, March 15, 2021, (time 9:06), https://pawsandreward.com/episode17/..
2. Suzanne Clothier, "The Bitey End of the Dog", An Aggressivedog.com Podcast via *Apple Podcasts*, March 15, 2021 (time 44:37), https://podcasts.apple.com/us/podcast/suzanne-clothier/id1521311807?i=1000513262837.
3. Check out Lili Chin's work at www.doggiedrawings.net.

Chapter 22. Social Support Equals Social Success
1. Robin Dunbar, "It's Not What You Say, It's How You Say It," *The Society for Personality and Social Psychology*, January 22, 2022. https://spsp.org/news-center/character-context-blog/its-not-what-you-say-its-how-you-say-it.

Chapter 23. From Ownership to Relationship
1. https://www.merriam-webster.com/dictionary/anthropomorphic
2. Susan Friedman, PhD, "Parrot Hero," *PisttaScene* 25.1, no. 94 (February 2013), 13, https://www.behaviorworks.org/files/articles/WPT%20Interview%20-%20Parrot%20Hero.pdf.
3. Friedman, "Parrot Hero," 15.
4. Scott Abraham Miller, "Little Robots," *Why We Do What We Do* podcast, episode 213 (time 24:30), https://wwdwwdpodcast.com/episodes/2021/0609-episode-213-aba-pt-3-little-robots-why-we-do-what-we-do?rq=213.
5. Oprah Winfrey Network (OWN), "The Powerful Lesson Maya Angelou Taught Oprah," Aired October 19, 2011. https://www.oprah.com/oprahs-lifeclass/the-powerful-lesson-maya-angelou-taught-oprah-video.

Chapter 25. Breathing

1. Yu-Fen Chen et al., "The Effectiveness of Diaphragmatic Breathing Relaxation Training for Reducing Anxiety," *Perspectives in Psychiatric Care* 53, no. 4 (October 2017): 333. https://doi.org/10.1111/ppc.12184.
2. Recall that cortisol is the fight, flight, or freeze hormone.
3. Christopher Bergland, "Longer Exhalations Are an Easy Way to Hack Your Vagus Nerve," *Psychology Today*, May 9, 2019. https://www.psychologytoday.com/us/blog/the-athletes-way/201905/longer-exhalations-are-easy-way-hack-your-vagus-nerve.
4. Andrew Weil, M.D. "How to Perform the 4-7-8 Breathing Exercise," accessed May 7, 2024, https://youtu.be/YRPh_GaiL8s?si=6Nw5Egiqfrz4g9rb/.

Chapter 26. Relaxing Your Muscles

1. Loren Toussaint et al., "Effectiveness of Progressive Muscle Relaxation, Deep Breathing, and Guided Imagery in Promoting Psychological and Physiological States of Relaxation," *Evidence-Based Complementary and Alternative Medicine* 2021, no. 6 (July 2021): 7.
2. Michael Ussher, et al., "Immediate Effects of a Brief Mindfulness-Based Body Scan on Patients with Chronic Pain," *Journal of Behavioral Medicine*, 37, no. 1 (November 2014): 132–133.
3. Christina Corbett, Jonathan Egan, and Monika Pilch, "A Randomised Comparison of Two 'Stress Control' Programmes: Progressive Muscle Relaxation versus Mindfulness Body Scan," *Mental Health and Prevention* 15 (May 2019): 200163.
4. This technique, widely used by play therapists, was adapted from classroom instruction by Elizabeth Hamilton, PhD.

Chapter 27. Focusing Your Mind

1. "Getting Started with Mindfulness," *Mindful*, accessed May 7, 2024, https://www.mindful.org/meditation/mindfulness-getting-started/.
2. Kendra Cherry, "Benefits of Mindfulness," *Verywell Mind*, September 2, 2022, https://www.verywellmind.com/the-benefits-of-mindfulness-5205137.
3. Ronald Siegel, *The Science of Mindfulness: A Research-Based Path to Well-Being* (Chantilly, VA: The Great Courses, 2014), 17.
4. DBT Tools, "STOP Skill," 2024, https://dbt.tools/emotional_regulation/stop.php.
5. Russ Harris, and Steven C. Hayes, *ACT Made Simple: An Easy-to-Read Primer on Acceptance and Commitment Therapy* (Oakland, CA: New Harbinger Publications, 2019), 174.
6. Tricia Case, *Child and Dog Interaction Guide*, "Trailblazing Tails," accessed May 7, 2024, https://www.trailblazingtails.com/products/child-and-dog-interactions?_pos=1&_sid=10c15131a&_ss=r.

Chapter 28. Reciting Mantras and Practicing Meditation
1. Recall that cortisol is the fight, flight, or freeze hormone.
2. Daniel Goleman and Richard R. Davidson, *The Science of Meditation: How to Change Your Brain, Mind and Body* (London: Penguin Random House UK, 2017), 6.
3. Brené Brown with Russell Brand, "Are People Doing the Best They Can?" *Under the Skin with Russell Brand*, June 18, 2019, https://www.youtube.com/watch?v=w5TkA7d7eTw.
4. Christopher Pachel, blog post message to author, September 4, 2022.
5. Jack Kornfield, "How to Do Metta," *Lion's Roar: Buddhist Wisdom for Our Time*, November 15, 2022, https://www.lionsroar.com/how-to-do-metta-january-2014/.
6. See Goleman and Davidson's work published in 2017.

Chapter 29. Putting Pen to Paper
1. Keita Umejima et al. "Paper Notebooks vs. Mobile Devices: Brain Activation Differences during Memory Retrieval," *Frontiers in Behavioral Neuroscience* 15, 2021 (March 19, 2021): 634158, https://doi.org/10.3389/fnbeh.2021.634158.
2. James W. Pennebaker and Joshua M. Smyth, *Opening Up by Writing it Down* (New York: Guilford Press, 2016), 75–76.
3. "Why Everyone Should Keep a Journal—7 Surprising Benefits," *Thrive*, March 24, 2020, https://thrive.kaiserpermanente.org/thrive-together/live-well/everyone-keep-journal-7-surprising-benefits.
4. Kaiser, "Why Everyone."
6. Pennebaker, *Opening Up*, 26.
7. Pennebaker, 156.
8. Feelings charts can be downloaded from https://www.freeprintablebehaviorcharts.com/feeling_charts.htm.

Chapter 30. Ending on a Positive Note
1. Mark Stibich, "10 Big Benefits of Smiling, *Verywell Mind*, February 17, 2023, https://www.verywellmind.com/top-reasons-to-smile-every-day-2223755.
2. Recall that cortisol is the fight, flight, or freeze hormone.
3. Jaewon Kang et al., "The Effect of Creative Arts Therapy For Veterans: A Comparison between In-Person and Hybrid-Based Therapy," *Archives of Physical Medicine and Rehabilitation* 103, no. 3 (March 2022): e11, https://doi.org/10.1016/j.apmr.2022.01.029.
4. "Music Quotes," *Keep Inspiring Me*, September 12, 2022, https://www.keepinspiring.me/music-quotes/.
5. Alan Yu, "Which Animals Play, and Why?" interview with Maiken Scott, *The Pulse*, NPR August 15, 2019. https://whyy.org/segments/which-animals-play-and-why/#:~:text=Play%20is%20important%20for%20social,aggression%20or%20a%20mating%20display.

Bonus for Timeouts

1. "Healthy Sleep Habits," American Academy of Sleep Medicine, accessed May 7, 2024, https://sleepeducation.org/healthy-sleep/healthy-sleep-habits/.
2. William R. Miller et al, from the *University of New Mexico Department of Psychology Update*: 2011. In the public domain. No license required for usage.
3. Elizabeth Coombes, "Anxiety: A Playlist to Calm the Mind from a Music Therapist," The Conversation US, November 22, 2019. https://theconversation.com/anxiety-a-playlist-to-calm-the-mind-from-a-music-therapist-121655.
4. Jeanette Settembre, "Your stressed-out dog wants to hear Mozart, not 'Harry Potter': study," *New York Post*, August 23,2022. https://nypost.com/2022/08/23/stressed-out-dogs-want-to-hear-mozart-not-harry-potter-study/.

Acknowledgments

By Charlene:
I'd like to thank those whose names I remember and whose names I've forgotten who helped me build timeouts into my life beginning at an early age. During childhood, my parents, camp counselors, and youth convention speakers all played an important role in helping me find my quiet place. In the business world, my managers, mentors, and professional associates helped me shape techniques for taking a timeout from professional stressors. By applying self-care strategies throughout my lifetime, I now have something to offer others.

I owe coauthors Shaun and Kelsey a debt of gratitude for participating in this project. Thanks especially to Shaun who kept us grounded in evidence-based practices and contributing insights based on her therapy practice. And thanks to Kelsey who added expertise beyond her knowledge of animal care. Not only does she understand animals, she understands organizational content and helped ensure that we stuck to our themes and avoided tangents. Their contributions far exceeded original expectations and their fingerprints can be found on every page of the book.

I soon learned that I needed to create my village to successfully publish a book of this length. Early support came from Richard Byron's parents, Earl and Barbara, who were thrilled he'd been trusted to illustrate a larger work. Ongoing support came from my husband Richard who reviewed early drafts, provided suggestions, and never complained about the hours I spent at the keyboard or on Zoom calls. My daughter Charlotte was eager to share her perspective on the stressors facing young adults and what she and her friends were doing to deal with them.

As the work progressed, it became obvious that I needed additional expertise. My editors Kathy Ide, Rachel McKinley, and Janet F. Williams tightened up our content, fixed our misplaced modifiers, and moved our commas to their proper locations. Following their suggestions resulted in a polished work. They've helped turn a brainstorm into a useful, physical book.

The legal services of Mallory King at Breathe Brand Protection assisted us with copyright laws and registration. Book designer Drew Stevens talked us out of our amateur formatting ideas and guided us toward publishing industry standards. Thanks, Drew, for making us look professional.

Many others touched the manuscript at some point and encouraged the team along the way. To all, I express my gratitude.

By Shaun:
When the idea of this book was first proposed it sounded so fun I couldn't possibly say no. Three years later I have learned much more about the book writing process and the sweat, tears, and determination it takes to bring a project to completion. And I'm not only talking about my effort. I have deep appreciation for my family and friends who encouraged me along the way. They brought me tea and treats during my writing phases and helped me carve out the quiet times I needed for reviewing, rewriting, and editing. To my husband and daughters: thank you for letting me use our family stories as part of the project. I value your trust. Thank you for reminding me to practice what I preach. To my grandchildren: you light up my life and inspire me to take on new adventures. To Jesse and Krispin: you read the earliest versions and provided helpful feedback such as reminding me not to write a parenting textbook. And to Julia, who read a more polished version and quieted my doubts with her kind words. I am blessed beyond measure to call you my colleagues and friends.

Finally, this book absolutely would not have been completed without my coauthors, Charlene and Kelsey. Kelsey, you were ferocious with your insistence that we hone our work to perfection. Your tenacity and eye for detail were key in bringing our three different styles together in a cohesive manner. Thank you for not going easy on me when I was tempted to just "get it done." Also, I never again want to have to think so hard about whether to use bullet points or not … just saying. Charlene, you were the engineer and the engine of this project. You kept us grounded and on track from start to finish. You brought the resources, did the research, and managed Kelsey and I with respect even when I know at times we must have driven you crazy. I don't know where you found the patience. Thank you for not giving up on me when it seemed like my efforts were lagging. Thank you for not giving up on the mission. This has been a journey and a privilege. Thank you for making it happen.

By Kelsey:
I am so incredibly grateful that Shaun and Charlene brought me along for the crazy ride that has been the creation of this book. As Shaun mentioned, my perfectionism can be a gift on a project like this, but it can also get in the way, and Charlene was a lovely manager of my process. Shaun, I am adding an extra layer of appreciation for kicking my imposter syndrome to the curb. It was a bit scary putting my thoughts into a published work, but I think the three of us (along with our editors, illustrator, and designer) managed to produce something pretty amazing.

As an enthusiastic project starter—not always a project finisher—I often struggled to find the right moment to sit down and write. My wonderful husband, Zach, made this possible by being endlessly supportive and even pushy at times. My dear friend, Ariel, was my primary sounding board as I teased apart my complex ideas and found the words to put on the page. My brilliant mentors, Catherine Comden and Kim Brophey, never let me forget how important it was to get this content out of my head and into the world. My enthusiastic clients were eager to see the finished copy and kept me focused on producing a product that could truly make a difference in their lives. My LIMA Beings Membership community helped me continue to tend to myself and my personal growth, even when things were stressful, complicated, and confusing throughout the pandemic. It's interesting how as the coauthor of a self-care book, I can need a little help applying these concepts for myself. Thank you to all my friends, family, and community—you continue to inspire me to grow, learn, and evolve.

Meet the Authors

Shaun Davis, PsyD
Shaun is a licensed psychologist working in private practice and is a certified EAGALA mental health professional (equine-assisted therapy). She earned her doctorate in clinical psychology at George Fox University. Her training included work in a rural school district and several years as a behavioral health provider in a medical clinic. Prior to that she worked as a guidance counselor in a small private school and attempted to be a super mom by volunteering for everything from being a Girl Scout Leader to a basketball stats person. Her personal and professional work is distinguished by her focus on relationships. Because the need to be a super mom never dies, Shaun is invested in her grandchildren, works as a clinical mentor at her alma mater, supervises therapist trainees, teaches community classes, and enrolls in endless training events. Self-care powers her engine so she can continue to maintain her many passions.

Shaun has a wide array of timeout activities that restore her body and soul: spending time with her husband (the most patient man on the planet!), traveling to the ocean to feel the sand between her toes, reading, creative arts, and most of all, spending time with her children, grandchildren, and therapy animals.

To learn more about Shaun, visit her website at www.shaundavispsyd.com or check out her Dr. Mema Facebook page at https://www.facebook.com/AskDrMema. (You can also search for #drmema.)

Charlene A. Derby, MA

Charlene is a freelance writer focused on non-fiction and creative writing projects. She holds a BA in English and Secondary Education from Spring Arbor University in Spring Arbor, Michigan. She earned her MA in Management from the University of Redlands in Redlands, California.

Charlene's business career was divided between traditional employment and independent contracting. As an employee, she held job titles as a Training Specialist and Manager of Training Program Development in the manufacturing and food service sectors. As an independent contractor, she was instrumental in helping organizations transition to office automation in the late 1990s and early 2000s. She has worked on projects for the utility, automotive, healthcare, hospitality, and communication industries. She has also developed curriculum for academic publishers and universities.

During her free time, you may find her taking a timeout by experimenting with new recipes or by reading a crime mystery. She resides with her husband in Southern California. They have one grown daughter.

To learn more about Charlene's writing projects, visit her website at www.charlenederby.com, her Facebook page at @CharleneADerbyAuthor, and her Amazon Author Page. For details about her business career, see her LinkedIn profile.

Kelsey Weber, ABCDT, CPDT-KA, LFDM-T

Kelsey is a Certified Dog Trainer and Licensed Family Dog Mediator who lives in the gorgeous Willamette Valley outside Portland, Oregon. She and her husband are surrounded by animals on their small hobby farm, and she happily spends any free time in the garden.

As a teenager, Kelsey volunteered raising service dog puppies for Guide Dogs for the Blind and worked as a horse trainer throughout her high school and college years. She attended Cal Poly, San Luis Obispo and pursued courses in agricultural sciences, education, animal science, and animal behavior. Soon thereafter, she began working professionally with dog owners, and has spent her career continuing her education in the fields of ethology, neurobiology, and psychology.

Over the years, Kelsey has worked with hundreds of animals of various species and has partnered with shelters, rescues, daycare facilities, breeders, pet stores, and veterinarians. In her business, Pawsitively Trained, LLC, she focuses on helping pets and their people coexist peacefully and to better understand and enjoy each other. Since all behavior happens for a reason, she ensures her clients can discover the underlying cause(s) of their pet's problematic behaviors and follows up with a training plan to produce lasting results and strengthened relationships. Because the animal training industry is unregulated, Kelsey strives to provide pet owners with updated, evidence-driven strategies, and her numerous certifications in the industry demonstrate her dedication to maintaining high standards for animal training practices.

You can find out more about what Kelsey is up to by checking out her training website www.pawsitivelytraineddogs.com or searching for Pawsitively Trained, LLC on Facebook and Instagram.

Richard Byron
Illustrator
Richard is a freelance illustrator and designer born and raised in California's Central Valley. At a young age he fell in love with newspaper comics, which influenced his bold, cartoony style. In high school he created and managed a comics page for the school newspaper. Drawing expressions and making people laugh are what motivate him to learn new styles and techniques as he improves his work. Richard received his BA from the University of California, Davis, where he studied graphic design and traditional drawing. He spends his free time catching up with friends and working on personal art projects.

To learn more about his projects, visit his website at https://www.richardbyron.com/.